Communication Studies

an introductory reader

Edited by John Corner and Jeremy Hawthorn

Edward Arnold

Selection and editorial material
copyright © John Corner and Jeremy Hawthorn 1980

First published 1980 by
Edward Arnold (Publishers) Ltd
41 Bedford Square, London WC1B 3DQ

British Library Cataloguing in Publication Data
Communication studies.
   1. Communication—Addresses, essays, lectures
   I Corner, John II. Hawthorn, Jeremy
   001.5′08   P21.25
   ISBN 0-7131-6278-3 Pbk

Contents

Acknowledgements

Our grateful thanks are due to those colleagues and friends who have helped us with advice and criticism during the compiling of this Reader. In particular, members of the BA Communication Studies course team at Sunderland Polytechnic have provided invaluable assistance to us.

The publisher wishes to thank the following for permission to use their copyright material:

Universe Books, New York and Hutchinson (Publishers) Ltd, London for Jean Aitchison's 'Defining Language' from *The Articulate Mammal*; Penguin Books Ltd for 'Verbal and Non-Verbal Communication' from Michael Argyle's *The Psychology of Interpersonal Behaviour* (Pelican Original, 3/e 1978) © Michael Argyle, 1967, 1972, 1978; Jonathan Cape Ltd for Roland Barthes's 'The Poor and the Proletariat', 'Striptease' and an extract from 'Language and Speech (*Langue* and *Parole*)' from *Elements of Semiology*, translated by Annette Lavers and Colin Smith. These Barthes extracts are also reprinted with the permission of Hill and Wang (now a division of Farrar, Straus and Giroux Inc.) from *Elements of Semiology*, translated from the French by Annette Lavers and Colin Smith; Routledge & Kegan Paul Ltd for 'Social Class, Language and Socialization' from Basil Bernstein's *Class, Codes and Control*, Vol. I; The MIT Press, Mass. for 'What is Communication' from Colin Cherry's *On Human Communication*; Hutchinson Publishing Co. for an extract from Umberto Eco's *Towards a Semiotic Inquiry into the Television Message*, trans. by P. Splendore, which appeared in *Resistance through Rituals* by Hall, Stuart and Jefferson; Mouton Publishers, The Hague for 'Historical Changes in Gestural Behaviour' from David Efron's *Gesture, Race and Culture*; Chatto & Windus, London and New Directions, New York for William Empson's 'Analysis of Gerard Manley Hopkins' poem

"Spring and Fall" ' from *Seven Types of Ambiguity*; Association for Educational Communications and Technology, Washington for George Gerbner's 'Basic Generalized Graphic Model of Communication' from 'On content-analysis and critical research in mass communications' in *Audio-Visual Communication Review* (AVCR) Vol. 6, No. 3, Spring 1958, pp. 85–108; Penguin Books Ltd (Allen Lane, the Penguin Press, 1969 Pelican Books, 1971) © Irving Goffmann 1959 and Doubleday & Co. Inc., NY © Irving Goffman 1958) for 'Introduction' *To the Presentation of Self in Everyday Life* by Irving Goffman; Harper & Row, NY and Penguin Books Ltd for Irving Goffman's 'The Radio Drama Frame' from *Frame Analysis*; New Science Publications for an extract from Stuart Hall's *A World at one with Itself* ('New Society' 18 June 1970); Addison-Wesley Publishing Company. for 'The Issues in Person Perception' from *Person Perception* (© 1970) by A. H. Hastorf, D. J. Schneider and J. Polefka; Sage Publications, Calif. for Elihu Katz, J. G. Blumler and Michael Gurevitch's (Eds) 'Utilization of Mass Communication by the Individual' from *Uses of Mass Communication*; Cambridge University Press for 'Problems of Terminology' from Edmund Leach's *Problems of Terminology*; Harvard University Press, Cambridge, Mass. for 'Education, Generalization and Abstraction' and 'Cultural Factors in Human Perception' from A. R. Luria's *Cognitive Development* © 1976 by the President and Fellows of Harvard College; British Film Institute for 'The Narrator as Guarantor of Truth' from Colin McArthur's *Television and History*; Trevor Pateman for 'Impossible Discourse' from *Language, Truth and Politics*; Cambridge University Press for 'Expression, Meanings and Speech Acts' from J. R. Searle's *Speech Acts*; W. W. Norton & Co. Inc. NY for 'The Impossibility of Not Communicating' from P. Watzlawick, J. H. Beavin and D. D. Jackson's *Pragmatics of Human Communication* (© 1967 by W. W. Norton & Co, Inc.) and Fontana Paper Backs and Schocken Books Inc. NY, for 'Effects of the Technology and Its Uses' from *Television: Technology and Cultural Form* © Schocken Books 1974.

Introduction

This Reader has grown out of the editors' experience of teaching on a new Communication Studies degree, and is primarily intended for students of such courses. Communication Studies is an interdisciplinary subject, and this can create special problems: the student, even in the first year, will be expected to read articles and books which have been produced in different academic contexts, and which presuppose different levels—and sorts—of understanding. Right from the start, students need to organize and relate their work within some overall sense of their intended field of study yet they may well find the important, early task of arriving at a working definition of communication difficult and even disabling if they search for a set of agreed, universal characteristics.

Does communication include interaction, or is interaction different from communication? Is it possible to communicate unintentionally, or is that a contradiction in terms? When we talk of animals or machines 'communicating', are we using the word metaphorically, or are these processes equivalent to human communication?

Any discussion of these and similar questions must acknowledge that in different contexts and different academic traditions people use the word itself differently, but that nevertheless the things they are talking about both have important elements in common and important resemblances and relations. Communication Studies explores these connections and we hope that this Reader provides students with a helpful and stimulating selection of work in the field.

Studying communication

The student will obviously look on this Reader more as a book to be dipped into than as one to be read through in strict sequence. Nevertheless we strongly recommend that the first section be read, as a complete section, before any of the other material in the book is studied. This first section raises questions which will help the student to become aware of certain issues that should inform his or her subsequent reading of other sections. You need, early on, to become sensitive to the problems involved in the use of concepts such as 'code', 'language', 'information', 'culture', 'ideology', 'connotation and denotation', and even 'meaning'. This is not just a questions of learning a vocabulary (although it does involve this), but of engaging with the ways in which writers coming from a range of academic backgrounds deal with important, related questions.

To give a simple example: whether one decides to define 'communication' so as to include or exclude 'intention to communicate', one still has to come to terms with the complex relationship between the reception of intended messages and the reading-off of unintended ones. When you talk to a person whose verbal behaviour displays aggression but whose non-verbal behaviour indicates fear, you are affected by both of these elements. Whether we choose to call one 'communication' and one 'behaviour', or one 'communication' and one 'interaction', or both 'communication' does not alter this fundamental point. It may, however, affect the way we choose, as students, to give such characteristics of human behaviour further attention.

Because Communication Studies is an interdisciplinary subject— what we would call a field of study—students must in their early work spend a fair amount of time familiarizing themselves with 'foundations': basic assumptions, theories, approaches and concerns of constituent disciplines. Initial study can thus sometimes appear both 'bitty' and over-abstract: the student may well feel that time could be better spent in looking at practical examples of communication rather than discussing how best to study such practical examples. Patience is a virtue at this stage, however, for the clarification of such issues can be of great value in the long run.

A note on the selection of extracts

We have not attempted to achieve anything like a blanket coverage of any given topic in this Reader. Nor have we attempted to provide readers with the most authoritative or up-to-date material in each case. We have, rather, tried to balance a number of different criteria when deciding what should be included.

Firstly, we have sought to select pieces which help to define areas of inquiry by raising questions and discussing problems. We believe that an important early stage in the development of any subject is to make it problematic, to go underneath the problem-free surface of things to reveal those difficulties that familiarity and inattention often hide. We have also tried to include pieces which in addition to raising questions also suggest answers, in the belief that even if the answers are wrong the reader will be encouraged to seek more satisfying ones. Thus, to take one example, there are certainly more recent works concerned with gestural behaviour than David Efron's *Gesture, Race and Culture*, which was first published in 1941. But we have included an extract from this particular work in our second section because it advances hypotheses to explain changes in gestural behaviour, hypotheses which we have found stimulating.

From this it can be seen that the main function of this Reader is not to provide students with detailed or comprehensive *information*, but rather to help the student construct a framework which can be used to organize subsequent, more detailed information and to make it coherent. To give another example: our concern with language has generally been of the order of encouraging students to think *about* language. Detailed descriptive or empirical linguistics should be studied by reference to more specialist sources.

Secondly, we have favoured, wherever possible, extracts or articles which indicate or explore points of connection between different academic areas, disciplines, and methods of study. On occasion we have tried to achieve this by juxtaposition: thus the existence of a section entitled *Meaning and interpretation* which includes writing by a literary critic, two semioticians and a sociologist should, we hope, cause readers to explore similarities and dissimilarities in the products of such different academic approaches.

Thirdly, we have tried to include material which has been particularly influential in those different academic areas which have contributed to the development of Communication Studies. Thus our chosen extract from the work of Basil Bernstein is one which summarizes the most influential of his contributions to the field of study, contributions which have had reverberations in many different parts of the field.

Finally, we have favoured pieces which have a bias in the direction of situating their study in the contexts of society and culture and, to perhaps a lesser degree, history. We believe such a bias to be fruitful both because it allows for the integration of work from different disciplines and also because it makes particular studies richer through an engagement with social experience and its constituents.

A note on presentation

In the extracts following, presentation has wherever possible been standardized so that (i) minor references in an extract to other parts of the book or article from which the extract has been taken have been deleted; (ii) references have in general been standardized in accordance with the Harvard system; (iii) a common house-style of punctuation and presentation has been adopted.

John Corner

Jeremy Hawthorn

Section I

Communication: definitions and approaches

The terms, definitions and general frameworks of inquiry which we employ when we go about any piece of investigation have a considerable bearing on what in the end we find out. To note this much does not require us to adopt the sceptical view that we will only discover what our procedures of inquiry have somehow manufactured (there is a vast amount of complex discussion about this in both the natural and social sciences) but it does remind us that knowledge is usefully seen as a product of human activity.

So, what definitions of communication might we employ to identify the phenomena we want to study and to distinguish them from those we don't? And what concepts and basic propositions will serve as the tools with which we can begin to think about the range of activities and processes involved in human communication?

Here, it is important to avoid constructing a false unity called 'communication' by taking from different activities only those aspects which appear to have a resemblance and studying these while ignoring the rest. Some attempts to produce a 'general theory of communication' seem to us to consist precisely of this type of coercive categorization.

Colin Cherry's discussion of possible working definitions is useful because he is aware of these dangers. His opening remark 'Communication is essentially a social affair' needs to be remembered at every stage of a Communication Studies programme and to be effectively present throughout a student's reading, thinking and writing.

Cherry directs our attention to the fundamental point that in dealing with activities involving meaning-production we are concerned with notions of 'language', that is to say systematic procedures (rules, conventions, perhaps we might want to say codes) through which meaning-units (e.g. words, images, symbols, gestures) can be organized into enablers of communicational behaviour. Cherry develops a lucid and, we find, helpful investigation into just what the key terms variously indicate and offers a number of examples to show the sorts of social activity he has in mind when he employs them. His stress on communication as a 'sharing of rules' keeps the emphasis on social convention; the generation of meaning through culturally produced patterns. Later on in the Reader you will find work which relates this idea of 'sharing' to other social factors like power, social class, educational choice and the uses of technology, factors which complicate any ideas one might have about a simple equality in human communication.

Our second extract is from the work of the Cambridge anthropologist Edmund Leach. Leach has been greatly influenced by the writings of those continental researchers who have related linguistic to social research by investigating the ways in which both languages and societies are formed into systematic wholes (or 'structures') of a similar kind. This latter point is very important because it gives a high priority to the study of language in any social inquiry, that is to say it has implications for such disciplines as Sociology, Psychology and Anthropology not simply for the discipline of Linguistics. This will be taken up later in the Reader.

Leach offers us a detailed discussion of terminology but, like Cherry, he is careful to provide particular examples of what he means. You may find that this extract needs very close attention but it will repay this since the problems and terms considered by Leach are to be found elsewhere in this collection, often in the context of particular analyses rather than theoretical reflections. Leach's approach is a far more technically complex one than Cherry's. It is informed by a way of thinking not only about language (in the sense of English, French, Hindi etc.) but about all meaning-systems, one which is still very controversial. This general approach—Semiotics—raises some important issues regarding the extent to which different types of human communication can be seen and studied as *systems of transformation* of a fundamentally similar kind.

In the third extract, Watzlawick, Beavin and Jackson discuss 'The impossibility of not communicating'. They point to interaction as a central aspect of communication and this places an emphasis which we can also find present in both Cherry's and Leach's arguments. The main thesis in this extract is a useful counter to the easy use of explanatory phrases like 'communication breakdown' where these are not accompanied by any sense of the need for further contextual inquiry into the social relationships, and possibly conflicts of interest, involved. By asking questions about the idea of an 'intention to communicate' they add further to our sense of the subtleties of interaction constituting human communication.

Finally, we have reproduced a model (in academic work, a diagram of process and relationship) devised by George Gerbner to aid the discussion of what he sees as general characteristics of communication. The model is accompanied by a quite detailed textual note so no comments need to be made here except a brief one on models. We have generally eschewed the diagrammatic representations which so frequently appeared in early studies of communication. This is because we believe models of this kind generally do little more than stress some very simplified and general notions, often in such a boldly graphic manner as to impair the student's consideration of complexity, context and change. Gerbner's model we consider to be an exception.

The four treatments of communication in this section come from, in order, a telecommunications engineer, an anthropologist, a team of psychologists and a sociologist. Each writer clearly displays a mode of thought and academic imagination which is truly interdisciplinary. In this, the authors stand as representative of the intellectual project of Communication Studies.

Further reading

Students are advised to use the references contained in the extracts and articles to further their knowledge of specific areas. The following list offers, however, a useful development of the topics and discussions suggested in this section of the Reader.

Cherry, Colin 1966: *On human communication* (second edition). Massachusetts: The MIT Technology Press.
A very influential though highly technical survey of communication theory drawing heavily on cybernetic research and attempting an interdisciplinary approach to informational aspects of language. Develops mathematical inquiries to a very high level, perhaps at the expense of sociological detail.
Dance, F. E. 1970: The concept of communication. *Journal of Communication* **20**, 201–10.
A short but helpful discussion of some basic definitional problems.
Gerbner, George 1956: Towards a general model of communication. *Audio Visual Communication Review* **IV.3.**
A clearly written and very suggestive argument about the general characteristics of communication processes.

Leach, Edmund 1976: *Culture and communication*. London: Cambridge University Press.
    Though intended primarily as an introductory text in Social Anthropology this is the best short account of the structuralist method of relating linguistic and symbolic forms to social organization. Well provided with examples.

Lin, N. 1973: *The study of human communication*. New York: Bobbs-Merrill.
    A highly regarded survey which deals thoroughly with a number of preliminary matters and goes on to offer advanced and original arguments about the social psychology of language processes.

Mortensen, C. D. 1972: *Communication: the study of human interaction*. New York: McGraw-Hill.
    An excellent textbook with a fine use of diagrams and visual illustration. The attempted comprehensiveness leads to some rather patchy 'overviews' from time to time but the volume has much to offer and is written in a format and style designed for the student reader. Very well referenced throughout.

Shannon, C. E. and Weaver, W. 1949: *The mathematical theory of communication*. Illinois: University of Illinois Press.
    A classic, early argument about the way in which the study of communication might be aided by theories drawn from work on telecommunications systems. One of the first studies to use terms such as 'feedback', 'channel', 'noise' etc. in the discussion of human communication. The book as a whole remains difficult for those not trained in Technology, though the early chapters are quite accessible and should be read by students who want to understand and evaluate for themselves the criticisms concerning reductiveness and sociological inadequacy which have now gathered around the volume. See Cherry 1966 above for a re-working of the technological appproach.

Watzlawick, P., Beavin, J. and Jackson, D. 1968: *Pragmatics of human communication*. London: Faber.
    A study based on work carried out at the Mental Research Institute, Palo Alto, California, which was an attempt to deal with behaviour disorders in terms of Linguistics and communication theory. A closely argued and frequently witty book with an excellent layout enabling students to locate particular arguments and topics very quickly. The emphasis on psycho-pathology makes the volume a rather specialized and advanced one but selective reading could profitably be undertaken by students at all levels.

I

What is communication?
Colin Cherry

From Cherry, Colin 1957: *On human communication*. Cambridge, Mass: MIT Press, 3–9.

Communication is essentially a social affair. Man has evolved a host of different systems of communication which render his social life possible—social life not in the sense of living in packs for hunting or for making war, but in a sense unknown to animals. Most prominent among all these systems of communication is, of course, human speech and language. Human language is not to be equated with the sign systems of animals, for man is not restricted to calling his young, or suggesting mating, or shouting cries of danger; he can with his remarkable faculties of speech give utterance to almost any thought. Like animals, we too have our inborn instinctive cries of alarm, pain, et cetera: we say *Oh!*, *Ah!*; we have smiles, groans, and tears; we blush, shiver, yawn, and frown.[1] A hen can set her chicks scurrying up to her, by clucking—communication established by a releaser mechanism—*but human language is vastly more than a complicated system of clucking*.

The development of language reflects back upon thought; for with language thoughts may become organized, new thoughts evolved. Self-awareness and the sense of social responsibility have arisen as a result of organized thoughts. Systems of ethics and law have been built up. Man has become self-conscious, responsible, a social creature.

Inasmuch as the words we use disclose the true nature of things, as truth is to each one of us, the various words relating to personal communication are most revealing. The very word 'communicate' means 'share', and inasmuch as you and I are communicating at this moment, we are one. Not so much a union as a unity. Inasmuch as we agree, we say that we *are of one mind*, or, again, that we understand *one another*. This one another is the unity. A group of people, a society, a culture, I would define as 'people in communication'. They may be thought of as 'sharing rules' of language, custom, of habit; but who wrote these rules? These have evolved out of those people themselves—rules of conformity. Inasmuch as that conformity is the greater or the less, so is the unity. The degree of communication, the sharing, the conformity, is a measure of one-mindedness. After all, what we share, we cannot each have as our own possession, and no single person in this world has ever been born and bred in utter isolation. 'No man is an island, entire of itself.'[2]

Speech and writing are by no means our only system of communication. Social intercourse is greatly strengthened by habits of gesture—little movements of the hands and face. With nods, smiles, frowns, handshakes, kisses, fist shakes, and other gestures we can convey most subtle understanding.[3] We also have economic systems for trafficking not in ideas but in material goods and services; the tokens of communication are coins, bonds, letters of credit, and so on. We have conventions of dress, rules of the road, social formalities, and good manners; we have rules of membership and function in businesses, institutions, and families. But life in the modern world is coming to depend more and more upon 'technical' means of communication, telephone and telegraph, radio and printing. Without such technical aids the modern city-state could not exist one week, for it is only by means of them that trade and business can proceed; that goods and services can be distributed where needed; that railways can run on a schedule; that law and order are maintained; that education is possible. Communication renders true social life practicable, for communication means organization. Communications have enabled the social unit to grow, from the village to the town, to the modern city-state, until today we see organized systems of mutual dependence grown to cover whole hemispheres (McDougall, 1927).

The development of human language was a, tremendous step in evolution; its power for organizing thoughts, and the resulting growth of social organizations of all kinds, has given man, wars or no wars, street accidents or no street accidents, vastly increased potential for survival.

As a start, let us now take a few of the concepts and notions to do with communication, and discuss them briefly, not in any formal scientific sense, but in the language of the market place. A few dictionary definitions may serve as a starting point for our discursive approach here; later we shall see that such definitions are not at variance with those more restricted definitions used in scientific analysis. The following have been drawn from the *Concise Oxford English Dictionary*:[4]

> *Communication*, n.   Act of imparting (esp. news); information given; intercourse; ... (Military, Pl.) connexion between base and front.

Message, n.   Oral or written communication sent by one person to another.

Information, n.   Informing, telling; thing told, knowledge, items of knowledge, news, (on, about); ...

Signal, n., v.t. & i.   Preconcerted or intelligible sign conveying information ... at a distance. ...

Intelligence, n.   ... understanding, sagacity ... information, news.

News, n. pl.   Tidings, new information. ...

Knowledge, n.   ... familiarity gained by experience, person's range of information. ...

Belief, n.   Trust or confidence (*in*); ... acceptance as true or existing (of any fact, statement, etc.; ...). ...

Organism, n.   Organised body with connected interdependent parts sharing common life, ...; whole with interdependent parts compared to living being.

System, n.   Complex whole, set of connected things or parts, organized body of material or immaterial things ...; method, organization, considered principles of procedure, (principle of) classification; ...

Such dictionary definitions are the 'common usages' of words; scientific usage frequently needs to be more restricted but should not violate common sense—an accusation often mistakenly levelled against scientific words by the layman.

The most frequent use of the words listed above is in connection with *human* communication, as the dictionary suggests. The word 'communication' calls to mind most readily the sending or receipt of a letter, or a conversation between two friends; some may think of newspapers issued daily from a central office to thousands of subscribers, or of radio broadcasting; others may think of telephones, linking one speaker and one listener. There are systems too which come to mind only to specialists; for instance, ornithologists and entomologists may think of flocking and swarming, or of the incredible precision with which flight manœuvres are made by certain birds, or the homing of pigeons—problems which have been extensively studied, yet are still so imperfectly understood. Again, physiologists may consider the communicative function of the nervous system, coordinating the actions of all the parts of an integrated animal. At the other end of the scale, the anthropologist and sociologist are greatly interested in the communication between large groups of people, societies and races, by virtue of their cultures, their economic and religious systems, their laws, languages, and ethical codes. Examples of 'communication systems' are endless and varied.

When 'members' or 'elements' are in communication with one

another, they are associating, cooperating, forming an 'organization', or sometimes an 'organism'. Communication is a social function. That old cliché, 'a whole is more than the sum of the parts', expresses a truth; the whole, the organization or organism, possesses a structure which is describable as a set of *rules*, and this structure, the rules, may remain unchanged as the individual members or elements are changed. By the possession of this structure the whole organization may be better adapted or better fitted for some goal-seeking activity. Communication means a *sharing* of elements of behaviour or modes of life, by the existence of sets of rules. This word *rule* will be discussed later.

.   .   .

Perhaps we may be permitted to comment upon a definition of communication, as given by a leading psychologist (Stevens, 1950): '*Communication is the discriminatory response of an organism to a stimulus.*'[5] The same writer emphasizes that a definition broad enough to embrace all that the word 'communication' means to different people may risk finding itself dissipated in generalities. We would agree; such definitions or descriptions serve as little more than foci for discussion. But there are two points we wish to make concerning this psychologist's definition. First, as we shall view it in our present context, communication is not the response itself but is essentially the *relationship* set up by the transmission of stimuli and the evocation of responses. Second, it will be well to expand somewhat upon the notion of a stimulus; we shall need to distinguish between human language and the communicative signs of animals, between languages, codes, and logical sign systems, at least.

The study of the signs used in communication, and of the rules operating upon them and upon their users, forms the core of the study of communication. There is no communication without a system of signs—but there are many kinds of 'signs'. Let us refer again to the *Concise Oxford English Dictionary*:

> *Sign*, n.   ... written mark conventionally used for word or phrase, symbol, thing used as representation of something ... presumptive evidence or indication or suggestion or symptom *of* or *that*, distinctive mark, token, guarantee, password ... portent ...; natural or conventional motion or gesture used instead of words to convey information. ...
>
> *Language*, n.   A vocabulary and way of using it. ...
>
> *Code*, n., and v.t.   Systematic collection of statutes, body of laws so arranged as to avoid inconsistency and overlapping; ... set of rules on

any subject; prevalent morality of a society or class ...; system of mil. or nav. signals. ...

Symbol, n. ... Thing regarded by general consent as naturally typifying or representing or recalling something by possession of analogous qualities or by association in fact or thought. ...

We shall use the word *sign* for any physical event used in communication—human, animal, or machine—avoiding the term *symbol*, which is best reserved for the Crown, the Cross, Uncle Sam, the olive branch, the Devil, Father Time, and others 'naturally typifying or representing or recalling ... by association in fact or thought', religious and cultural symbols interpretable only in specified historical contexts. The term *language* will be used in the sense of human language, 'a vocabulary [of signs] and way of using it'; as a set of signs and rules such as we use in everyday speech and conversation, in a highly flexible and mostly illogical way. On the other hand, we shall refer to the strictly formalized systems of signs and rules, such as those of mathematics and logic, as *language systems* or *sign systems*.

The term *code* has a strictly technical usage which we shall adopt here. Messages can be coded *after* they are already expressed by means of signs (e.g. letters of the English alphabet); then a code is an agreed transformation, usually one to one and reversible, by which messages may be converted from one set of signs to another. Morse code, semaphore, and the deaf-and-dumb code represent typical examples. In our terminology then, we distinguish sharply between *language*, which is developed organically over long periods of time, and *codes*, which are invented for some specific purpose and follow explicit rules.

Apart from our natural languages (English, French, Italian, etc.), we have many examples of *systems* of signs and rules, which are mostly of a very inflexible kind. A pack of playing cards represents a set of signs, and the rules of the game ensure communication and patterned behaviour among the players. Every motorist in Britain is given a book of rules of the road called the *Highway Code*, and adherence to these signs and rules is supposed to produce concerted, patterned behaviour on British roads. There are endless examples of such simple sign systems. A society has a structure, definite sets of relationships between individuals, which is not formless and haphazard but organized. Hierarchies may exist and be recognized, in a family, a business, an institution, a factory, or an army—functional relationships which decide to a great extent the patterned flow of communication. The communication and the structure are subject to sets of rules, rules of conduct, authoritarian dictates, systems of law; and the structures may be highly complex and varied in form. A 'code' of ethics is more like a language, having developed organically; it is a set of guiding rules concerning 'ought situations', generally accepted, whereby people in a society associate together and have social coherence. Such codes are different in the various societies of the world, though there is an overlap of varying degrees. When the overlap is small a gulf of misunderstanding may open up. Across such a gulf communication may fail; if it does, the organization breaks down.

The whole broad study of language, and sign systems has been called, by Charles Morris, the theory of signs (Morris, 1938, 1946), and owes much to the earlier philosophy of Charles Peirce.[6] Morris distinguishes three types of rule operating upon signs, (*a*) *syntactic* rules (rules of syntax; relations between signs); (*b*) *semantic* rules (relations between signs and the things, actions, relationships, qualities—*designata*); (*c*) *pragmatic* rules (relations between signs and their users).

2

Problems of terminology
Edmund Leach

From Leach, Edmund 1976: *Culture and communication*. London: Cambridge University Press, 9–16.

When we are in the company of close friends and neighbours we all take it for granted that communication is a complex continuous process which has many non-verbal as well as verbal components. It is only when we meet with strangers that we suddenly become aware that, because all customary behaviours (and not just acts of speech) convey information, we cannot understand what is going on until we know the code. How then should we set about decoding other people's customs?

We can usefully distinguish three aspects of human behaviour:

(1) *natural biological activities of the human body*—breathing, heart-beat, metabolic process and so on;
(2) *technical actions*, which serve to alter the physical state of the world out there—digging a hole in the ground, boiling an egg;
(3) *expressive actions*, which either simply say something about the state of the world as it is, or else purport to alter it by metaphysical means.

Besides ordinary verbal utterances, expressive actions obviously include gestures, such as nodding the head, pulling faces and waving the arms, but they also include such behaviours as wearing a uniform, standing on a dais, and putting on a wedding ring.

My three *aspects* of behaviour are never completely separable. Even the act of breathing is 'expressive'—it 'says' that I am still alive. Even the simplest technical action has both biological and expressive implication. If I make myself a cup of coffee it not only alters the state of the world out there, it also stimulates my internal metabolic processes, and it 'says' something. The way I prepare the coffee and the instruments which I use in the process give information about my cultural background.

The modes and channels through which we communicate with one

another are very diverse and very complex but as a first approxima-
tion, for purposes of initial analysis, I shall assert that:

Human communication is achieved by means of expressive actions
which operate as *signals*, *signs* and *symbols*. Most of us do not distinguish these three commonplace words at all precisely, and even those
who do may use them in widely different ways,[1] but in this essay
they will be given specially defined meaning which I shall presently
spell out.

In some forms of communication the expressive action of the
sender is directly interpreted by the receiver. I speak, you listen; I
nod my head, you see me do so. But in other cases the link is indirect.
I write a letter and produce a pattern of signs and symbols on a piece of
paper; some time later you receive the paper and interpret what I
wrote.

The scope of indirect communication of this latter sort is very wide.
We spend our whole time interpreting the results of the past expressive actions of other people. I can recognize that a church is not just
an ordinary dwelling house simply by looking at it, but the 'expressive
actions' which built in the distinction in the first place took place a
long time ago.

In what follows I shall assume that *all* the various non-verbal dimensions of culture, such as styles in clothing, village layout, architecture,
furniture, food, cooking, music, physical gestures, postural attitudes
and so on are organized in patterned sets so as to incorporate coded
information in a manner analogous to the sounds and words and sentences of a natural language. I assume therefore it is just as meaningful
to talk about the grammatical rules which govern the wearing of
clothes as it is to talk about the grammatical rules which govern speech
utterances.

Clearly this is a very sweeping kind of assumption and I shall not
attempt to justify it in detail. The basic argument is that the messages
which we receive in different modes (through our various senses of
touch, sight, hearing, smell, taste, etc.) are readily transformed into
other modes. Thus we can visualize what we hear in words; we can
convert written texts into speech; a musician can transform the visual
patterns of a musical score into movements of the arms, mouth
and fingers. Evidently, at some deeply abstract level, all our different
senses are coded in the same way. There *must* be some kind of
'logical' mechanism which allows us to transform sight messages
into sound messages or touch messages or smell messages, and vice
versa.

However, it is also important to recognize that there are major differences between the way individuals convey information to one another by the use of ordinary speech and by the written word, and the way we communicate with one another by coded conventions of non-verbal behaviour and non-verbal signs and symbols.

The grammatical rules which govern speech utterances are such that anyone with a fluent command of a language can generate spontaneously entirely new sentences with the confident expectation that he will be understood by his audience. This is *not* the case with most forms of non-verbal communication. Customary conventions can only be understood if they are familiar. A private symbol generated in a dream or in a poem, or a newly invented 'symbolic statement' of a non-verbal kind, will fail to convey information to others until it has been explained by other means. This shows that the syntax of non-verbal 'language' must be a great deal simpler than that of spoken or written language. Indeed, were this not the case, a short essay such as this on such a complex theme would be a complete waste of time.

So in reading what follows you need to remember that there is only an analogic similarity between the generation of new sentences by an individual engaged in spontaneous discourse and the generation of new customs by a cultural community over a period of time. In point of fact we understand very little about either.

My starting point is arbitrary. Let us call any unit of communication a 'communication event'. Any such event is dyadic (two-faced) in at least two senses:

(1) There must always be two individuals: X, the 'sender', the originator of the expressive action, and Y, the 'receiver', the interpreter of the product of the expressive action. X and Y may be in the same place at the same time or they may not.

(2) The expressive action itself always has two aspects, simply because it transmits a message. On the one hand there is the action itself or the product of the action, the nodding of the head or the written letter, on the other there is the message which is encoded by the sender and decoded by the receiver.

The complexities of terminology which I have set out in Fig. 2.1 are analytically useful because the relationship between the 'message bearing entity A' and the 'message B' may assume a variety of forms. In reading the next few paragraphs I suggest that you refer repeatedly to Fig. 2.1.

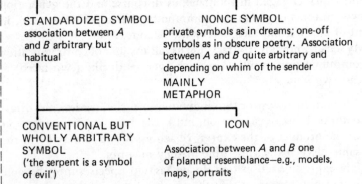

COMMUNICATION DYAD – 'The Communication Event'

Message-bearing entity *A* conveys information about message *B*

INDEX
A indicates *B*

SIGNAL
A causes *B* by trigger response

SIGNUM
A stands for *B* as
a result of arbitrary
human choice

NATURAL INDEX
A associated with *B* by nature, but
selected as an index of *B* by human choice
('smoke is an index of fire')
MAINLY
METONYMY

SYMBOL
A stands for *B* by
arbitrary association

SIGN
A stands for *B* as part for whole (metonymy)
('a crown is a sign for royalty')

STANDARDIZED SYMBOL
association between *A*
and *B* arbitrary but
habitual

NONCE SYMBOL
private symbols as in dreams; one-off
symbols as in obscure poetry. Association
between *A* and *B* quite arbitrary and
depending on whim of the sender
MAINLY
METAPHOR

CONVENTIONAL BUT
WHOLLY ARBITRARY
SYMBOL
('the serpent is a symbol
of evil')

ICON
Association between *A* and *B* one
of planned resemblance—e.g., models,
maps, portraits

Figure 2.1

The key distinctions in this schema are as follows:

SIGNAL   The relationship *A : B* is mechanical and automatic. *A*
triggers *B*. The message and the message-bearing entity
are simply two aspects of the same thing. All animals including human beings are constantly responding to a great
variety of signals all the time.

INDEX '*A* indicates *B*'. Signals are dynamic; indices static. Signals are causal; indices descriptive. Within this general class, *natural indices* are those in which the association is natural—'smoke is an index of fire', *signa* are those in which the association is a cultural convention; *symbols* and *signs* are then contrasted as sub-categories of *signa*.

So far I have more or less followed Mulder and Hervey (1972, 13–17). But the concern of these authors is to produce a rigorous analysis of the concept of *sign* in *linguistics*, and their lack of interest in non-verbal modes of communication limits the utility of the rest of their terminological system so far as my present purposes are concerned.

Mulder and Hervey distinguish *symbols* as '*signa* dependent on a separate (occasional) definition for their correct interpretation—e.g. *x*, *y*, *z* in an algebraic equation', and *signs* as '*signa* with wholly fixed conventional denotation, e.g. +, −, = in an algebraic equation'. According to these definitions proper names are symbols while classi-fying nouns are signs. For example in the statement: 'That man is called John', *John* is a symbol for *that man*, but in 'those animals are pigs', *pigs* is a sign for *those animals*. Although this distinction between 'separately defined denotation' and 'wholly fixed conventional denotation' applies also to the *symbol/sign* contrast in my own Fig. 2.1, I am interested in a different aspect of this contrast and I shall spell out my definitions in a different way.

However, before I do that, it may be noted that Mulder and Hervey's algebraic example immediately makes it clear that any particular 'symbolic statement' is likely to be a combination of both symbols and signs, e.g. $x + y = z$.

It is also evident that whether a particular *signum* is to be regarded as a *sign* or a *symbol* will depend upon how it is used. The letters of the Roman alphabet when used in mathematical equations are *symbols* but when used in the context of verbal transcription they have approximately fixed conventional phonetic values and become *signs*. In this latter context, any particular letter standing by itself is mean-ingless, yet in combination sub-sets of the twenty-six available letter-signs can be made to represent hundreds of thousands of different words in hundreds of different languages.

For my purposes this is the heart of the matter. The two key points are (i) signs do not occur in isolation; a sign is always a member of a set of contrasted signs which function within a specific cultural con-text; (ii) a sign only conveys information when it is combined with other signs and symbols from the same context. Example: $x + y = z$ implies a mathematical context. Outside that context the signs $+$ and $=$ would convey no information. Putting the same point differently: *signs* are always *contiguous* to other signs which are members of the same set.

This gives us the definitions shown on Fig. 2.1.

(1) A *signum* is a *sign* when there is an intrinsic prior relationship between A and B because they belong to the same cultural context.

Examples:

(i)   Given the context of the sound transcription of spoken English by means of letters of the Roman alphabet, each letter or pair of letters is a *sign* for a particular sound.

(ii) Given the conventions of English spelling, the letter sequence APPLE is a *sign* for a particular fruit.

(iii) In the expression '*A* stands for APPLE' *A* is a *sign* for APPLE and hence also a *sign* for the fruit.

(iv) Given the context of European political traditions in which the principal item of the ruling monarch's regalia was a crown, a crown is a *sign* for sovereignty.

This kind of relationship is sometimes described as *metonymy* and this is the sense in which I shall be using this word in this essay. Very roughly, as my last two examples suggest, *metonymy* is where 'a part stands for a whole'; the index which functions as a sign is contiguous to and part of that which is signified. Note that natural indices (e.g. 'smoke indicates fire') entail *metonymic* relationships as well as signs.

(2) Correspondingly: a *signum* is a *symbol* when *A* stands for *B* and there is *no* intrinsic prior relationship between *A* and *B*, that is to say *A* and *B* belong to different cultural contexts.

Examples:

(i)   In the algebraic proposition 'Let *x* stand for the price of cheese, *y* for the price of butter, and *z* for the price of bread ...' *x*, *y* and *z* are symbols. Here, *x*, *y*, *z* belong to the context of mathematics, the prices belong to the context of the market place.

(ii) Where a crown is used as a trade mark for a brand of beer, it is a symbol not a sign. There is no prior intrinsic relationship. Crowns and beer come from different contexts.

(iii) In the Bible story the Serpent in the Garden of Eden is a symbol for Evil. The zoological context of serpents has no *intrinsic* relationship to the moral context of the concept of Evil.

In my Fig 2.1, as is shown by the two dotted rectangles, the contrast between the *intrinsic* relationships entailed in natural indices and signs and the *non-intrinsic* relationships entailed in symbols corresponds to the distinction between *metonymy* and *metaphor*. Where *metonymy* implies contiguity, *metaphor* depends upon asserted similarity.

Within the general category *symbol*, my schema again partly follows Mulder and Hervey. *Standardized symbols* which convey information in the public domain are distinguished from *nonce symbols*, i.e. private one-off symbols, such as may appear in dreams or in poetry, which convey no public information until they are provided with an additional gloss. Within the broad category of *standardized symbols*, I distinguish *icons*, where the relation A/B is one of planned resemblance—e.g. models, maps, portraits—from *conventional but wholly arbitrary symbols*. This is a normal usage (see, e.g. Firth, 1973).

My point that *sign* relationships are contiguous and thus mainly *metonymic* while *symbol* relationships are arbitrary assertions of similarity and therefore mainly *metaphoric* needs further elaboration.

Almost everyone who has made a careful study of the processes of human communication is agreed that a distinction of this sort is analytically important, but again there are wide differences of terminology.

The usage *metaphor/metonymy* is due to Jakobson (1956). Lévi-Strauss (1966), in the tradition of de Saussure, describes almost the same distinction by the terms *paradigmatic/syntagmatic*. We meet much the same contrast in music when *harmony*, in which different instruments make simultaneous noises which are heard in combination, is distinguished from *melody* in which one note follows another to form a tune.

In music we are familiar with the idea of a melody being transposed into a different key so that it can be played by a different instrument, but this is simply a special case of a very general process by which syntagmatic chains of signs linked by metonymy can be shifted by paradigmatic transposition (metaphor) into a different manifest form. Prototype examples of *syntagmatic chains* are the letters forming a written word, or the words forming a sentence, or the sequence of musical notes written on a musical score to indicate a 'tune'.

An example of *paradigmatic association* is provided by the simultaneous transposition which occurs when a sequence of musical notes is interpreted as a sequence of finger movements across the keyboard of a piano, which, by further conversion, become a sequential pattern of sound waves reaching the ear of the listener. The relation between the written score, the finger movements and the sound waves is *paradigmatic*.

The jargon is tiresome but at times useful. Approximately, but not exactly, the following equivalents apply:

Symbol/Sign = Metaphor/Metonymy =
Paradigmatic association/Syntagmatic chain = Harmony/Melody.

It is our common experience that all kinds of human action, and not just speaking, serve to convey information. Such modes of communication include writing, musical performance, dancing, painting, singing, building, acting, curing, worshipping and so on. The whole argument of this essay rests on the proposition that, at some level, the 'mechanism' of these various modes of communication must be the same, that each is a 'transformation' of every other in much the same sense as a written text is a transformation of speech. If this really is the case then we need a language in which to discuss the attributes of this common code. That is where my jargon comes in.

3

The impossibility of not communicating

P. Watzlawick, J. Beavin and D. Jackson

From Watzlawick, P., Beavin, J. and Jackson, D. 1968: *Pragmatics of human communication*. London: Faber, 48–51.

First of all, there is a property of behaviour that could hardly be more basic and is, therefore, often overlooked: behaviour has no opposite. In other words, there is no such thing as non-behaviour or, to put it even more simply: one cannot *not* behave. Now, if it is accepted that all behaviour in an interactional situation[1] has message value, i.e. is communication, it follows that no matter how one may try, one cannot *not* communicate. Activity or inactivity, words or silence all have message value: they influence others and these others, in turn, cannot *not* respond to these communications and are thus themselves communicating. It should be clearly understood that the mere absence of talking or of taking notice of each other is no exception to what has just been asserted. The man at a crowded lunch counter who looks straight ahead, or the aeroplane passenger who sits with his eyes closed, are both communicating that they do not want to speak to anybody or be spoken to, and their neighbours usually 'get the message' and respond appropriately by leaving them alone. This, obviously, is just as much an interchange of communication as an animated discussion.[2]

Neither can we say that 'communication' only takes place when it is intentional, conscious, or successful, that is, when mutual understanding occurs. Whether message sent equals message received is an important but different order of analysis, as it must rest ultimately on evaluations of specific, introspective, subject-reported data, which we choose to neglect for the exposition of a behavioural theory of communication. On the question of misunderstanding, our concern, given certain formal properties of communication, is with the development of related pathologies, aside from, indeed in spite of, the motivations or intentions of the communicants.

2.22

In the foregoing, the term 'communication' has been used in two ways: as the generic title of our study, and as a loosely defined unit of behaviour. Let us now be more precise. We will, of course, continue to refer to the pragmatic aspect of the theory of human communication simply as 'communication'. For the various units of communication (behaviour), we have sought to select terms which are already generally understood. A single communicational unit will be called a *message* or, where there is no possibility of confusion, a communication. A series of messages exchanged between persons will be called *interaction*. (For those who crave more precise quantification, we can only say that the sequence we refer to by the term 'interaction' is greater than one message but not infinite.) Finally, in Chapters 4–7,* we will add *patterns of interaction*, which is a still higher-level unit of human communication.

Further, in regard to even the simplest possible unit, it will be obvious that once we accept all behaviour as communication, we will not be dealing with a monophonic message unit, but rather with a fluid and multifaceted compound of many behavioural modes— verbal, tonal, postural, contextual, etc.—all of which qualify the meaning of all the others. The various elements of this compound (considered as a whole) are capable of highly varied and complex permutations, ranging from the congruent to the incongruent and paradoxical. The pragmatic effect of these combinations in interpersonal situations will be our interest herein.

2.23
The impossibility of not communicating is a phenomenon of more than theoretical interest. It is, for instance, part and parcel of the schizophrenic 'dilemma'. If schizophrenic behaviour is observed with aetiological considerations in abeyance, it appears that the schizophrenic tries *not to communicate*. But since even nonsense, silence, withdrawal, immobility (postural silence), or any other form of denial is itself a communication, the schizophrenic is faced with the impossible task of denying that he is communicating and at the same time denying that his denial is a communication. The realization of this basic dilemma in schizophrenia is a key to a good many aspects of schizophrenic communication that would otherwise remain obscure. Since any communication, as we shall see, implies commitment and thereby defines the sender's view of his relationship with the receiver, it can be hypothesized that the schizophrenic behaves as if he would avoid

* Not included in this Reader.

commitment by not communicating. Whether this is his purpose, in the causal sense, is of course impossible of proof.

2.24
To summarize, a metacommunicational axiom of the pragmatics of communication can be postulated: *one cannot* not *communicate*.

4

Basic generalized graphic model of communication
George Gerbner

From Gerbner, George 1956: Towards a general model of communication in *Audio-Visual Communication Review* **IV.3**, 1956.

Editors' note on Gerbner's model of communication (opposite page)
Gerbner's model is an attempt to depict diagrammatically some of the issues of perception and representation which must be taken into account in any study of communicational activity as a dynamic, social process.

The flow is from right to left in the diagram.

An event (E) is perceived by someone (M). The event-as-perceived (E^1) is the product of perceptual *activity* and thus the mediations and transformations of particular selective and contextual factors introduce the difference between E and E^1.

The vertical arm of the model shows the *representation* of the event ('statement about event') by the perceiver to be partly a product of the available meaning systems (e.g. print, speech, photograph, film) and of the particular conventions of use of such systems (here it is important to stress the social and historical contingency of these conventions). These formal elements (S) combine with event-related elements (E).

Finally, the lower horizontal arm shows this representation, the statement about the event (SE), being perceived (heard, read, viewed) by a second person (M^2). This perceptual activity will involve, as it did in the earlier case, a *transformation* such that the difference SE/SE^1 will occur.

All academic models must be seen as argued accounts of the world rather than diagrams of its processes (indeed Gerbner's own model draws our attention to just this point!); as such they invite not only our understanding but also our criticism. The processes which Gerbner treats graphically (and, we think, usefully) are the subject of very complex arguments, some of which you will find elsewhere in this Reader.

The relation of language to reality, the nature of different representing practices, the advisability of considering 'form' as separate from

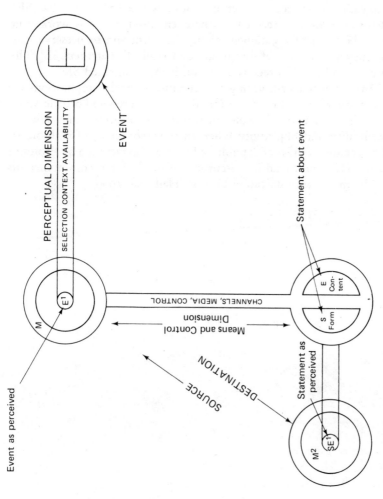

PERCEPTUAL DIMENSION

SELECTION CONTEXT AVAILABILITY

EVENT

Event as perceived

M

E¹

CHANNELS, MEDIA, CONTROL

Means and Control
Dimension

SOURCE

DESTINATION

Statement as
perceived

Statement about event

S
Form

E
Con-
tent

M² SE¹

Basic generalized graphic model of communication

'content', the extent to which the perception and representation of events in, say, the natural sciences involve problems and possibilities different from those in, say, sports journalism—questions such as these should be borne in mind when using and discussing the model.

We would also suggest that the diagram designations are slightly misleading in so far as M's representation is called SE rather than SE^1. It is the event-as-perceived *not* the event itself which is worked up into the form of a statement about the event and to preserve consistency it would therefore appear best to call M's statement SE^1. This would lead to M^2's received version being designated SE^2.

Finally, it is worth noting that the model carries implications for the study of mass communication (notably the press and broadcasting) since it suggests the difficulty in realizing such professional goals as 'neutrality' and 'objectivity' where these are conceived of as absolutes. The version of the model published here was in fact used by Professor James Halloran to aid his discussion of professional communicators in the mass communication process (Halloran, 1969).

Section II

Perception, behaviour, interaction

At first glance the title of this section may suggest an easy progression: perception—how the individual makes sense of his or her world; behaviour—how he or she acts within that perceived world; interaction—how he or she influences and is influenced by other people. If this chapter achieves nothing else we hope that it will dispel such a simplistic view. It is the interconnectedness of the processes being studied here that is, for us, crucial. We do not perceive the world passively but actively, and the more active our role in the world the more developed our perceptions are; we do not 'behave' in isolation but on the basis of our perceptions of and our relations with other people; we do not interact with other isolated and autonomous individuals—we interact on the basis of shared perceptions and common as well as disputed goals. Thus each term in our title both implies and is in part constituted by the others.

This section clearly relies heavily on the work of psychologists and social psychologists, and yet it has to be admitted that at least two of our chosen extracts—those of Luria and Efron—are somewhat outside the mainstream of Anglo-American psychology. In both cases our choice has been motivated by the stress on the social, cultural and historical determinants of perception and behaviour to be found in these contributions, a stress which in our opinion is a necessary counterbalance to a tendency within the dominant practices of Anglo-American psychology to study 'the individual' in relative isolation from such determinants. We do not deny the value of descriptive accounts of individual human behaviour, or of study of the biological and physiological factors involved in, for example, perception. But we believe that in isolation such studies avoid crucial questions about the factors which are privileged in the determination of how human beings make sense of their world by acting together within it.

The extract from Luria's *Cognitive Development* is thus an appropriate starting point, for it is based on the study of the differences in the perception of even simple optical illusions on the part of people within the same society who have been subject to variable social and cultural influences. Luria's work here is based on research in Soviet Uzbekistan and Kirghizia in the late 1920s and early 1930s, when enormous changes were taking place in these regions: a largely illiterate, peasant population was being involved in the collectivization of the farms and receiving, in most cases for the first time, formal education. Other, cultural factors were also being revolutionized; the position of women—to cite a striking example—was being radically transformed. Here was a society-wide laboratory, and Luria and his colleagues set out to discover whether these changes in the social and cultural situation of those concerned were apparent in their perceptual processes.

In brief, Luria argues for a conception of perception as culturally saturated if not determined, and against a view of it as in any sense purely physiological. We should note that this conclusion ties in with the positions outlined by Hastorf *et al.* (later in this section), and Bernstein (see section III). For if the former are correct to assert that perception is at least in part reliant on categories provided by language, and the latter is correct to uphold the view that our use of language is impregnate with social factors, then it follows logically that social factors constitute at least in part the framework around which our perceptions are structured and formed. This is not to suggest that there are no innate predispositions involved in human perception, or that there are no extra-cultural, universal perceptual processes (although it is revealing that psychologists who argue that there are seem mostly to adduce studies of babies to make their point). We would suggest, however, that the reader remember the ability of which human beings are possessed to adapt, subdue and even rid themselves of such innate predispositions. Most of us appear to have an innate predisposition to be afraid of heights but many people—including one of the editors of this book—have adapted such a predisposition so as to enable it to constitute, in its adapted form, a pleasurable aspect of the pastime of rock-climbing.

Efron's piece is both scholarly and polemical. The former aspect perhaps explains what may appear as a rather excessive use of references, which the present reader is asked to be tolerant towards in view of the distorting effects of selecting a small extract; the latter aspect reminds us that the questions confronted in this section are not merely 'academic'. Efron was replying to the theorists of Nazi 'anthropology' such as Hans Günther and Fritz Lenz, who had claimed that the amount and manner of gesticulation, and the bodily posture of the individual, were racially determined. In common with Luria, Efron chooses a fascinating real-life laboratory: the United States of America with its population composed of generations of immigrants all at various stages of social and cultural integration. Efron concentrates in the bulk of his book on study of the gestural habits of first-generation and 'assimilated' Jews and Italians, and demonstrates that culture rather than race is the determining factor in gestural behaviour. In the piece we have selected here, he gives a brief historical survey of the gestural changes in different European societies—changes that can hardly be explained racially or biologically. Our own contention is that factors such as industrialization and colonialism have to be taken into account in explaining changes in gestural behaviour on the part of the English: the Industrial Revolution involved in many areas of life a suppression of personal, expressive behaviour in favour of the development of disciplined habits obedient to the needs of highly organized productive processes; the habits of the English with their 'stiff upper lip' are similarly related to the need to maintain a posture of authority in front of 'subordinate' peoples—compare the typical behaviour of policemen and customs officials.

Hastorf, Schneider and Polefka move very interestingly from an examination of people's perception of objects to that of people's perceptions of one another. The most stimulating aspect of their piece is its stress on the *active* nature of our perceptions: we are not blank sheets of paper receiving impressions passively, but active agents who, individually and collectively, shape our own perceptions. This is not to say that we 'make our own reality', but that reality makes us work to 'seize' and control it, and that through such activity alone can we become cognizant of its true nature. Hastorf *et al.* claim that 'The categories we use are derived from our past history and are dependent on our language and our cultural background.' It is interesting that the extract from their work given here contains evidence to substantiate this assertion: why, we may ask, should the alternative interpretations of the ambiguous figure taken from Robert W. Leeper's work (see p. 45 following) be labelled 'old hag' and 'attractive young woman'? Why not 'old woman' and 'young woman'? A change in our social and cultural situation has perhaps made us aware of the ways in which the society of Hastorf, Schneider and Polefka (or of Leeper) has provided them with a particular set of perceptual categories which we now find unsatisfactory.

Argyle, finally, gives us a useful inventory of the variety of verbal and non-verbal communicative means of which we are possessed. We find a certain unreadiness on Argyle's part to explain *why* cultural differentiation occurs, and perhaps too prompt a willingness to accept notions of innate communicational elements in human behaviour. This is, none the less, a piece which should open the reader's eyes to the variety of communicative resources which human beings have at their disposal.

Further reading

There are so many books on such topics as perception, non-verbal communication, interaction and ideology that students may well find selection difficult. Many of these books suffer from being based on rather behaviourist approaches, or from preferring description to explanation. In our opinion researchers in the areas of, say, perception and ideology—to choose two examples—would often benefit from an understanding of the lines of research being pursued by each other.

Berger, J. 1972: *Ways of seeing*. Harmondsworth: Penguin.
  A book which arose from a series of television programmes. Although it concentrates on examining the ways in which fine-art paintings have been and can be seen, it raises a number of crucially important questions about the cultural dimensions of human perception.
Gombrich, E. H. 1960: *Art and illusion*. New York: Pantheon.
  Another book in which human perception is studied through analysis of our response to works of art. Gombrich explores the paradox that the world does not look like a picture, but a picture can look like the world.
Gregory, R. L. 1966: *Eye and brain*. London: Weidenfeld & Nicolson.
Gregory, R. L. 1970: *The intelligent eye*. London: Weidenfeld & Nicolson.
  Both of these books are intelligent and readable introductions to the study of perception. Gregory makes much use of visual illusions so that the reader can examine his or her own perceptual processes.
Hinde, R. A. (ed) 1972: *Non-verbal communication*. Cambridge: Cambridge University Press.
  An excellent book that is strongly recommended for all Communication Studies students. In addition to sections on *Communication in animals* and *Non-verbal communication in man* there is an interesting introductory section which discusses various problems of defining

communication. Contributors include John Lyons, Michael Argyle, Edmund Leach, Jonathan Miller and E. H. Gombrich.

Kuhn, T. S. 1970: *The structure of scientific revolutions*. (Second edition.) London: University of Chicago Press.

A book that has been very influential in showing that what Kuhn calls 'paradigms'—unified sets of assumptions governing scientific investigation—are crucial in determining what scientists 'see' in their research. Weaker in explaining where paradigms come from and why they change.

Laing, R. D. 1969: *Knots*. Harmondsworth: Penguin.

Laing is a controversial figure, and his claim that mental disorders such as schizophrenia are socially determined—or do not exist at all—is now treated with increasing scepticism. Laing does, however, have an undeniable insight into the dialectical complexities of human relationships, and this book is one of the most economical explorations into the 'knots' we get into through the connections between our self-concepts, our perceptions of others, and our behaviour.

Morris, D., Collett, P., Marsh, P. and O'Shaughnessy, M. 1979: *Gestures: their origins and distribution*. London: Jonathan Cape.

A book primarily concerned with the geographical distribution, origin, and meaning of a number of 'key gestures'. Research into these matters for the book was conducted in various centres throughout Western Europe and the Mediterranean coast, and the book includes some historical and theoretical discussion. The bibliography is extremely comprehensive and very useful.

5

Cultural factors in human perception
A. R. Luria

From Luria, A. R. 1976: *Cognitive development*. Cambridge, Mass., and London: Harvard University Press, 41–5.

For a long time the notion that optical illusions differ in some cultures and that they might result from causes other than elementary physiological laws remained entirely alien to psychologists of perception. As a consequence, the literature on perception contains little data to confirm the view that optical illusions are historically conditioned.

The first investigator to suggest the cultural origins of optical illusions was W. H. R. Rivers (1901), who pointed out that the Toda people of India were much less subject to visual illusions than Europeans. He claimed that there are different classes of illusions, some more closely dependent on cultural conditions than others (for example, the illusion of vertical and horizontal line length was more frequent among the Toda people than the Müller–Lyer illusion).

The cultural and historical conditioning of illusions has received more attention during the past decade. Illusions about geometrical perspective are much more frequent among city-dwellers; among Zulus inhabiting dense forests the trapezoidal-window illusion occurs in only 14 per cent of the population, whereas it occurs in 64 per cent of the Zulus living in more open environments (Allport and Pettigrew, 1957). Psychologists have advanced the hypothesis that many optical illusions appear only under the economic conditions of city culture (the 'carpentered world'), and are encountered much less frequently among forest-dwellers living in circular wattle-and-daub huts. Hence the roots of optical illusions should be sought less in the physiological laws of visual perception than in external social and historical conditions (Segall, Campbell and Herskovits, 1963, 1966; and others).

In our study (in which Mordkovich and Gazaryants also participated), subjects in different groups observed figures that usually give rise to optical illusions, so as to determine whether these illusions appear in all cases.

We presented various types of illusions (Fig. 5.1). Some contained

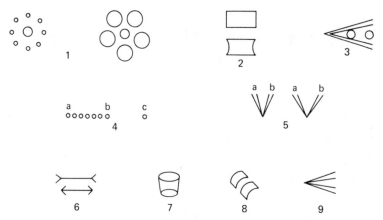

Figure 5.1 Optical illusions presented to subjects in different groups

differing figure–ground relationships; in others, some distances were 'filled in' or not; and still others involved misevaluations of some common area.

We attempted to determine whether the familiar illusion phenomena were present in all our subjects. If optical illusions were not universal, which ones specifically were retained under which conditions, and which ones were not?

It turned out that optical illusions are not universal. The number of illusions fluctuated strongly, increasing to 75.6 per cent as the educational level of the subjects rose (Table 5.1). It became apparent that even among the teachers' school students illusions did not always occur (only in 70–80 per cent of the subjects). The number of cases dropped proportionately in groups whose educational qualifications were lower. Thus the data clearly show that *optical illusions are linked to complex psychological processes that vary in accordance with sociohistorical development.*

As Table 5.1 indicates, the presence of a particular illusion varies from group to group. We can readily distinguish specific geometrical structures that yield a high percentage of illusions among subjects with a higher educational level but that give rise to no such illusions among illiterate subjects.

The Müller–Lyer illusion appears among almost all subjects (see Fig. 5.1), even among ichkari women* (two-thirds of them). Hence,

---

* Women living according to Islamic law in separate quarters which they could leave only if veiled, and who enjoyed only a very limited circle of contacts. [Editorial note]

Table 5.1   Number of optical illusions (percentages)

Group	Number of subjects	Illusion number (see Fig. 5.1)									Mean
		1	2	3	4	5	6	7	8	9	
Ichkari women	9	33.3	66.6	0	33.3	11.1	66.6	0	11.1	33.3	29.2
Peasants	25	20.8	36.8	10.5	37.5	25.0	95.8	16.6	29.1	20.8	44.7
Women in preschool courses	25	64.0	60.0	24.0	60.8	36.0	92.0	—	—	—	50.4
Collective-farm activists	40	85.0	72.5	45.0	62.5	77.5	100.0	52.5	47.5	70.0	70.2
Women at teachers' school	38	92.1	68.4	39.4	81.5	71.0	89.9	—	—	—	75.6

we may assume that the illusion is fairly elementary and independent of cognitive activity. Recent studies (Yarbus, 1967) indicate that eye motion arises from the reflex movement of the eyes over the general area occupied by the figure. This lends a fairly clear explanation to our results.

The illusions perceived primarily by educated subjects include the perspective illusion (3) and others associated with the perception of relationships among geometrical structural elements (5, 7 and 9). There is reason to assume that these illusions result from more complex mental processes and habits acquired through specialized instruction. The perception of perspective, for example, is related to education (Deregowski, 1968a and 1968b).

Our data, however, are preliminary. The mechanisms underlying these illusions might become clearer if we could hit upon a special experiment in which we could vary conditions to produce illusions at will or make them disappear. In our opinion, however, our data clearly show how perceptual processes hitherto regarded as purely physiological (and thus universal) are influenced by sociohistorical development.

We began our analysis of how history shapes consciousness by investigating particular psychological processes, specifically forms of perception usually regarded as fairly elementary and suited only to physiological analysis.

The data show that even relatively simple processes involved in perception of colours and geometrical shapes depend to a considerable extent on the subjects' practical experience and their cultural milieu.

The facts thus suggest to us that the conclusions of most current investigations of the perception of colour and shape apply in fact only to individuals shaped by cultural and academic influences, that is, persons with a system of conceptual codes for which such perception is adapted. In other sociohistorical conditions in which life experience is basically determined by practical experience and the shaping influence of school has not yet had effect, the encoding process is different because colour and shape perception fit into a different system of practical experiences, are denoted by a different system of speech terms and are subject to different laws.

6

Historical changes in gestural behaviour
David Efron

From Efron, D. 1972: *Gesture, race and culture*. Paris and The Hague: Mouton, 44–7, 53–5. (Originally published 1941 as *Gesture and environment*. New York: King's Crown Press.)

The problem of determining the factors that condition the gestural behaviour of a given human group cannot be solved by speculative assumptions nor by vague generalizations. There are only two legitimate ways of approaching it: (a) the experimental, (b) the historical.

Space forbids description of all the historical material on gestural conduct we have been able to assemble. Tempting as it is, such a description would make up a book in itself. All we can do now is to give a few examples.[1]

> Foreigners talk with their arms and hands as auxiliaries to the voice. The custom is considered vulgar by us calm Englishmen.... You have no need to act with the hands, but, if you use them at all, it should be very slightly and gracefully, never bringing down a fist upon the table, nor slapping one hand upon another, nor poking your fingers at your interlocutor. Pointing, too, is a habit to be avoided, especially pointing with the thumb over the shoulder, which is an inelegant action.... You should not be too lively in your actions....

Thus reads a passage in a treatise on good manners of the Victorian period.[2] Similar passages may be found in many other social codes of that period.

Unlike Mr Günther *et al.*, the English gentleman of 1870 does not seem to have considered gesticulation an innate impropriety, characteristic only of certain non-'Nordic' groups, but merely a 'foreign' vulgar custom, disliked by 'us calm Englishmen'. He seems to have assumed, however, that *all* Englishmen of all times were as calm and parsimonious in their expressive bodily motions as were apparently the habitués of his club. Had he spent some time looking through the window of history, instead of leisurely watching from his club window the sidewalks of an exclusive section of Victorian London, he might have learned that a good many of his ancestors of the Georgian epoch used to gesticulate as warmly as the 'foreigners' of his own lifetime. Again, had he taken the pains of visiting the British Parliament in the seventies, his belief might have been weakened before the large amount and the forcefulness of gestural movement displayed by the leading orators of that house. This may be ascertained from documents like the following. The first is an excerpt from a satirical description by Steele of a tendency apparently prevalent among the habitués of the coffee-houses of his time to manipulate the wearing apparel of the conversational partner, and to bring him over 'by force of arms'. It is taken from *The Guardian*, 13 and 15 June 1713.

There is a silly habit among many of our minor orators, who display their eloquence in the several coffee-houses of this fair city, to the no small annoyance of considerable numbers of her majesty's spruce and loving subjects, and that is a humour they have got of twisting off your buttons. These ingenious gentlemen are not able to advance three words until they have got fast hold of one of your buttons; but as soon as they have procured such an excellent handle for discourse, they will indeed proceed with great elocution. I know not how well some may have escaped, but for my part I have often met with them to my cost; having I believe within these three years last past been argued out of several dozens; insomuch that I have for sometime ordered my taylor to bring me home with every suit a dozen of spare ones, to supply the place of such as from time to time are detached as an help to discourse by the vehement gentlemen before mentioned. This way of holding a man in discourse is much practised in the coffee-houses within the city, and does not indeed so much prevail at the politer end of the town. It is likewise more frequently made use of among the small politicians, than any other body of men; I am therefore something cautious of entering into a controversy with this species of statesmen, especially the younger fry; for if you offer in the least to dissent from any thing that one of these advances, he immediately steps up to you, takes hold of one of your buttons, and indeed will soon convince you of the strength of his argumentations....

Besides the gentlemen before mentioned, there are others who are no less active in their harangues, but with gentle services rather than robberies. These while they are improving your understanding, are at the same time setting off your person; they will new-plait and adjust your neck-cloth.

But though I can bear with this kind of orator, who is so humble as to aim at the good will of his hearer by being his valet de chambre, I must rebel against another sort of them. There are some, sir, that do not stick to take a man by the collar when they have a mind to persuade him. It is your bunsiness, I humbly presume, Mr Ironside, to interpose that man is not brought over his opponent by force of arms. It were requisite therefore that you should name a certain interval, which ought to be preserved between the speaker and him to whom he speaks. For sure no man has a right, because I am not of his opinion, to take any of my clothes from me, or dress me according to his own liking. I am of the opinion that no orator or speaker in public or private has any right to meddle with anybody's clothes but his own. I indulge men in the liberty of playing with their own hats, fumbling in their own pockets, settling their own periwigs, tossing or twisting their heads, and all other gesticulations which may contribute to their elocution; but pronounce it an infringement of the English liberty of a man to keep his neighbour's person in custody in order to force a hearing; and further declare, that all assent given by an auditor under such constraint, is void and of no effect.[3]

That the gestural behaviour of many of the habitués of the London coffee-houses of Steele's time was not restricted to button-twisting and to the manipulation of the interlocutor's wearing apparel we learn from several sketches of some of these people, drawn from life by William Hogarth. Several of these will be found in Samuel Ireland's *Graphic Illustrations of Hogarth* (Vol. I, London, 1794).

. . .

Amusingly enough—and with reference to the racist theory of gestural behaviour propounded by Messrs Günther *et al.*—the Jew Disraeli, in contrast to a good many of his 'Nordic' parliamentary colleagues, 'indulged in little gesticulation. . . . He would hook his fingers in his armholes while speaking.'[4] As a matter of fact, it was precisely Lord Beaconsfield who introduced the 'Victorian' style of public delivery—that of 'matter-of-factness'—which in years to come made of gestural taciturnity an oratorical virtue.

According to some of the proponents of the racist interpretation of gesture, the French people have a natural propensity to accompany their speech with lively bodily motions. This tendency, they claim, is determined by a hereditary emotional overtness, as contrasted with what they consider a congenital affective restraint in the Anglo-Saxons.

It is rather amusing to learn that diametrically opposite 'natural' theory was held by a prominent French linguist of the sixteenth century. We are referring to Henri Estienne who, in his book on the 'italianization' of the French language, makes the categorical statement that 'Frenchmen are not gesturers by nature and dislike gesticulation'.

Estienne was engaged at that time in fustigating the upper circles of French society for having succumbed to the Italian idioms and mann- ners which were imported into France (particularly into the court of Henri II) by the Florentine retinue of Catherine de Medici. The two satirical dialogues which he wrote to that effect deal also with gestural asssimilation. The document is especially interesting in that it indicates that the French courtiers, and apparently also the Frenchmen of other social strata, of the preceding period, considered gesticulation an impolite and 'vulgar' form of behaviour. The habit of the upper-class Frenchmen of Catherine's time to use gestural movement in conversa- tion is resentfully ascribed by Estienne to the strong influence exerted in Paris by the forms of social demeanour of the Italian courtiers of the niece of Clement VII. This may be gathered from statements like the following:

Celtophile.—Voulez-vous dire qu'il-y-a du changement des personnes, non
   seulement en ce qui concerne le corps, mais aussi quant à l'esprit?
Philasvone.—Qui, quant à plusieurs, et principalement des courtisans. Car
   ils n'ont pas seulement changé d'habits ... mais aussi de gestes et con-
   tenance, mesmement d'alleure, et quasi de toutes façons de faire visitées
   en la conversation ordinaire. Voire ils en sont venus jusques à faire de
   grands vices des vertus, et de vertus en faire des vices. Et s'est faicte une
   telle revolution en leurs cerveau: qu'ils aiment ce qu'ils ont hay, et
   hayssent: ce qu'ils ont aimé. Vela pourquoi il ne vous faudra pas estonner
   quand vous serez à la court, si vous voyez que plusieurs choses qui
   estoyent trouvés fort inciuiles le temps passé, et qui aussi vraiment sentent
   leur grobianisme, y sont maintenant les fort bien venues.
Celtophile.—Et les françois italianizent-ils en [les] gestes?...
Philasvone.—... ie-ay souuenance de ce que ie vous vay dir: c'est que plusieurs s'accomodent à la mine Italiennée....[5]

Like the Victorian gentleman, the patriotic Frenchman thought that only 'foreigners' talk with their hands. Had he lived long enough to witness the development of the 'honnête homme' and the 'société polie' in France, with their 'bienséances du corps', and their norms of moderate and graceful gestural conduct, he would have probably been greatly shocked by the fact that also in that case the change was due to no small extent to Italian influence, although of an opposite character, namely: the tradition of 'regola e misura' in expressive movement, transplanted into the upper layers of seventeenth-century French society through the translated works on courteous demeanour of Castiglione, Guazzo, Grimaldi, della Casa, etc.[6] His belief in the 'natural' disinclination of the French people to gestural movement would have strongly been shaken, on the other hand, had he been able to foresee the enthusiastic liking for manual rhetorics of his co-nationals of the revolutionary and the post-Napoleonic periods, when no foreign influence was operative in that respect at all.

7

The perceptual process
Albert H. Hastorf, David J. Schneider and Judith Polefka

From Hastorf, A. H., Schneider, D. J. and Polefka, J. 1970: *Person perception*. Reading, Mass., and London: 1970, 3–9.

Both philosophers and psychologists have long been intrigued with the nature of the human perceptual process. One explanation for their interest is that man is naturally curious about his contact with the outside world and wonders how his experiences are caused and to what degree they reflect the world accurately. Beyond general curiosity, the reason for the interest stems from an apparent paradox, the basis of which lies in the difference between the nature of our experiences and our knowledge of how those experiences are caused.

Anyone who takes the trouble to think about and to describe his own experiences usually finds himself overwhelmed with both their immediacy and their structure. One's experience of the world is dominated by objects which stand out in space and which have such attributes as shape, colour, and size. The immediacy of such experiences becomes obvious if one closes his eyes, turns his head in a new direction, and then opens his eyes again. A structured world of objects is immediately present in awareness, without delay and without any consciousness of interpretative or inferential activity. The world appears to be given to us in experience. Yet a causal analysis of these events indicates a very different state of affairs.

You have opened your eyes and you experience a blue vase about six inches high situated on a table. The vase appears to be at a certain distance, and its shape and colour are equally clear. Let us remind ourselves of the causal events that are involved. Light waves of a certain wavelength are reflected off the vase. Some of them impinge on the retina of your eye, and if enough retinal cells are irritated, some visual nerves will fire and a series of electrical impulses will be carried through the sensory apparatus, including the subcortical centres, and will finally arrive at the cortex. This description paints a picture of a very indirect contact with the world: light waves to retinal events to sensory nerve events to subcortical events and finally to cortical events, from which visual experiences result. What is especially important is that this causal description reveals a very different picture than does our naive description of experience. (This causal description led a famous German physiologist to remark that 'we are aware of our nerves, not of objects'.) Thus we have a conflict between our everyday-life experiences of objects together with their properties and an analysis of how these experiences come to exist. How *does* the human being create a coherent perceptual world out of chaotic physical impingements?

Our world of experience has structure

Let us begin with this fact of experience and explore how the structure may be achieved. First of all, we know that our experiences are ultimately dependent on our sensory apparatus, which for visual experiences would include both the retina of the eye and the sensory neurons connecting the retina to the visual areas of the cortex. This apparatus plays, in a manner of speaking, the role of translator Light waves impinge on the eyes and we experience colour. Sound waves impinge on the ear and we experience pitch. Without the sensory apparatus we would have no contact with the external world. There remains, however, the question of the nature of this translation.

A number of philosophers and psychologists have conceived of the translation process as an essentially passive one, completely determined by the physical properties of the stimulus and by the structure of the receptors and sensory nervous system. They conceive of our sensory apparatus as working somewhat like a high-speed translation device. Physical impingements are looked up and the proper experiential attribute is read out. This conception has led to arguments as to how much of this dictionary is present at birth and how much is the product of our learning history. One reason for the popularity of the passive recording view of perception is the immediacy and 'givenness' of our experience. Our experiences are immediate and they feel direct. These feelings led to the belief that the translation process must be automatic and built in.

The primary argument against that position stems from the fact that our experience of the world is highly selective. If we passively translated and recorded stimuli, our world would be a jumble of experiences; while you were reading a book, you would also be aware of the pressure of your clothes on your body and of all the sounds around you. Actually, from a myriad of impinging stimuli, we are aware of only certain objects and certain attributes of the objects.

Anyone who has asked two different persons to describe the same scene has been struck by the fact that they often describe it very differently; each selects different events and different attributes of the events. Given this phenomenon, we must be more than passive translators. In fact, we must be active processors of information. The world is not merely revealed to us; rather, we play an active role in the creation of our experiences.

Let us take an example from the research of Robert W. Leeper to illustrate our point (Leeper, 1935). The stimulus he used was an ambiguous picture which can be seen as either an old hag or an atttactive young woman (Fig. 7.1a). Continued inspection of the picture usually

(a) (b) (c)

Figure 7.1

permits an observer to see first one and then the other. Leeper had the original picture redrawn so that one version emphasized the young woman (b) and another emphasized the old hag (c). Subjects who had been exposed to one or the other of these redrawings found themselves 'locked in' on that view when the original ambiguous picture was presented. One hundred per cent of the subjects who had had prior experience with the version emphasizing the hag saw the hag and only the hag in their first look at the ambiguous picture; 95 per cent of the subjects who had had prior experience with the version emphasizing the young woman saw only the young woman when first looking at the same ambiguous picture. The subjects had been given a set to process the input stimuli in a certain way, and they created a structure consistent with that set. Although our experiences are both immediate and structured, extremely complex participation by the organism, including the active selection and processing of stimulus impingements, is involved in their creation.

One of the most salient features of the person's participation in structuring his experiential world can be described as a categorizing process. He extracts stimuli from the world and forces them into a set of categories. We have here a powerful example of the effects of linguistic coding on the structuring of experience. The subjects in Leeper's experiment did not see a complex pattern of light and dark nor even 'a person' (a possible category); they saw an old hag or a young woman. The categories we use are derived from our past history and are dependent on our language and our cultural background. Some of these categories are markedly ubiquitous and well agreed on by perceivers. Classification of objects according to the attributes of size and shape seems obvious, but some persons may employ different sets of categories. For example, they may perceive in terms of colour and softness. Moreover, there are occasions when all of us change categories in perceiving objects. Instead of size and colour, we may see things in terms of function: the large blue pen and the small green pencil are suddenly similar when we want only to jot down a telephone number. Whatever the nature of the categories we use, they play an important role in the processing of information.

We have begun with the experiential fact that our perceptions are both structured and organized. This structure is immediate and appears to be given by the world of objects. We have argued that a causal analysis of the situation clearly indicates that structured perceptions are the outcome of the organism's engaging in active processing of information, which includes the translation of physical impingements to nerve impulses and the active selection and categorizing of the inputs.

Our world of experience has stability

When we open our eyes and look at a scene, we are not overwhelmed with constant shifts in the picture as our eyes and our attention wander. There is a certain enduring aspect to our experience. We select certain facets of the situation and stick with them. Check this statement against your own experience with the ambiguous picture in Fig. 7.1. If it was like the experience of most people, the first organization of the picture, whether it was the old hag or the young woman, continued to demand your attention. It was hard to 'find' the other one. You made various attempts to shift the focus of attention by blinking your eyes or by concentrating on a certain part of the picture, but those strategems did not always work. Although stability in a case of this kind may frustrate us to such an extent that it deserves to be given a different and more pejorative label—rigidity—the example demonstrates that we do *not* experience a world of chaotic instability.

The most obvious example of the maintenance of stability in our experience has been termed *the constancies* in perception. Constancy phenomena have been most carefully described in regard to the perception of size, colour, shape, and brightness. Let us consider an example. You are sitting in a chair in your living room. Another person walks into the room, moves over to a table by the window, picks up a magazine, and then goes across the room to sit down and read it. What are the successive visual-stimulus events impinging on your retina and your successive experiences? Every time the person moves closer to you, the impingement, or *proximal stimulus*, gets larger; in fact, if he moves from 20 feet away to 10 feet away, the height of the image on your eye doubles in size. The opposite occurs as he moves away from you because the size of the retinal image is inversely proportional to the distance of the object from you. Furthermore, when the person moves near the window, more light is available and more light is reflected to the retina. Yet your perception does not fit this description of the stimulus events. While the person is moving about the room, you experience him as remaining relatively constant in size and brightness. In spite of dramatic alterations in the proximal stimulus, you experience a stable world. Given this discrepancy between proximal-stimulus events and experience, the organism must actively process information to produce the stability in his world of experience.

Psychologists are not in total agreement as to how this information-processing takes place, but certain general characteristics of the organism's contribution are apparent. The organism seems to seek *invariance*; that is, he perceives as constant those aspects of the physical world which are most enduring, e.g. size and shape, even though the information he has about them may change radically. The perceived invariance seems to depend on the ability of the organism to combine information from different sources, and to result from the application of equations which define proximal stimulation as a joint function of the distal stimulus (the object) and environmental mediating factors, such as distance and incident illumination. For example, our person moving about the room is always the same height, say six feet. The height of the retinal image, on the other hand, varies, but it is always a constant direct function of his height and an inverse function of his distance from the observer. An invariant function exists:

$$\text{Proximal size} = K \times \frac{\text{Distal size}}{\text{Distance}}$$

Figure 7.2 illustrates the relationships. Note that K is the distance from the lens to the retina, which is assumed to be constant. The invariant relationship allows the formula to be 'solved' by the perceiver; e.g., knowing retinal size and estimating distance, one can arrive at an estimate of the size of the object. By applying this invariant relationship to a particular case, the perceiver can account for variation in proximal size and perceive the object as of a constant size, as he knows from other experiences it must be. Finding invariance by applying relationships such as the above requires the processing of considerable

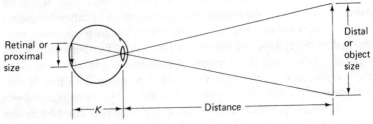

Figure 7.2

amounts of information, including the physical size of the object, distance, and illumination; and the information-processing involved in this kind of perceptual act must be quite complicated.

Let us think of the perceptual act as a complex form of problem-solving, the goal of which is to create a stability in which our perceptions bear some relationship to external events. We can then draw an analogy between perceptual problem-solving and scientific problem-solving. Just as the scientist attempts to reduce a complex jumble of events to a small set of variables which serve as a set of determining conditions for a particular event, so we search out the invariant aspects of a situation to produce stable perceptions. The scientist searches for invariance in order to understand and to predict the world; we as perceivers also seek to understand and to predict the world in order that we may behave in it to our advantage. In other words, the perceptual act can be said to generate a prediction that we can use as a basis for action. The goal in both cases is predictability of the environment, and the means to the goal is the specification of causal relationships.

Our world of experience is meaningful

The connotation of 'meaningful' here is that structured and stable events are not isolated from one another but appear to be related in some orderly fashion over time. Both structure and stability are probably necessary for meaning to exist. It is so common for the world of experience to make sense to us that the most powerful way to point out the importance of the phenomenon is to suggest trying to conceive of a world that does not make sense. Events would follow each other with no apparent causal relationships. Almost every event would entail surprise. Nothing would seem familiar. The general experience would be one of chaos. Such a state of affairs is so alien to our everyday-life experience that it is extremely difficult to imagine. Our experiences usually *are* meaningful in that they are structured and they are stable; they are related in the sense that they seem familiar, but particularly in the sense that events have implications for one another.

We must look at the organism as an active processor of input stimuli who categorizes stimulus events and relates them to both past and present events. One property of the organism as an information processor is that he possesses a linguistic coding system which possesses a set of implicative relationships. The impinging stimuli provide the raw material; the organism, with the aid of language, produces the meaning. The organism exists in time: he has a past and he anticipates the future. Past experience, language, and present motivational state or goals for the future influence our perceptions of the present. Our past learning has a significant influence on perception, but it always operates within a framework of purposive activity. The experience-derived rules we apply are selected by the purposes we are trying to accomplish. The perceptual process is an achievement by the organism, and perception would not exist without active problem-solving on the part of the perceiver. Our perceptions do have meaning, they do make sense; and meaning and sense derive from both our own past experiences and our present purposes. Without the presence of meaning and sense as active, organizing agents, perception, as we know it, would not exist.

8

Verbal and non-verbal communication
Michael Argyle

From Argyle, M. 1972: *The psychology of interpersonal behaviour*. Harmondsworth: Penguin Books (Pelican Original), 37–50.

Different kinds of social act

1. *Bodily contact* is of interest since it is the most primitive kind of social act, and is found in all animals. In addition to aggressive and sexual contacts there are various methods of influence, as when others are pushed, pulled or led. There are symbolic contacts, such as patting on the back, and the various ways of shaking hands. Outside the family, bodily contact is mainly restricted to the hands. Jourard (1966) has surveyed who has been touched by whom and where, and his results for American students are shown in Fig 8.1. It can be seen that there are great differences in who is touched by whom, and on which parts of their anatomy.

There are great cross-cultural differences in bodily contact, and this form of social behaviour is less common in Britain than almost anywhere else. It usually conveys intimacy, and occurs at the beginning and end of encounters. There has been some interest in 'encounter groups' in the USA and Britain during recent years. The greater use of bodily contact here is found to be exciting and disturbing—but it must be remembered that those concerned have been brought up in cultures in which there are strong restraints against bodily contact, and will have internalized these restraints.

2. *Physical proximity* is important mainly in relation to intimacy and dominance. It is one of the cues for intimacy, both sexual and between friends of the same sex. The normal degree of proximity varies between cultures and every species of animal has its characteristic social distance. The significance of physical proximity varies with the physical surroundings—proximity to the point of bodily contact in a lift has no affiliative significance, and it is noteworthy that eye-contact and conversation are avoided here. If A sits near B, it makes a difference whether there are other places where A could have sat, whether he is directly facing B or at an angle, and whether there is

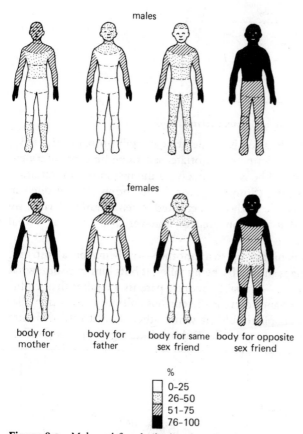

males

females

body for
mother

body for
father

body for same
sex friend

body for opposite
sex friend

%
☐ 0-25
▦ 26-50
▨ 51-75
■ 76-100

Figure 8.1 Male and female 'bodies-for-others', as experienced through the amount of touching received from others (Jourard, 1966)

any physical barrier. Closer distances are adopted for more intimate conversations: at the closest distances different sensory modes are used—touch and smell come into operation, and vision becomes less important (Hall, 1963). It is found that people sit or stand closer to people that they like. There are also large cross-cultural differences— Arabs and Latin Americans stand very close, Swedes and Scots are the most distant (Lott *et al.*, 1969). *Changes* of proximity are of course used to signal the wish to begin or end an encounter, accompanied by other appropriate messages.

3. *Orientation* signals interpersonal attitudes. If person A is sitting at a table, as shown in Fig. 8.2, B can sit in several different places. If

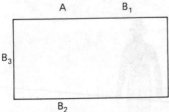

Figure 8.2 Orientation in different relationships

he is told that the situation is cooperative he will probably sit at B_1; if he is told he is to compete, negotiate, sell something or interview A, he will sit at B_2; if he is told to have a discussion or conversation he usually chooses B_3 (Sommer, 1965). This shows (a) that one can become more sensitive to the cues emitted, often unintentionally, by others, and (b) that one can control non-verbal as well as verbal signals.

If one person is higher up than another—by being on a rostrum, standing, or perhaps simply by being taller, it puts him in a somewhat dominating position—probably because parents are taller than children. On the other hand, there is the curious cultural convention that more important people should sit while others have to stand. Hutte and Cohen in Holland made silent films of managers entering offices

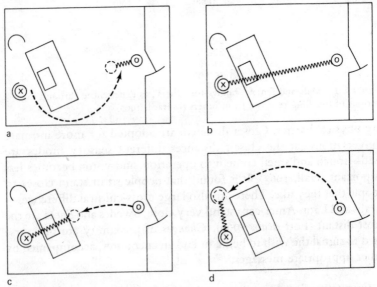

Figure 8.3 Key movements between men in an office indicating their relationship (Burns, 1964)

of other managers. It was quite clear to subjects who were shown these films which manager was the senior (in a and c), and how friendly they were (in b and d) (Burns, 1964; see also Fig. 8.3).

4. *Bodily posture* is another signal which is largely involuntary, but which can communicate important social signals. There are distinctive 'superior' (or dominant) and 'inferior' (or submissive) postures. The desire or intention to dominate can be signalled by standing erect, with the head tilted back, and with hands on hips, for example. There are also friendly, and hostile postures. (See Fig. 8.4.)

Figure 8.4 The meaning of bodily postures (Sarbin and Hardyck, 1953)

By his general bodily posture a person may signal his emotional state, e.g. tense versus relaxed. He can show his attitude to the others present—as when a person sits in a different way from the others, or puts his feet on the table.

People also have general styles of expressive behaviour, as shown in the way they walk, stand, sit and so on. This may reflect past or present roles—as in the case of a person who is or has been a soldier; it also reflects a person's self-image, self-confidence, and emotional state. It is very dependent on cultural fashions:

> In a street market I watched a working-class mum and her daughter. The mother waddled as if her feet were playing her up. Outside a Knightsbridge hotel I watched an upper-class mum and her daughter come out from a wedding reception and walk towards Hyde Park Corner, the mother on very thin legs slightly bowed as though she had wet herself. She controlled her body as if it might snap if moved too impulsively. Both daughters walked identically (Melly, 1965).

5. *Gestures* are movements of hands, feet or other parts of the body. Some are intended to communicate definite messages; others are involuntary social cues which may or may not be correctly interpreted by others.

Communicating emotional states. When a person is emotionally aroused he produces diffuse, apparently pointless, bodily movements. A nervous lecturer may work as hard as a manual labourer. More specific emotions produce particular gestures—fist clenching (aggression), face-touching (anxiety), scratching (self-blame), forehead-wiping (tiredness) etc. (Ekman and Friesen, 1969).

Completing the meaning of utterances. It has been found that while a person speaks he moves his hands, body and head continuously, that these movements are closely coordinated with speech, and that they form part of the total communication. He may (1) display the structure of the utterance by enumerating elements or showing how they are grouped, (2) point to people or objects, (3) provide emphasis, and (4) give illustrations of shapes, sizes or movements (Scheflen, 1965; Kendon, 1972).

Replacing speech. When speech is impossible for one reason or another, gesture languages develop.

6. *Head-nods* are a rather special kind of gesture, and have two distinctive roles. They act as 'reinforcers', i.e. they reward and encourage what has gone before, and can be used to make another talk more, for example. Head-nods also play an important role in controlling

the synchronizing of speech—in Britain a nod gives the other permission to carry on talking, whereas a rapid succession of nods indicates that the nodder wants to speak himself.

7. *Facial expression* can be reduced to changes in eyes, brows, mouth, and so on. The face is an area which is used by animals to communicate emotions and attitudes to others; for humans it does not work so well since we control our facial expression, and may smile sweetly while seething within. Emotions can be recognized to some extent from

Figure 8.5   The dimensions of facial expression (Schlosberg, 1952)

facial expression alone, as is shown by studies using still photographs of actors. Emotions can be recognized in terms of broad categories—for example, the pleasant and unpleasant ones—but those which are similar are harder to tell apart. The above circle (Fig. 8.5) shows which are seen as most similar to one another—those furthest apart are the easiest to distinguish. In addition to these states, it is possible to recognize degrees of emotional tension—by perspiration on the forehead and expansion of the pupils of the eyes.

Facial expression works rather better as a way of providing feedback on what another is saying. The eyebrows provide a continuous running commentary, going from:

fully raised   —disbelief
half raised   —surprise
normal   —no comment
half lowered   —puzzled
fully lowered—angry.

The area round the mouth adds to the running commentary by varying between being turned up (pleasure) and turned down (displeasure).

8. *Eye movements* have an effect quite out of proportion to the physical effort exerted. When A looks at B, in the region of the eyes, B knows that A is attending primarily to him, and that interaction can proceed. If A gazes for a long time at B, this can have a variety of meanings, depending on A's facial expression and on the situation—it can be an amorous, friendly, aggressive or curious gaze—in each case revealing something of A's feelings towards B. Glances can be long or short, furtive or open, and can combine together to form complex strategies of eye-play. Eye movements play an important part in sustaining the flow of interaction: while A is speaking he looks up to get feedback on how B is responding, and he ends a long utterance with a gaze which tells B that it is his turn to speak. When there is eye-contact between two people this is experienced as a heightening of interpersonal emotions, usually in the sense of greater intimacy.

9. *Appearance*. Many aspects of personal appearance are under voluntary control, and a great deal of effort is put into controlling them—clothes, hair and skin; other aspects can be modified to some extent by clothes and plastic surgery. The main purpose of this manipulation of appearance is self-presentation—signalling how the presenter sees himself and would like to be treated.

10. *Non-linguistic aspects of speech*. The same words may be said in quite different ways, conveying different emotional expressions, and even different meanings, as when 'yes' is used as a polite way of saying 'no'. Davitz (1964) found that when actors read out an emotionally neutral passage to express different emotional states, these were recognizable by judges about 60 or 70 per cent of the time. The emotions

in question were: admiration, affection, amusement, anger, boredom, cheerfulness, despair, disgust, dislike, fear, impatience, joy, satisfaction and surprise. The author has used this method as a means of sensitivity training. Some people are much better at making such judgements than others. Several aspects of voice quality are involved—loudness, pitch, speed, voice quality (such as breathiness, or breaking to incipient tears), and smoothness. These aspects of speech are correlated, though not perfectly, with emotional states. For example, an anxious person tends to talk faster than normal and at a higher pitch. A depressed person talks slowly, and at a lower pitch; an aggressive person talks loudly.

The pattern of pauses, stress and pitch is really part of the verbal utterance itself. Pauses provide punctuation (instead of saying 'full stop' as when dictating); stress and pitch show whether a question is being asked and provide emphasis, thus showing which of several possible meanings is intended (Crystal, 1969).

There are non-linguistic aspects of the conversation as a whole— the patterns of speech and silence—how much of the time each person talks, how fast, how soon after the other stops, and so on. Chapple (1956) has shown that people have characteristic ways of reacting to interruption and silence on the part of another. In his 'standard interview' the subject is first interviewed in a relaxed manner; later follows a period in which the interviewer fails to respond to twelve successive utterances by the subject, and another period during which the interviewer interrupts twelve successive speeches by the subject. Some people yield at once if interrupted, while others try to talk the interrupter down. Some people cannot tolerate silence, and will speak again if the interviewer is silent.

Another non-verbal aspect of speech is the rate of speech errors. These are of two main kinds—'ah's and 'er's, and 'non-ah' errors like changes of sentence, repetitions, stutters, etc. 'Non-ah' errors are caused by anxiety; 'ah's and 'er's are not, and seem to be used to create time to think and decide what to say next (Cook, 1969).

11. *Speech* is the most complex, subtle and characteristically human means of communication. Most animal noises simply communicate emotional states. Human speech is different in that it is learned, can convey information about external events, and has a grammatical structure. But it still consists of a set of learned social techniques which are used to influence others. There are great differences in the skill of individuals at using language, mainly associated with intelligence,

education and training, and social class. A large part of most social skills lies in putting together utterances which are tactful, persuasive, or whatever is required.

Speech is used to ask questions. These are of interest as they lead to further interaction, and to information about others. Some forms of encounter, such as the interview, consist entirely of questions and the answers to them. Questions vary in the extent to which they are open or closed—an open-ended question requires a lengthy explanation rather than a choice between alternatives; the best way to get someone to talk is to ask this kind of question.

Speech can be used to convey information to others, in answer to questions, as part of the work of committees or work-teams, in lectures, and elsewhere. The speaker may be reporting facts, giving his opinions, or arguing on the basis of these. Such communications are often imperfectly received, because the speaker has not made himself sufficiently clear, or because the hearer attaches different meaning to words or phrases. Ideally, both should speak exactly the same language, i.e. where every sentence carries the identical penumbra of meanings and implications.

Thirdly, speech is used more directly to influence the behaviour of others, by means of instructions or orders, persuasion and propaganda, as well as by aggressive remarks – which may be used when all else fails. Aggressive speech occurs in a variety of forms, of which the milder ones are gentle ridicule and teasing, and the more severe are direct insults.

A lot of speech is not primarily intended to communicate anything very serious, or to solve any problems. Informal speech, as it is called, is more concerned with establishing, sustaining and enjoying social relationships – chat, idle gossip, and joke-telling between friends or family members, or during coffee breaks at work. It has been found that about half of the very expensive conversation over the trans-Atlantic telephone is of this kind. Formal speech, as in a well-delivered lecture, is more concise, conveys information clearly, and is more like written language in structure.

Speech can also be concerned with the process of social interaction itself. This may be acceptable in clinical or training situations, but can be very disturbing in other encounters, when for example someone says 'There's an awkward silence, isn't there.' Words may be used to provide rewards and punishments; in fact this happens continually in the course of interaction, but is largely unintended.

Utterances vary in a number of ways; they can be intimate or impersonal, easy, abstract or technical, interesting or boring to the hearer. In specialized forms of social encounter particular kinds of utterance may be important, like 'interpretation' during psycho-analysis, 'follow-up questions' in an interview, etc. The joke is a special kind of verbal utterance, which has the effect of relieving ten-sion and creating euphoria in social situations. Speeches may have latent meanings, as when the speaker reveals something additional to the main message. This may be unintended, as with the speaker who was asked if he had ever been to Nigeria and replied 'that's a place I've not been to' (Brown, 1965). Or it may be intentional as when a schoolboy says 'Please, Sir, the board's shining' (when it isn't).

Three roles of non-verbal communication

Non-verbal communication (NVC) functions in three rather dif-ferent ways (Argyle, 1972).

1. *Communicating interpersonal attitudes and emotions.* Animals conduct their entire social life by means of NVC—they make friends, find mates, rear children, establish dominance hierarchies, and cooperate in groups, by means of facial expression, postures, gestures, grunting and barking noises, etc. It looks as if much the same is true of humans too. Argyle *et al.* (1970) carried out an experiment in which superior, equal and inferior verbal messages were delivered in superior, equal and inferior non-verbal styles, nine combinations in all, by speakers recorded on video-tapes. Two of the verbal messages were as follows:

> (1) It is probably quite a good thing for you subjects to come along to help in these experiments because it gives you a small glimpse of what psychological research is about. In fact the whole process is far more com-plex that you would be able to appreciate without a considerable training in research methods, paralinguistics, kinesic analysis, and so on.
>
> (2) These experiments must seem rather silly to you and I'm afraid they are not really concerned with anything very interesting and impor-tant. We'd be very glad if you could spare us a few moments afterwards to tell us how we could improve the experiment. We feel that we are not making a very good job of it, and feel rather guilty about wasting the time of busy people like yourself.

Some of the results are shown in Fig. 8.6 on p. 60.

It can be seen that the non-verbal style had more effect than the verbal contents, in fact about five times as much; when the verbal and non-verbal messages were in conflict, the verbal contents were virtually

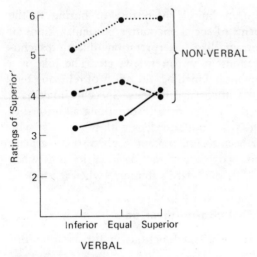

Figure 8.6   Interactions between verbal and non-verbal cues (Argyle *et al.*, 1970) ......, superior; -----, equal; ——, inferior

disregarded. Much the same results were obtained in another experiment on the friendly–hostile dimension.

The explanation of these results is probably that there is an innate biological basis to these NV signals, which evoke an immediate and powerful emotional response—as in animals. In human social behaviour it looks as if the NV channel is used for negotiating interpersonal attitudes, while the verbal channel is used primarily for conveying information.

2. *Supporting verbal communication.* Linguists recognize that timing, pitch and stress are integral to the meaning of utterances, e.g. by providing punctuation. A few linguists recognize that NVC plays a more extensive part—'We speak with our vocal organs, but we converse with our whole body (Abercrombie, 1968).

Completing the meaning of utterances. In addition to the *vocal* signals of timing, pitch and stress, *gestural* signals also add to meaning—by illustrating, pointing, displaying structure, etc. Frame-by-frame analysis of conversations has shown that there is a linkage between gesture and speech down to the level of the word, and that there is a hierarchical structure of gesture, where the larger movements correspond to larger verbal units, like paragraphs (Kendon, 1972). These fine movements are unintended, often unseen, and idiosyncratic, so that their full explanation is not known.

Controlling synchronizing. When two or more people are conversing they must take it in turns to speak, and usually achieve a fairly smooth pattern of synchronizing. This is done by the use of non-verbal signals such as shifts of gaze, head-nods, and grunts.

Obtaining feedback. When a person is speaking he needs feedback on how the others are responding, so that he can modify his remarks accordingly. He needs to know whether his listeners understand, believe him, are surprised or bored, agree or disagree, are pleased or annoyed. This information could be provided by *sotto voce* muttering, but is in fact obtained from careful study of the other's face, especially his eyebrows and mouth.

Signalling attentiveness. For an encounter to be sustained, those involved must provide intermittent evidence that they are still attending to the others. They should not fall asleep, look out of the window, or read the paper; they should be at the right distance, in the right orientation, look up frequently, nod their heads, adopt an alert, congruent position, and react to the speaker's bodily movements.

3. *Replacing speech.* When speech is impossible, gesture languages develop. This happens in noisy factories, the army, racecourses, and underwater swimming. Some of these languages are complex and enable elaborate messages to be sent, though rather slowly, as in deaf-and-dumb language, and the sign language used by some Australian aboriginals.

It has been suggested by some psychiatrists that the symptoms of certain mental patients are a kind of NVC used when speech has failed—in pursuit of attention or love.

Section III
Language, thought, culture

Our intention in this section is not to concentrate narrowly upon language as a 'medium' of communication—language treated almost as a transport system for ideas, a transport system which can be subjected to detailed analysis and description. The section is, rather, concerned to investigate the relationship between language, distinctively human capacities and qualities, and social, cultural and historical factors. Thus we start off with an extract which we hope will set the reader thinking about the extraordinary richness and uniqueness of language by contrasting it with the communication systems of various animals. Language is so close to us—it is a necessary part of what we are—that it is often difficult to think about it without comparing it with systems which lack many of its attributes. We hope that this section will help the reader to appreciate that language does not just allow human beings to *do* certain things, but to *be* human in the first place. Human beings have complex and unique interlocking relationships with their environment, their history, one another, and themselves which are constituted by as well as mediated through language.

Amongst the characteristics of language which are discussed in our first extract by Aitchison we would draw particular attention to *displacement* and *cultural transmission*, as these are important for a full understanding of later discussions in this section. Aitchison points out—albeit with a certain amount of deliberate humour—that the lack of displacement in bee-communication systems is one of the reasons why a bee cannot say such things as 'I wonder whether there's good nectar in Siberia'. Interestingly enough this example calls to mind some of the abilities which, according to Luria, those without the skills of literacy or formal education also lack. We can surmise that one effect of formal education is that the potentialities implicit in this quality of displacement are developed, with a resultant development of mental powers and, in particular, of creative imagination.

Cultural transmission, to take our second characteristic, means that human language is more responsive to social and cultural changes, less to be understood purely in terms of the operation of a biological mechanism.

Language study has traditionally concentrated upon two separate approaches—the *synchronic* (language seen as a complete system at a given instant of time) and the *diachronic* or historical (language as it evolves over time). The former approach has been very influential in a number of fields in the present century, including several outside of the study of language—the anthropological study of complete cultures for instance. Our second extract from Barthes is representative of this approach, and details very briefly the key contribution to the study of language of Saussure. The positive aspect of such an approach, in our opinion, is that it stresses the social rather than the purely individual aspects of language. Its shortcoming, again in our opinion, is that it is vulnerable to a certain formalism, abstracting language from the *particular* social and temporal contexts within which it has to be set to be understood. Study of language independent of such contexts is, we believe, much like a study of a motor-car which neglects the contexts in which cars were invented, used, developed, and which they in turn affected. Such a study—by Martians, who had taken a car back to Mars after a fleeting visit—might *describe* in great detail, but it could hardly *explain*. Indeed, even the description might be hopelessly inappropriate: there are thousands of ways one can describe a wheel, but without knowing what it has been developed to do one has no means of choosing between them.

To extend our simile, we can say that if our Martians assumed that the car had been designed and built 'at a stroke', rather than having evolved through painful trial and error in a changing set of contexts, then again they might misunderstand why it was as it was. This, at any rate, is the sort of criticism that has been levelled at the more formalist of synchronic approaches. Geoffrey Sampson (1978), discussing Chomsky's work, has suggested that Chomsky's adoption of the 'simplifying assumption' that 'learning can be conceptualized as an instantaneous process' is enormously question-begging; we would agree, and add that in our view such an assumption misrepresents rather than simplifies, as it ignores crucial, determining relationships between language, culture and history. The Soviet writer V. N. Vološinov (1973, 95) expresses cogently the objection to any isolated study of abstract 'systems' alone:

> The actual reality of language-speech is not the abstract system of linguistic forms, not the isolated monologic utterance, and not the psycho-

physiological act of its implementation, but the social event of verbal interaction implemented in an utterance or utterances.

Our extract from Searle's *Speech Acts*, therefore, follows logically on from the Barthes piece as it complements Barthes's synchronic approach by an investigation which approaches a consideration of language through the study of utterances, or speech acts. The individual speech act is, in our opinion, just one of the interlocking contexts which constitute language and in which language must be studied. To ignore such contexts is to run the risk of being led to explain all language characteristics as innate, and it would seem that some writers have fallen into the trap of explaining language purely biologically precisely because without culture, society and history, biology is all that they have left to explain why languages should be as they are.

Searle's emphasis on speech acts is a timely reminder that for the contemporary, literate individual as well as for the human race historically, speech has always preceded writing. Indeed, Vološinov has argued that language study has been distorted by the historical emphasis on the examination of written records from dead languages. Speech always takes place within a determining context which is more or less apparent; writing, on the other hand, is more displaced than speech, it involves none of those paralinguistic and non-verbal features informing speech about which Michael Argyle talks in the extract in our previous section.

Certainly, if it is dangerous to abstract language absolutely from the context of *individual* speech utterances, it is disastrous to abstract it from culture and history. The pieces from Luria, Bernstein and Pateman all consider the ways in which language, through the development of specific language practices, habits and abilities, is involved in the process whereby we internalize different attitudes and relationships to the world, other people and ourselves. It should be stressed that, in Saussure's terminology (see the Barthes extract), all the above are talking of *parole* rather than *langue*. Leonard Jackson (1974) has pointed out that Bernstein's 'codes' (a bad choice of term in our view) are not *linguistic*: a linguistician could not find any formal linguistic capacities of which Bernstein's 'middle-class children' were possessed but which his 'working-class children' lacked. Bernstein is wise, we feel, to modify the terminology he uses in the extract given so as to allow him to talk of *socio-linguistic* rather than *linguistic* codes. It is not that people of different social classes somehow speak different languages but rather that social and cultural factors of power and knowledge are internalized in the individual's language habits and capacities. These social and cultural factors which are related to social structure act on and through the individual not as simple one-stage 'causes', but through complex processes of reinforcement, alone or in conjunction with others, at different times.

Pateman's piece can be seen as a development of Bernstein's assertion that:

> Historically, and now, only a tiny percentage of the population has been socialized into knowledge at the level of the meta-languages of control and innovation, whereas the mass of the population has been socialized into knowledge at the level of context-tied operations.
>
> (See p. 92 following)

Similarly, although in one sense Luria's untutored subjects speak the same language as their interviewer, they too have been socialized into knowledge at the level of context-tied operations, while their newly educated, younger compatriots are being socialized into at least some of the meta-languages of control and innovation of which Bernstein speaks. There are some things that the person lacking both literacy and formal education appears not to be able to think, and this inability is both a function of the society to which he or she belongs and in which he or she has an ascribed role, and also, at the same time, is a realization of the language resources available to him or her.

Further reading

One of the more encouraging developments in the general area of the study of language is that work crossing single-discipline frontiers is becoming far more widespread. Linguisticians are likely nowadays to be well versed in the philosophy of language; psycholinguistics is increasingly informed by a knowledge of research into the social aspects of language acquisition and use. A developing interest in language in use—*parole* rather than *langue*—is perhaps both cause and result of such a movement. In spite of this the student should remember that the study of language involves a number of different areas of research each with their traditions, foci of interest, and vocabulary. All of the following, however, should be found accessible to the relatively uninformed inquirer.

Chao, Y. R. 1968: *Language and symbolic systems*. Cambridge: Cambridge University Press.
   One of the most accessible general introductions to language, which

covers such topics as phonetics, phonemics, language change, writing and the languages of the world. The chapter on symbolic systems will interest many Communication Studies students.

Chomsky, N. 1959: Review of Skinner's *Verbal behavior, Language* **35**, 26–58.

Of all Chomsky's work this is perhaps that which comes closest to the issues dealt with in this section of the Reader. In it Chomsky sets out most clearly his objections to empiricist approaches.

Boyle, D. G. 1971: *Language and thinking in human development*. London: Hutchinson.

Written by a psychologist, this book offers a useful survey of psychological approaches to the study of language and its relationship with mental processes and human growth. Boyle suggests that Piaget's work 'offers a more consistent and comprehensive attempt to give an account of man in relation to his environment than any other at the present time'.

Halliday, M. A.K. 1978: *Language as social semiotic*. London: Edward Arnold.

A useful collection of essays in which the author attempts to interpret linguistic processes in the context of the social order, in contrast to what he sees as the prevailing mode of studying language through concern with the individual mind. There are various interesting comments on the work of Bernstein and Labov, and on the difference between dialect and register.

Levitas, M. 1974: *Marxist perspectives in the sociology of education*. London: Routledge.

Contains a very useful chapter on language and deprivation in which Levitas suggests that Bernstein diverges from Vygotsky (one of his acknowledged sources) by failing to stress that 'a restricted code is an inferior one' because (according to Vygotsky and Luria) it 'is a lower stage of linguistic development'.

Luria, A. R. and Yudovich, F. La. 1971: *Speech and the development of mental processes in the child*. Edited by Joan Simon and with a new introduction by James Britton. Harmondsworth: Penguin.

Extremely readable account of 'Luria's twins': two brothers whose language development is impaired by their ability to communicate non-verbally. Luria's success in effecting a significant improvement in their linguistic and mental development through separating them and giving them formal instruction has important implications.

Open University language and learning course team (eds) 1972: *Language in education*. London: Routledge.

A very useful collection of key essays and extracts, with sections on (among other things) *Language and social reality, Social relationships and language codes,* and *Language acquisition: language and thought.* Includes W. Labov's important critique of Bernstein's theories: 'The logic of nonstandard English'.

Open University E201 course team 1976: Language as a mould to thought? In *Cultural influences on cognition and attainment.* Open University course E201 block 8 section 4. Milton Keynes: Open University Press.

A clear and succinct critique of the theories of Whorf and Sapir which raises some of the most important questions and problems involving the relationship between language and thought.

Vygotsky, L. 1962: *Thought and language.* Translated by Eugenia Hanfmann and Gertrude Vakar. Cambridge, Mass.: MIT Press.

One of the most influential books on this subject which laid foundations which have been built on by many later writers—especially in the Soviet Union. First published in Russian in 1934 the book argues for a complex and shifting relationship between thought and language, whereby developments in each are built on, and facilitate, developments in the other.

9

Defining language
Jean Aitchison

From Aitchison, J. 1976: *The articulate mammal*. London: Hutchinson, 36–43.

A useful first step might be to attempt to define 'language'. This is
not as easy as it sounds. Most of the definitions found in elementary
textbooks are too wide. For example: 'The faculty of language consists in man's ability to make noises with the vocal organs and marks
on paper or some other material, by means of which groups of people
"speaking the same language" are able to interact and cooperate as
a group' (Robins, 1971, 12). This definition, if one ignores the word
'man' and the phrase involving 'marks on paper', might equally well
apply to a pack of wolves howling in chorus.

Perhaps the most promising approach is that suggested by the linguist Charles Hockett. In a series of articles stretching over ten years
he has attempted to itemize out the various 'design features' which
characterize language. For example: '*Interchangeability:* Adult
members of any speech community are interchangeably transmitters
and receivers of linguistic signals'; '*Complete Feedback:* The transmitter
of a linguistic signal himself receives the message' (Hockett, 1963, 9).
Of course, such an approach is not perfect. A list of features may even
be misleading, since it represents a random set of observations which
do not cohere in any obvious way. To use this list to define language
is like trying to define a man by noting that he has two arms, two
legs, a head, a belly button, he bleeds if you scratch him, and shrieks
if you tread on his toe. But in spite of this, a definition of language
based on design features or 'essential characteristics' seems to be the
most useful proposed so far.

But how many characteristics should be considered? Two? Ten?
A hundred? The number of design features Hockett considers important has changed over the years. The longest list contains sixteen
(Hockett, 1963), though perhaps most people would consider that
eight features capture the essential nature of language: *use of the vocal-
auditory channel*, *arbitrariness*, *semanticity*, *cultural transmission*, *duality*,
displacement, *structure-dependence* and *creativity*.

Let us discuss each of these features in turn, and see whether it is present in animal communication. If any animal naturally possesses *all* the design features of human language, then clearly that animal can talk.

The use of the *vocal-auditory channel* is perhaps the most obvious characteristic of language. Sounds are made with the vocal organs, and a hearing mechanism receives them—a phenomenon which is neither rare nor particularly surprising. The use of sound is widespread as a means of animal communication. One obvious advantage is that messages can be sent or received in the dark or in a dense forest. Not all sound signals are vocal—woodpeckers tap on wood, and rattlesnakes have a rattle apparatus on their tail. But vocal-auditory signals are common and are used by birds, cows, apes and foxes, to name just a few. The advantages of this method of producing the sound are that it leaves the body free to carry on other activities at the same time, and also requires relatively little physical energy. But this design feature is clearly neither unique to humans, nor all-important, since language can be transferred without loss to visual symbols (as in deaf-and-dumb language, or writing) and to tactile symbols (as in Braille). Patients who have had their vocal cords removed, and communicate mainly by writing, have not lost their language ability. It follows that this characteristic is of little use in an attempt to distinguish animal from human communication. So let us proceed to the second feature, arbitrariness.

Arbitrariness means that human languages use neutral symbols. There is no connection between the word 'dog' and the four-legged animal it symbolizes. It can equally be called UN CHIEN (French), EIN HUND (German), or CANIS (Latin). GÜL (Turkish) and RHODON (Greek) are equally satisfactory names for a 'rose'. As Juliet notes:

What's in a name? that which we call a rose
By any other name would smell as sweet.
(Shakespeare)

Onomatopoeic words such as CUCKOO, POP, BANG, SLURP and SQUISH are exceptions to this. But there are relatively few of these in any language. On the other hand, it is normal for animals to have a strong link between the message they are sending and the signal they use to convey it. A crab which wishes to convey extreme aggression will extend a large claw. A less angry crab will merely raise a leg: 'Extending a major chaliped is more effective than raising a single ambulatory leg in causing the second crab to retreat or duck back into its shell' (Marshall, 1970). However, arbitrary symbols are not unique to man. Gulls, for example, sometimes indicate aggression by turning away from their opponent and uprooting beakfuls of grass. So we are forced to conclude that arbitrariness cannot be regarded as a critical distinction between human and animal communication.

Semanticity, the third suggested test for language ability, is the use of symbols to 'mean' or refer to objects and actions. To a human, a CHAIR 'means' a four-legged contraption you can sit on. Humans can generalize by applying this name to all types of chairs, not just one in particular. Furthermore, semanticity applies to actions as well as objects. For example, to JUMP 'means' the act of leaping in the air. Some writers have claimed that semanticity is exclusively human. Animals may only be able to communicate about a total situation. A hen who utters 'danger' cries when a fox is nearby is possibly conveying the message 'Beware! beware! there is terrible danger about!' rather than using the sound to 'mean' FOX. But, as was shown by the call of the vervet monkey who might or might not mean 'snake' when he *chutters*, it is difficult to be certain. We must remain agnostic about whether this feature is present in animal communication.

Cultural transmission or *tradition* indicates that human beings hand their languages down from one generation to another. The role played by teaching in animal communication is unclear and varies from animal to animal—and even within species. Among birds it is claimed that the song-thrush's song is largely innate, but can be slightly modified by learning, whereas the skylark's song is almost wholly learned. Birds such as the chaffinch are particularly interesting: the basic pattern of the song seems to be innate, but all the finer detail and much of the pitch and rhythm have to be acquired by learning (Thorpe, 1961, 1963). However, although the distinction between man and animals is not clear-cut as regards this feature, it seems that a far greater proportion of communication is genetically inbuilt in animals than in man. If a child is brought up in isolation, away from human beings, he does not acquire language. In contrast, birds reared in isolation sing songs that are sometimes recognizable (though almost always abnormal).

The fifth property, *duality* or *double-articulation*, means that language is organized into two 'layers': the basic sound units of speech, such as P, I, G, are normally meaningless by themselves. They only become meaningful when combined into sequences such as P—I—G PIG. This property is sometimes claimed to be unique to humans. But this is not so. Duality is also present in bird song, where each individual note is itself meaningless—it is the combination of notes which convey meaningful messages. So once again we have not found a critical difference between animals and humans in the use of this feature.

A more important characteristic of language is *displacement*, the ability to refer to things far removed in time and place. Humans frequently say things such as 'My Aunt Matilda, who lives in Australia, cracked her knee-cap last week.' It may be impossible for an animal to convey a similar item of information. However, as in the case of other design features, it is sometimes difficult to decide whether displacement is present in an animal's communication system. A bird frequently continues to give alarm cries long after the disappearance of a cat which was stalking it. Is this displacement or not? The answer is unclear. Definite examples of displacement are hard to find. But it is undoubtedly found in bee communication (von Frisch, 1950, 1954, 1967). When a worker bee finds a source of nectar she returns to the hive to perform a complex dance which informs the other bees of its location. She does a 'round dance', which involves turning round in circles if the nectar is close to the hive, and a 'waggle dance' in which she wiggles her tail from side to side if it is far away. The other bees work out the distance by noting the tempo of her waggles, and discover what kind of flower to look for by smelling its scent on her body. After the dance, they unerringly fly to the right place, even if it is several miles away, with a hill intervening.

This is an unusual ability—but even this degree of displacement is considerably less than that found in human speech. The bee cannot inform other bees about anything further removed than the nectar patch she has just visited. She cannot say 'The day before yesterday we visited a lovely clump of flowers, let's go and see if they are still there'—she can only say, 'Come to the nectar I have just visited.' Nor can she communicate about anything further away in place. She could not say 'I wonder whether there's good nectar in Siberia.' So displacement in bee communication is strictly limited to the number of miles a bee can easily fly, and the time it takes to do this. At last, it seems we may have found a feature which seems to be of importance in human language, and only partially present in non-human communication.

The seventh feature, *structure-dependence*, was discussed [earlier in the book]. Humans do not just apply simple recognition or counting techniques when they speak to one another. They automatically recognize the patterned nature of language, and manipulate 'structured chunks'. For example, they understand that a group of words can sometimes be the structural equivalent of one:

SHE THE OLD LADY WHO WAS WEARING A WHITE BONNET	GAVE THE DONKEY A CARROT

and they can rearrange these chunks according to strict rules:

A CARROT	WAS GIVEN TO THE DONKEY	BY THE OLD LADY WHO WAS WEARING A WHITE BONNET

As far as we know, animals do not use structure-dependent operations. We do not know enough about the communication of all animals to be sure, but no definite example has yet been found.

Finally, there is one feature that seems to be of overwhelming importance, and unique to humans—the ability to produce and understand an indefinite number of novel utterances. This property of language has several different names. Chomsky calls it *creativity*, others call it *openness* or *productivity*. A human can talk about anything he likes—even a platypus falling backwards downstairs—without causing any linguistic problems to himself or the hearer. He can say *what* he wants *when* he wants. If it thunders, he does not automatically utter a set phrase, such as 'It's thundering, run for cover'. He can say 'Isn't the lightning pretty?' or 'Better get the dog in' or 'Thunder is two dragons colliding in tin tubs, according to a Chinese legend.'

In contrast, most animals have a fixed number of signals which convey a set number of messages, sent in clearly definable circumstances. A North American cicada can give four signals only. It emits a 'disturbance squawk' when it is seized, picked up or eaten. A 'congregation call' seems to mean 'Let's all get together and sing in chorus!' A preliminary courtship call (an invitation?) is uttered when a female is several inches away. An advanced courtship call (a buzz of triumph?) occurs when the female is almost within grasp (Alexander and Moore, quoted in McNeill, 1966). Even the impressive vervet monkey has only thirty-six distinct vocal sounds in its repertoire. And as this total includes sneezing and vomiting, the actual number used for communication is several fewer. Within this range, choice is limited, since circumstances generally dictate which call to use. An infant separated from its mother gives the lost *rrah* cry. A female who wishes to deter an amorous male gives the 'anti-copulatory squeal-scream' (Struhsaker, 1967).

But perhaps it is unfair to concentrate on cicadas and monkeys. Compared with these, bees and dolphins have extremely sophisticated communication systems. Yet researchers have reluctantly concluded that even bees and dolphins seem unable to say anything new. The bees were investigated by the famous 'bee-man', Karl von Frisch (1954). He noted that worker bees normally give information about the *horizontal* distance and direction of a source of nectar. If bee communication is in any sense 'open', then a worker bee should be able to inform the other bees about *vertical* distance and direction if necessary. He tested this idea by placing a hive of bees at the foot of a radio beacon, and a supply of sugar water at the top. But the bees who were shown the sugar water were unable to tell the other bees where to find it. They duly performed a 'round dance', indicating that a source of nectar was in the vicinity of the hive—and then for several hours their comrades flew in all directions *except* upwards, looking for the honey source. Eventually, they gave up the search. As von Frisch noted, 'The bees have no word for "up" in their language. There are no flowers in the clouds' (von Frisch, 1954, 139). Failure to communicate this extra item of information means that bee communication cannot be regarded as 'open-ended' in the same way that human language is open-ended.

The dolphin experiments carried out by Dr Jarvis Bastian were considerably more exciting—though in the long run equally disappointing. Bastian tried to teach a male dolphin Buzz and a female dolphin Doris to communicate across an opaque barrier.

First of all, while they were still together, Bastian taught the dolphins to press paddles when they saw a light. If the light was kept steady, they had to press the right paddle first. If it flashed, the left-hand one. When they did this correctly they were rewarded with fish.

As soon as they had learned this manœuvre, he separated them. They could now hear one another, but they could not see one another. The paddles and light were set up in the same way, except that the light which indicated which paddle to press first was seen only by Doris. But in order to get fish both dolphins had to press the levers in the correct order. Doris had to *tell* Buzz which this was, as only she could see the light. Amazingly, the dolphins 'demonstrated essentially perfect success over thousands of trials at this task' (Evans and Bastian, 1969, 432). It seemed that dolphins could *talk*! Doris was conveying novel information through an opaque barrier!

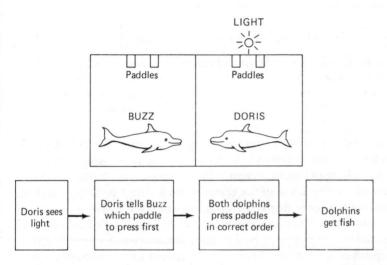

But it later became clear that the achievement was considerably less clever. Even while the dolphins were together Doris had become accustomed to making certain sounds when the light was flashing and different sounds when it was continuous. When the dolphins were separated she continued the habit. And Buzz had, of course, already learnt which sound of Doris's to associate with which light. Doris was therefore not 'talking creatively'.

So not even dolphins have a 'creative' communication system, it seems—though it is always possible that more is known about 'dolphinese' than has been made public. The high intelligence of dolphins has obvious implications for naval warfare, and so has attracted the attention of military authorities, with the result that much research is shrouded in official secrecy. But on the whole it seems unlikely that there exist hidden tanks of 'talking dolphins' (as was suggested in a recent film). Most researchers would agree with the comment of the psychologist John Morton: 'On the question as to whether dolphins have a language, I would like to comment parenthetically from the evidence I have seen, if they do have a language they are going to extraordinary lengths to conceal the fact from us' (Morton, 1971, 83).

It seems, then, that animals cannot send truly novel messages, and that Ogden Nash encapsulates a modicum of truth in his comment:

The song of canaries
Never varies.

And so does Alice in her complaint about kittens:

It is a very inconvenient habit of kittens that, whatever you say to them, they always purr. If they would only purr for 'yes' and mew for 'no', or any rule of that sort, so that one could keep up a conversation! But how *can* you talk with a person if they *always* say the same thing?

(Lewis Carroll)

It is now possible to answer the question, can animals talk? If, in order to qualify as 'talkers' they have to utilize all the design characteristics of human language 'naturally', the answer is clearly 'no'. Some animals possess some of the features. Bird song has duality, and bee dancing has some degree of displacement. But, as far as we know, no animal communication system has duality *and* displacement. No animal system can be proved to have semanticity or to use structure-dependent operations. Above all, no animal can communicate creatively with another animal.

But although animals do not 'naturally' talk, this does not mean that they are *incapable* of talking. Perhaps they have just never had the chance to learn language.

10

Language and speech (*langue* and *parole*)
Roland Barthes

From Barthes, R. 1967: *Elements of semiology*. Translated by Annette Lavers and Colin Smith, London: Cape, 13–17.

I.1.1. *In Saussure:* The (dichotomic) concept of *language/speech* is central in Saussure* and was certainly a great novelty in relation to earlier linguistics which sought to find the causes of historical changes in the evolution of pronunciation, spontaneous associations and the working of analogy, and was therefore a linguistics of the individual act. In working out this famous dichotomy, Saussure started from the 'multiform and heterogeneous' nature of language, which appears at first sight as an unclassifiable reality[1] the unity of which cannot be brought to light, since it partakes at the same time of the physical, the physiological, the mental, the individual and the social. Now this disorder disappears if, from this heterogeneous whole, is extracted a purely social object, the systematized set of conventions necessary to communication, indifferent to the *material* of the signals which compose it, and which is a *language (langue)*; as opposed to which *speech (parole)* covers the purely individual part of language (phonation, application of the rules and contingent combinations of signs).

I.1.2. *The language (langue):* A *language* is therefore, so to speak, language minus speech: it is at the same time a social institution and a system of values. As a social institution, it is by no means an act, and it is not subject to any premeditation. It is the social part of language, the individual cannot by himself either create or modify it; it is essentially a collective contract which one must accept in its entirety if one wishes to communicate. Moreover, this social product is autonomous, like a game with its own rules, for it can be handled only after a period of learning. As a system of values, a language is made of a certain

---

* The Saussurean notions of *langue* and *parole* present to the translator into English notorious difficulties, which their extension in the present work does nothing to alleviate. We have translated *langue* as 'a' or the '*the* language', except when the coupling with 'speech' makes the meaning clear. *Les paroles*, whether applied to several people or to several semiotic systems, has been translated by various periphrases which we hope do not obscure the identity of meaning.

number of elements, each one of which is at the same time the equivalent of a given quantity of things and a term of a larger function, in which are found, in a differential order, other correlative values: from the point of view of the language, the sign is like a coin[2] which has the value of a certain amount of goods which it allows one to buy, but also has value in relation to other coins, in a greater or lesser degree. The institutional and the systematic aspect are of course connected: it is because a language is a system of contractual values (in part arbitrary, or, more exactly, unmotivated) that it resists the modifications coming from a single individual, and is consequently a social institution.

I.1.3. *Speech (parole)*: In contrast to the language, which is both institution and system, *speech* is essentially an individual act of selection and actualization; it is made in the first place of the 'combination thanks to which the speaking subject can use the code of the language with a view to expressing his personal thought' (this extended speech could be called *discourse*), and secondly by the 'psycho-physical mechanisms which allow him to exteriorize these combinations'. It is certain that phonation, for instance, cannot be confused with the language; neither the institution nor the system are altered if the individual who resorts to them speaks loudly or softly, with slow or rapid delivery, etc. The combinative aspect of speech is of course of capital importance, for it implies that speech is constituted by the recurrence of identical signs: it is because signs are repeated in successive discourses and within one and the same discourse (although they are combined in accordance with the infinite diversity of various people's speech) that each sign becomes an element of the language; and it is because speech is essentially a combinative activity that it corresponds to an individual act and not to a pure creation.

I.1.4 *The dialectics of language and speech:* Language and speech: each of these two terms of course achieves its full definition only in the dialectical process which unites one to the other: there is no language without speech, and no speech outside language: it is in this exchange that the real linguistic *praxis* is situated, as Merleau-Ponty has pointed out. And V. Brøndal writes, 'A language is a purely abstract entity, a norm which stands above individuals, a set of essential types, which speech actualizes in an infinite variety of ways.'[3] Language and speech are therefore in a relation of reciprocal comprehensiveness. On the one hand, the language is 'the treasure deposited by the practice of speech, in the subjects belonging to the same community' and, since it is a collective summa of individual imprints, it must remain incomplete at the level of each isolated individual: a language does not exist perfectly except in the 'speaking mass'; one cannot handle speech except by drawing on the language. But conversely, a language is possible only starting from speech: historically, speech phenomena always precede language phenomena (it is speech which makes language evolve), and genetically, a language is constituted in the individual through his learning from the environmental speech (one does not teach grammar and vocabulary which are, broadly speaking, the language, to babies). To sum, a language is at the same time the product and the instrument of speech: their relationship is therefore a genuinely dialectical one. It will be noticed (an important fact when we come to semiological prospects) that there could not possibly be (at least according to Saussure) a linguistics of speech, since any speech, as soon as it is grasped as a process of communication, is *already* part of the language: the latter only can be the object of a science. This disposes of two questions at the outset: it is useless to wonder whether speech must be studied *before* the language: the opposite is impossible: one can only study speech straight away inasmuch as it reflects the language (inasmuch as it is 'glottic'). It is just as useless to wonder *at the outset* how to separate the language from speech: this is no preliminary operation, but on the contrary the very essence of linguistic and later semiological investigation: to separate the language from speech means *ipso facto* constituting the problematics of the meaning.

II

Expressions, meaning and speech acts

J. R. Searle

From Searle, J. R. 1969: *Speech acts*. Cambridge: Cambridge University Press, 22–6.

The hypothesis then of this work is that speaking a language is engaging in a rule-governed form of behaviour. To put it more briskly, talking is performing acts according to rules. In order to substantiate that hypothesis and explicate speech, I shall state some of the rules according to which we talk. The procedure which I shall follow is to state a set of necessary and sufficient conditions for the performance of particular kinds of speech acts and then extract from those conditions sets of semantic rules for the use of the linguistic devices which mark the utterances as speech acts of those kinds. That is a rather bigger task than perhaps it sounds, and this chapter* will be devoted to preparing the ground for it by introducing distinctions between *different kinds of speech acts*, and discussing the notions of *propositions, rules, meaning, and facts*.

Expressions and kinds of speech acts

Let us begin this phase of our inquiry by making some distinctions which naturally suggest themselves to us as soon as we begin to reflect on simple speech situations. (The simplicity of the sentences in our examples will not detract from the generality of the distinctions we are trying to make.) Imagine a speaker and a hearer and suppose that in appropriate circumstances the speaker utters one of the following sentences:

(1) Sam smokes habitually.
(2) Does Sam smoke habitually?
(3) Sam, smoke habitually!
(4) Would that Sam smoked habitually.

Now let us ask how we might characterize or describe the speaker's utterance of one of these. What shall we say the speaker is doing when he utters one of these?

* Only the first part of the chapter is included here.

One thing is obvious: anyone who utters one of these can be said to have uttered a sentence formed of words in the English language. But clearly this is only the beginning of a description, for the speaker in uttering one of these is characteristically saying something and not merely mouthing words. In uttering (1) a speaker is making (what philosophers call) an assertion, in (2) asking a question, in (3) giving an order, and in (4) (a somewhat archaic form) expressing a wish or desire. And in the performance of each of these four different acts the speaker performs certain other acts which are common to all four: in uttering any of these the speaker *refers to* or mentions or designates a certain object Sam, and he predicates the expression 'smokes habitually' (or one of its inflections) of the object referred to. Thus we shall say that in the utterance of all four the reference and predication are the same, though in each case the same reference and predication occur as part of a complete speech act which is different from any of the other three. We thus detach the notions of referring and predicating from the notions of such complete speech acts as asserting, questioning, commanding, etc., and the justification for this separation lies in the fact that the same reference and predication can occur in the performance of different complete speech acts. Austin baptized these complete speech acts with the name 'illocutionary acts', and I shall henceforth employ this terminology.[1] Some of the English verbs denoting illocutionary acts are 'state', 'describe', 'assert', 'warn', 'remark', 'comment', 'command', 'order', 'request', 'criticize', 'apologize', 'censure', 'approve', 'welcome', 'promise', 'object', 'demand', and 'argue'. Austin claimed there were over a thousand such expressions in English.[2]

The first upshot of our preliminary reflections, then, is that in the utterance of any of the four sentences in the example a speaker is characteristically performing at least three distinct kinds of acts. (*a*) The uttering of words (morphemes, sentences); (*b*) referring and predicating; (*c*) stating, questioning, commanding, promising, etc.

Let us assign names to these under the general heading of speech acts:

(*a*) Uttering words (morphemes, sentences) = performing *utterance acts*.

(*b*) Referring and predicating = performing *propositional acts*.

(*c*) Stating, questioning, commanding, promising, etc. = performing *illocutionary acts*.

I am not saying, of course, that these are separate things that speakers do, as it happens, simultaneously, as one might smoke, read and scratch one's head simultaneously, but rather that in performing an illocutionary act one characteristically performs propositional acts and utterance acts. Nor should it be thought from this that utterance acts and propositional acts stand to illocutionary acts in the way buying a ticket and getting on a train stand to taking a railroad trip. They are not means to ends; rather, utterance acts stand to propositional and illocutionary acts in the way in which, e.g., making an 'X' on a ballot paper stands to voting.

The point of abstracting each of these kinds is that the 'identity criteria' are different in each case. We have already seen that the same propositional acts can be common to different illocutionary acts, and it is obvious that one can perform an utterance act without performing a propositional or illocutionary act at all. (One can utter words without saying anything.) And similarly, if we consider the utterance of a sentence such as:

Mr Samuel Martin is a regular smoker of tobacco

we can see reasons for saying that in certain contexts a speaker in uttering it would be performing the same propositional act as in (1)–(4) (reference and predication would be the same), the same illocutionary act as (1) (same statement or assertion is made), but a different utterance act from any of the first four since a different sentence, containing none of the same words and only some of the same morphemes, is uttered. Thus, in performing different utterance acts, a speaker may perform the same propositional and illocutionary acts. Nor, of course, need the performance of the same utterance act by two different speakers, or by the same speaker on different occasions, be a performance of the same propositional and illocutionary acts: the same sentence may, e.g., be used to make two different statements. Utterance acts consist simply in uttering strings of words. Illocutionary and propositional acts consist characteristically in uttering words in sentences in certain contexts, under certain conditions and with certain intentions, as we shall see later on.

So far I make no claims for dividing things up this way, other than its being a permissible way to divide them—vague though this may be. In particular, I do not claim that it is the only way to divide things. For example, for certain purposes one might wish to break up what I have called utterance acts into phonetic acts, phonemic acts, morphemic acts, etc. And, of course, for most purposes, in the science of linguistics it is not necessary to speak of acts at all. One can just discuss phonemes, morphemes, sentences, etc.

To these three notions I now wish to add Austin's notion of the *perlocutionary act*. Correlated with the notion of illocutionary acts is the notion of the consequences or *effects* such acts have on the actions, thoughts, or beliefs, etc. of hearers. For example, by arguing I may *persuade* or *convince* someone, by warning him I may *scare* or *alarm* him, by making a request I may *get him to do something*, by informing him I may *convince him (enlighten, edify, inspire him, get him to realize)*. The italicized expressions above denote perlocutionary acts.

Correlative with the notion of propositional acts and illocutionary acts, respectively, are certain kinds of expressions uttered in their performance: the characteristic grammatical form of the illocutionary act is the complete sentence (it can be a one-word sentence); and the characteristic grammatical form of the propositional acts are parts of sentences: grammatical predicates for the act of predication, and proper names, pronouns, and certain other sorts of noun phrases for reference. Propositional acts cannot occur alone; that is, one cannot *just* refer and predicate without making an assertion or asking a question or performing some other illocutionary act. The linguistic correlate of this point is that sentences, not words, are used to say things. This is also what Frege meant when he said that only in the context of a sentence do words have reference—'Nur im Zusammenhang eines Satzes bedeuten die Wörter etwas.'[3] The same thing in my terminology: One only refers as part of the performance of an illocutionary act, and the grammatical clothing of an illocutionary act is the complete sentence. An utterance of a referring expression only counts as referring if one says something.

The parallel between kinds of expressions and propositional acts is not, of course, exact. If I say, e.g., 'He left me in the lurch', I am not referring to a particular lurch in which I was left, though phrases of the form 'the so-and-so' are characteristically referring expressions.

12

Education, generalization and abstraction
A. R. Luria

From Luria, A. R. 1976: *Cognitive development*. Cambridge, Mass., and London: Harvard University Press, 58–60.

Subject: Sher., age sixty, illiterate peasant from the village of Yardan. The task is explained through the example, *shirt–boots–skullcap–mouse*, and subject shown pictures of the following: *hammer–saw–log–hatchet*.

'They all fit here! The saw has to saw the log, the hammer has to hammer it, and the hatchet has to chop it. And if you want to chop the log up really good, you need the hammer. You can't take any of these things away. There isn't any you don't need!'

Replaces abstract classification with situational thinking.

But in the first example I showed you that the mouse didn't fit in.

'The mouse didn't fit in! But here all the things are very much alike [*ukhshaidi*]. The saw saws the log, and the hatchet chops it, you just have to hit harder with the hammer.'

But one fellow told me the log didn't belong here.

'Why'd he say that? If we say the log isn't like the other things and put it off to one side, we'd be making a mistake. All these things are needed for the log.'

Considers idea of utility more important than similarity.

But that other fellow said that the saw, hammer, and hatchet are all alike in some way, while the log isn't.

'So what if they're not alike? They all work together and chop the log. Here everything works right, here everything's just fine.'

Look, you can use one word—tools—for these three but not for the log.

'What sense does it make to use one word for them all if they're not going to work together?'

Rejects use of generalizing term.

What word could you use for these things?

'The words people use: saw, hammer, hatchet. You can't use one word for them all!'

Could you call them tools?

'Yes, you could, except a log isn't a tool. Still, the way we look at it, the log has to be here. Otherwise, what good are the others?'

Employs predominantly situational thinking again.

The examples cited indicate that we had no luck getting these subjects to perform the abstract act of classification. Even when they grasped some similarity among various objects, they attached no particular importance to the fact. As a rule, they operated on the basis of 'practical utility', grouping objects in practical schemes rather than categorizing them. When we referred to a generic term they could use to designate a distinct group of objects, they generally disregarded the information or considered it immaterial. Instead, they adhered to the idea that objects should be grouped in practical arrangements. They continued to do so even when we presented objects that, in our view, would be difficult to group together for some genuinely practical scheme. When we clarified the principle of abstract classification, they listened attentively enough to our explanation but failed to take it into account. The following examples illustrate this tendency.

Subject: Abdy-Gap., age sixty-two, illiterate peasant from remote village. After the task is explained, he is given the series: *knife–saw–wheel–hammer*.

'They're all needed here. Every one of these things. The saw to chop firewood, the others for other jobs.'

Evaluates objects in terms of 'necessity' instead of classifying them.

No, three of these things belong in one group. You can use one word for them that you can't for the other one.

'Maybe it's the hammer? But it's also needed. You can drive nails in with it.'

The principle of classification is explained: three of the objects are 'tools'.

'But you can sharpen things with a wheel. If it's a wheel from an *araba* [kind of bullock cart], why'd they put it here?'

Subject's ability to learn the principle of classification is tested through another series: *bayonet–rifle–sword–knife*.

'There's nothing you can leave out here! The bayonet is part of the gun. A man's got to wear the dagger on his left side and the rifle on the other.'

Again employs idea of necessity to group objects.

The principle of classification is explained: three of the objects can be used to cut but the rifle cannot.

'It'll shoot from a distance, but up close it can also cut.'

He is then given the series *finger–mouth–ear–eye* and told that three objects are found on the head, the fourth on the body.

'You say the finger isn't needed here? But if a fellow is missing an ear, he can't hear. All these are needed, they all fit in. If a man's missing a finger, he can't do a thing, not even move a bed.'

Applies same principle as in preceding response.

Principle is explained once again.

'No, that's not true, you can't do it that way. You have to keep all these things together.'

One could scarcely find a more clear-cut example to prove that for some people abstract classification is a wholly alien procedure. Even when we explained the principle of classification very thoroughly, the subjects persisted in their own approach.

13

Social class, language and socialization
Basil Bernstein

From Bernstein, B. 1971: *Class, codes and control*. Volume 1. London: Routledge. This extract taken from the Paladin edition, 193–205.

It may be helpful to make explicit the theoretical origins of the thesis I have been developing over the past decade. Although, initially, the thesis appeared to be concerned with the problem of educability, this problem was embedded in and was stimulated by the wider question of the relationships between symbolic orders and social structure. The basic theoretical question, which dictated the approach to the initially narrow but important empirical problem, was concerned with the fundamental structure and changes in the structure of cultural transmission. Indeed, any detailed examination of what superficially may seem to be a string of somewhat repetitive papers, I think would show three things:

(1) The gradual emergence of the dominance of the major theoretical problem from the local, empirical problem of the social antecedents of the educability of different groups of children.
(2) Attempts to develop both the generality of the thesis and to develop increasing specificity at the contextual level.
(3) Entailed in (2) were attempts to clarify both the logical and empirical status of the basic organizing concept, code. Unfortunately, until recently these attempts were more readily seen in the *planning* and *analysis* of the empirical research than available as formal statements.

Looking back, however, I think I would have created less misunderstanding if I had written about socio-linguistic codes rather than linguistic codes. Through using only the latter concept it gave the impression that I was reifying syntax and at the cost of semantics; or worse, suggesting that there was a one-to-one relation between meaning and a given syntax. Also, by defining the codes in a context-free fashion, I robbed myself of properly understanding, at a theoretical level, their significance. *I should point out that nearly all the empirical*

*planning was directed to trying to find out the code realizations in different
contexts.*

The concept of socio-linguistic code points to the social structuring
of meanings *and* to their diverse but *related* contextual linguistic realizations. A careful reading of the papers always shows the emphasis
given to the form of the social relationship, that is to the structuring
of relevant meanings. Indeed, role is defined as a complex coding
activity controlling the creation and organization of specific meanings
and the conditions for their transmission and reception. The general
socio-linguistic thesis attempts to explore how symbolic systems are
both realizations and regulators of the structure of social relationships.
The particular symbolic system is that of speech *not* language.

It is pertinent, at this point, to make explicit earlier work in the
social sciences which formed the implicit starting point of the thesis.
It will then be seen, I hope, that the thesis is an integration of different
streams of thought. The major starting points are Durkheim and
Marx, and a small number of other thinkers have been drawn into
the basic matrix. I shall very briefly, and so selectively, outline this
matrix and some of the problems to which it gave rise.

Durkheim's work is a truly magnificent insight into the relationships between symbolic orders, social relationships and the structuring
of experience. In a sense, if Marx turned Hegel on his head, then Durkheim attempted to turn Kant on his head. For in *Primitive Classification*
and in *The Elementary Forms of the Religious Life*, Durkheim attempted
to derive the basic categories of thought from the structuring of the
social relation. It is beside the point as to his success. He raised the
whole question of the relation between the classifications and frames
of the symbolic order *and* the structuring of experience. In his study
of different forms of social integration he pointed to the implicit, condensed, symbolic structure of mechanical solidarity and the more
explicit and differentiated symbolic structures of organic solidarity.
Cassirer, the early cultural anthropologists, and, in particular, Sapir
(I was not aware of von Humboldt until much later), sensitized me
to the cultural properties of speech. Whorf, particularly where he
refers to the fashions of speaking, frames of consistency, alerted me
to the selective effect of the culture (acting through its patterning of
social relationships) upon the *patterning* of grammar *together* with the
pattern's semantic and thus cognitive significance. Whorf more than
anyone, I think, opened up, at least for me, the question of the deep
structure of linguistically regulated communication.

In all the above work I found two difficulties. If we grant the fundamental linkage of symbolic systems, social structure and the shaping
of experience it is still unclear *how* such shaping takes place. The *processes* underlying the social structuring of experience are not explicit.
The second difficulty is in dealing with the question of change of symbolic systems. Mead is of central importance in the solution of the first
difficulty, the HOW. Mead outlined in general terms the relationships
between role, reflexiveness and speech and in so doing provided the
basis of the solution to the HOW. It is still the case that the Meadian
solution does not allow us to deal with the problem of change. For
the concept, which enables role to be related to a higher order concept,
'the generalized other', is, itself, not subject to systematic inquiry.
Even if 'the generalized other' is placed within a Durkheimian framework, we are still left with the problem of change. Indeed, in Mead
change is introduced only at the cost of the re-emergence of a traditional Western dichotomy in the concepts of the 'I' and the 'me'. The
'I' is both the indeterminate response to the 'me' and yet, at the same
time, shapes it. The Meadian 'I' points to the voluntarism in the affairs
of men, to the fundamental creativity of man, made possible by
speech; a little before Chomsky.

Thus Meadian thought helps to solve the puzzle of the HOW but
it does not help with the question of change in the structuring of experience; although both Mead implicitly and Durkheim explicitly
pointed to the conditions which bring about pathological structuring
of experience.

One major theory of the development of and change in symbolic
structures is, of course, that of Marx. Although Marx is less concerned
with the internal structure and the process of transmission of symbolic
systems, he does give us a key to their institutionalization and change.
The key is given in terms of the social significance of society's productive system and the power relationships to which the productive system gives rise. Further, access to, control over, orientation of and
change in critical symbolic systems, according to the theory, is governed by power relationships as these are embodied in the class
structure. It is not only capital, in the strict economic sense, which
is subject to appropriation, manipulation and exploitation, but also
cultural capital in the form of the symbolic systems through which
man can extend and change the boundaries of his experience.

I am not putting forward a matrix of thought necessary for the
study of the basic structure and change in the structure of cultural
transmission, *only* the specific matrix which underlies my own

approach. Essentially and briefly I have used Durkheim and Marx at the macro-level and Mead at the micro-level to realize a sociolinguistic thesis which could meet with a range of work in anthropology, linguistics, sociology and psychology.

I want first of all to make clear what I am not concerned with. Chomsky, in *Aspects of the Theory of Syntax*, neatly severs the study of the rule system of language from the study of the social rules which determine their contextual use. He does this by making a distinction between competence and performance. Competence refers to the child's tacit understanding of the rule system, performance relates to the essentially social use to which the rule system is put. Competence refers to man abstracted from contextual constraints. Performance refers to man in the grip of the contextual constraints which determine his speech acts. Competence refers to the Ideal, performance refers to the Fall. In this sense Chomsky's notion of competence is Platonic. Competence has its source in the very biology of man. There is no difference between men in terms of their access to the linguistic rule system. Here Chomsky, like many other linguists before him, announces the communality of man; all men have equal access to the creative act which is language. On the other hand, performance is under the control of the social—performances are culturally specific acts, they refer to the choices which are made in specific speech encounters. Thus, according to Hymes, Chomsky indicates the tragedy of man, the potentiality of competence and the degeneration of performance.

Clearly, much is to be gained in rigour and explanatory power through the severing of the relationship between the formal properties of the grammar and the meanings which are realized in its use. But if we are to study speech, *la parole*, we are inevitably involved in a study of a rather different rule system; we are involved in a study of rules, formal and informal, which regulate the options we take up in various contexts in which we find ourselves. This second rule system is the cultural system. This raises immediately the question of the relationship between the linguistic rule system and the cultural system. Clearly, specific linguistic rule systems are part of the cultural system, but it has been argued that the linguistic rule system in various ways shapes the cultural system. This very briefly is the view of those who hold a narrow form of the linguistic relativity hypothesis. I do not intend to get involved in that particular quagmire. Instead, I shall take the view that the code which the linguist invents to explain the formal properties of the grammar is capable of generating any number of speech codes, and there is no reason for believing that any one language code is better than another in this respect. On this argument, language is a set of rules to which all speech codes must comply, but which speech codes are realized is a function of the culture acting through social relationships in specific contexts. Different speech forms or codes symbolize the form of the social relationship, regulate the nature of the speech encounters, and create for the speakers different orders of relevance and relation. The experience of the speakers is then transformed by what is made significant or relevant by the speech form. This is a sociological argument because the speech form is taken as a consequence of the form of the social relation or, put more generally, is a quality of a social structure. Let me qualify this immediately. Because the speech form is initially a function of a given social arrangement, it does not mean that the speech form does not in turn modify or even change that social structure which initially evolved the speech form. This formulation, indeed, invites the question: under what conditions does a given speech form free itself sufficiently from its embodiment in the social structure so that the system of meanings it realizes points to alternative realities, alternative arrangements in the affairs of men? Here we become concerned immediately with the antecedents and consequences of the boundary-maintaining principles of a culture or subculture. I am here suggesting a relationship between forms of boundary maintenance at the cultural level and forms of speech.

I am required to consider the relationship between language and socialization. It should be clear from these opening remarks that I am not concerned with language, but with speech, and concerned more specifically with the contextual constraints upon speech. Now what about socialization? I shall take the term to refer to the process whereby a child acquires a specific cultural identity, *and* to his responses to such an identity. Socialization refers to the process whereby the biological is transformed into a specific cultural being. It follows from this that the process of socialization is a complex process of control, whereby a particular moral, cognitive and affective awareness is evoked in the child and given a specific form and content. Socialization sensitizes the child to the various orderings of society as these are made substantive in the various roles he is expected to play. In a sense, then, socialization is a process for making people safe. The process acts selectively on the possibilities of man by creating through time a sense of the inevitability of a given social arrangement, and through limiting the areas of permitted change. The basic agencies of socialization in contemporary societies are the family, the peer group, school and work. It is through these agencies, and in particular through their relationship to each other, that the various orderings of society are made manifest.

Now it is quite clear that given this view of socialization it is necessary to limit the discussion. I shall limit our discussion to socialization within the family, but it should be obvious that the focusing and filtering of the child's experience within the family in a large measure is a microcosm of the macroscopic orderings of society. Our question now becomes: what are the sociological factors which affect linguistic performances within the family critical to the process of socialization?

Without a shadow of doubt the most formative influence upon the procedures of socialization, from a sociological viewpoint, is social class. The class structure influences work and educational roles and brings families into a special relationship with each other and deeply penetrates the structure of life experiences within the family. The class system has deeply marked the distribution of knowledge within society. It has given differential access to the sense that the world is permeable. It has sealed off communities from each other and has ranked these communities on a scale of invidious worth. We have three components: knowledge, possibility and invidious insulation. It would be a little naïve to believe that differences in knowledge, differences in the sense of the possible, combined with invidious insulation, rooted in differential *material* well-being, would not affect the forms of control and innovation in the socializing procedures of different social classes. I shall go on to argue that the deep structure of communication itself is affected, but not in any final or irrevocable way.

As an approach to my argument, let me glance at the social distribution of knowledge. We can see that the class system has affected the distribution of knowledge. Historically, and now, only a tiny percentage of the population has been socialized into knowledge at the level of the meta-languages of control and innovation, whereas the mass of the population has been socialized into knowledge at the level of context-tied operations.

A tiny percentage of the population has been given access to the principles of intellectual change, whereas the rest have been denied such access. This suggests that we might be able to distinguish between two orders of meaning. One we could call universalistic, the other particularistic. Universalistic meanings are those in which principles and operations are made linguistically explicit, whereas particularistic orders of meaning are meanings in which principles and operation are relatively linguistically implicit. If orders of meaning are universalistic, then the meanings are less tied to a given context. The meta-languages of public forms of thought as these apply to objects and persons realize meanings of a universalistic type. Where meanings have this characteristic then individuals have access to the grounds of their experience and can change the grounds. Where orders of meaning are particularistic, where principles are linguistically implicit, then such meanings are less context-independent and *more* context-bound, that is, tied to a local relationship and to a local social structure. Where the meaning system is particularistic, much of the meaning is embedded in the context and may be restricted to those who share a similar contextual history. Where meanings are universalistic, they are in principle available to all because the principles and operations have been made explicit, and so public.

I shall argue that forms of socialization orient the child towards speech codes which control access to relatively context-tied or relatively context-independent meanings. Thus I shall argue that elaborated codes orient their users towards universalistic meanings, whereas restricted codes orient, sensitize, their users to particularistic meanings: that the linguistic realization of the two orders are different, and so are the social relationships which realize them. Elaborated codes are less tied to a given or local structure and thus contain the potentiality of change in principles. In the case of elaborated codes the speech may be freed from its evoking social structure and it can take on an autonomy. A university is a place organized around talk. Restricted codes are more tied to a local social structure and have a reduced potential for change in principles. Where codes are elaborated, the socialized has more access to the grounds of his own socialization, and so can enter into a reflexive relationship to the social order he has taken over. Where codes are restricted, the socialized has less access to the grounds of his socialization, and thus reflexiveness may be limited in range. *One of the effects of the class system is to limit access to elaborated codes.*

I shall go on to suggest that restricted codes have their basis in condensed symbols, whereas elaborated codes have their basis in articulated symbols; that restricted codes draw upon metaphor, whereas elaborated codes draw upon rationality; that these codes constrain the contextual use of language in critical socializing contexts and in this way regulate the orders of relevance and relation which the socialized takes over. From this point of view, change in habitual speech codes involves changes in the means by which object and person relationships are realized.

I want first to start with the notions of elaborated and restricted speech variants. A variant can be considered as the contextual constraints upon grammatical-lexical choices.

Sapir, Malinowski, Firth, Vygotsky and Luria have all pointed out from different points of view that the closer the identifications of speakers the greater the range of shared interests, the more probable that the speech will take a specific form. The range of syntactic alternatives is likely to be reduced and the lexis to be drawn from a narrow range. Thus, the form of these social relations is acting selectively on the meanings to be verbally realized. In these relationships the intent of the other person can be taken for granted as the speech is played out against a backdrop of common assumptions, common history, common interests. As a result, there is less need to raise meanings to the level of explicitness or elaboration. There is a reduced need to make explicit through syntactic choices the logical structure of the communication. Further, if the speaker wishes to individualize his communication, he is likely to do this by varying the expressive associates of the speech. Under these conditions, the speech is likely to have a strong metaphoric element. In these situations the speaker may be more concerned with how something is said, when it is said; silence takes on a variety of meanings. Often in these encounters the speech cannot be understood apart from the context, and the context cannot be read by those who do not share the history of the relationships. Thus the form of the social relationship acts selectively in the meanings to be verbalized, which in turn affect the syntactic and lexical choices. The unspoken assumptions underlying the relationship are not available to those who are outside the relationship. For these are limited, and restricted to the speakers. The symbolic form of the communication is condensed, yet the specific cultural history of the relationship is alive in its form. We can say that the roles of the speakers are communalized roles. Thus, we can make a relationship between restricted social relationships based upon communalized roles and the verbal realization of their meaning. In the language of the earlier part of this paper, restricted social relationships based upon communalized roles evoke particularistic, that is, context-tied, meanings, realized through a restricted speech variant.

Imagine a husband and wife have just come out of the cinema, and are talking about the film: 'What do you think?' 'It had a lot to say.' 'Yes, I thought so too—let's go to the Millers, there may be something going there.' They arrive at the Millers, who ask about the film. An hour is spent in the complex, moral, political, aesthetic subtleties of the film and its place in the contemporary scene. Here we have an elaborated variant; the meanings now have to be made public to others who have not seen the film. The speech shows careful editing, at both the grammatical and lexical levels. It is no longer context-tied. The meanings are explicit, elaborated and individualized. While expressive channels are clearly relevant, the burden of meaning inheres predominantly in the verbal channel. The experience of the listeners cannot be taken for granted. Thus each member of the group is on his own as he offers his interpretation. Elaborated variants of this kind involve the speakers in particular role relationships, and *if you cannot manage the role, you can't produce the appropriate speech.* For as the speaker proceeds to individualize his meanings, he is differentiated from others like a figure from its ground.

The roles receive less support from each other. There is a measure of isolation. *Difference* lies at the basis of the social relationship, and is made verbally active, whereas in the other context it is *consensus*. The insides of the speaker have become psychologically active through the verbal aspect of the communication. Various defensive strategies may be used to decrease potential vulnerability of self and to increase the vulnerability of others. The verbal aspect of the communication becomes a vehicle for the transmission of individuated symbols. The 'I' stands over the 'we'. Meanings which are discrete to the speaker must be offered so that they are intelligible to the listener. Communalized roles have given way to individualized roles, condensed symbols to articulated symbols. Elaborated speech variants of this type realize universalistic meanings in the sense that they are less context-tied. Thus individualized roles are realized through elaborated speech variants which involve complex editing at the grammatical and lexical levels and which point to universalistic meanings.

Let me give another example. Consider the two following stories which Peter Hawkins, Assistant Research Officer in the Sociological Research Unit, University of London Institute of Education, constructed as a result of his analysis of the speech of middle-class and working-class five-year-old children. The children were given a series of four pictures which told a story and they were invited to tell the story. The first picture showed some boys playing football; in the second the ball goes through the window of a house; the third shows a woman looking out of the window and a man making an ominous gesture, and in the fourth the children are moving away.

Here are the two stories:

1. Three boys are playing football and one boy kicks the ball and it goes through the window the ball breaks the window and the boys are looking at it and a man comes out and shouts at them because they've broken the window so they run away and then that lady looks out of her window and she tells the boys off.
2. They're playing football and he kicks it and it goes through there it breaks the window and they're looking at it and he comes out and shouts at them because they've broken it so they run away and then she looks out and she tells them off.

With the first story the reader does not have to have the four pictures which were used as the basis for the story, whereas in the case of the second story the reader would require the initial pictures in order to make sense of the story. The first story is free of the context which generated it, whereas the second story is much more closely tied to its context. As a result the meanings of the second story are implicit, whereas the meanings of the first story are explicit. It is not that the working-class children do not have in their passive vocabulary the vocabulary used by the middle-class children. Nor is it the case that the children differ in their tacit understanding of the linguistic rule system. Rather, what we have here are differences in the use of language arising out of a specific context. One child makes explicit the meanings which he is realizing through language for the person he is telling the story to, whereas the second child does not to the same extent. The first child takes very little for granted, whereas the second child takes a great deal for granted. Thus for the first child the task was seen as a context in which his meanings were required to be made explicit, whereas the task for the second child was not seen as a task which required such explication of meaning. It would not be difficult to imagine a context where the first child would produce speech rather like the second. What we are dealing with here are differences between the children in the way they realize in language-use apparently the same context. We could say that the speech of the first child generated universalistic meanings in the sense that the meanings are freed from the context and so understandable by all, whereas the speech of the second child generated particularistic meanings, in the sense that the meanings are closely tied to the context and would be fully understood by others only if they had access to the context which originally generated the speech.

It is again important to stress that the second child has access to a more differentiated noun phrase, but there is a restriction on its *use*.

Geoffrey Turner, Linguist in the Sociological Research Unit, shows that working-class, five-year-old children in the same contexts examined by Hawkins use fewer linguistic expressions of uncertainty when compared with the middle-class children. This does not mean that working-class children do *not* have access to such expressions, but that the eliciting speech context did not provoke them. Telling a story from pictures, talking about scenes on cards, *formally framed* contexts, do not encourage working-class children to consider the possibilities of alternate meanings and so there is a reduction in the linguistic expressions of uncertainty. Again, working-class children have access to a wide range of syntactic choices which involve the use of logical operators, 'because', 'but', 'either', 'or', 'only'. The constraints exist on the conditions for their *use*. Formally framed contexts used for eliciting context-independent universalistic meanings may evoke in the working-class child, relative to the middle-class child, restricted speech variants, because the working-class child has difficulty in managing the role relationships which such contexts require. This problem is further complicated when such contexts carry meanings very much removed from the child's cultural experience. In the same way we can show that there are constraints upon the middle-class child's use of language. Turner found that when middle-class children were asked to role-play in the picture story series, a higher percentage of these children, when compared with working-class children, initially refused. When the middle-class children were asked, 'What is the man saying?' or linguistically equivalent questions, a relatively higher percentage said 'I don't know.' When this question was followed by the hypothetical question, 'What do you think the man might be saying?' they offered their interpretations. The working-class children role-played without difficulty. It seems then that middle-class children at five need to have a very precise instruction to *hypothesize in that particular* context. This may be because they are more concerned here with getting their answers right or correct. When the children were invited to tell a story about some doll-like figures (a little boy, a little girl, a sailor and a dog) the working-class children's stories were freer, longer and more imaginative than the stories of the middle-class children. The latter children's stories were tighter, constrained within a strong narrative frame. It was as if these children were dominated by what they took to be the *form* of a narrative and the content was secondary. This is an example of the concern of the middle-class child with the structure of the contextual frame. It may be worthwhile to amplify this further.

A number of studies have shown that when working-class black child-ren are asked to associate to a series of words, their responses show considerable diversity, both from the meaning and form-class of the stimulus word. Our analysis suggests this may be because the children for the following reasons are less constrained. The form-class of the stimulus word may have reduced associative significance and this would less constrain the selection of potential words *or* phrases. With such a weakening of the grammatical frame there is a greater range of alternatives as possible candidates for selection. Further, the closely controlled, middle-class, linguistic socialization of the young child may point the child towards both the grammatical significance of the stimulus word and towards a tight logical ordering of semantic space. Middle-class children may well have access to deep interpretative rules which regulate their linguistic responses in certain formalized con-texts. The consequences may limit their imagination through the tightness of the frame which these interpretative rules create. It may even be that with *five*-year-old children, the middle-class child will innovate *more* with the arrangements of objects (i.e. bricks) than in his linguistic usage. His linguistic usage is under close supervision by adults. He has more *autonomy* in his play.

[The final eight pages of this essay are omitted.]

14

Impossible discourse
Trevor Pateman

From Pateman, T. 1975: *Language, truth and politics*. Newton Poppleford, Devon: Trevor Pateman and Jean Stroud, 70–84.

Note: *Language, truth and politics* will be published in a new, revised and enlarged edition in 1980. The extract that follows includes some amendments from this new edition, which can be obtained from Jean Stroud, PO Box 12, Lewes, East Sussex, England.

Language and logic

I don't understand physics because I don't know the language of physics. This is partly a question of *vocabulary*, partly one of *concepts*, partly one of the mental *organization* of vocabulary—and the last two aspects are interrelated, as I shall try to show. These are some of the obstacles to my understanding physics. Do some people face comparable obstacles to understanding radical or revolutionary politics?

Is it, first of all, that some people lack the *vocabulary* with which they could understand and within which they could think certain thoughts? Though not of central importance, the absence of vocabulary is, I think, of more importance than the logical possibility of paraphrase might make it seem. It is plausible for Orwell in *1984* to attribute considerable significance to the removal of words from the lexicon, for though paraphrase remains logically possible, to actively engage in paraphrase requires a greater commitment to thought than does the simple use of a ready-made word-concept. Words are things to think with, and without them one is obliged to produce the means of thought as well as thought itself.

However, even if a vocabulary is known, the concepts belonging to each word may not be fully or accurately known. 'Trotskyism', 'Anarchism', 'Soviet', 'commune', etc. are known to many people (though how many?), but perhaps in the majority of cases they will be known as the *names* of desirable or undesirable practices. They name objects, institutions and practices and they direct or discharge considerable emotional energy, but their conceptual content in use is small; they are used as *proper names*, which do no more than designate or refer. The words (no more than a proper name) cannot be used to think with about the practices to which they are used to refer. (This is perhaps what people are getting at when they object to *labelling*, that is, the use of an emotionally loaded proper name.) In addition, such words may be used inaccurately to refer, though this is not entailed by their being used as proper names.

The ways in which descriptive words are emptied of their conceptual content, and thereby become purely referential expressions, has been amply commented upon, for example, by Marcuse. I think that Anglo-American philosophers have compounded rather than counteracted this process in their analysis of political terms, since they have taken as the starting point for their analyses the actual occurrence of such words on the surface of discourse, where they are used as mere naming and 'boo' 'hooray' expressions. The results of such analysis are bound to be as disappointing as the discourse being analysed. (On this point, see my 1973a.) The results of such analysis for political philosophy have been disastrous, but no more so than such a use of words has been for the possibility of political thinking among the population at large.

If not by suppression, or emptying of content, then by other means can potentially critical concepts be rendered practically useless for critical thought. Marcuse has commented on such means in *One Dimensional Man* (1964). There he writes of the role of combining contradictory thoughts in a single expression. This occurs, for example, when a policy described in terms which would justify its designation as 'reactionary' is then named as 'revolutionary'. This could be a simple case in which 'revolution' has been emptied of meaning and is used simply to express an attitude or name an object, without giving rise to formally contradictory predication. On the other hand, there do appear to be more subtle cases (and it seems that Marcuse has these in mind) where one can speak of genuine contradiction, since the conceptual content of each of two terms is simultaneously predicated and denied. That is to say, the effectiveness of the statement made by A in persuading B to adopt an attitude towards *x* involves simultaneously evoking in B his understanding of the conceptual content of (say) 'revolution' whilst describing *x* in terms which indicate that it does not possess the properties which would justify the predication 'revolution'.

I think I can make this clearer with a concrete example from the sphere of trade names. In one sense, the trade name *Belair* for a brand of cigarette is an arbitrary proper name. If I ask for a packet of *Belair*, I use the name as a proper name and do not think of the name as having a conceptual content. On the other hand, *Belair* contributes to the task of selling the cigarette to the degree that the conceptual meaning (here, the literal meaning) and also the connotations of meaning (such as 'Frenchness') are known to the buyer.

But, with regard to the literal meaning, it might be questioned whether this would work as a selling force if the buyer became explicitly aware of the meaning. For if someone were to become explicitly aware of the literal meaning of *bel air*, would this not equal awareness of a characteristic so 'obviously' the opposite of the real characteristics of the product as to lead the potential buyer to ridicule the product? (In Orwell's *1984*, *Victory* is the brand name for the products with which a defeated population is drugged.)

Against this interpretation, consider what could happen if the potential buyer does not accept as 'obviously' true that 'Smoking can Damage your Health', that is to say, does not accept as obviously true the content of HM Government's Health Warning printed on the side of the packet. In such circumstances, conscious awareness of the meaning of *Belair* would produce a situation which could be characterized as follows: the packet of cigarettes carries, printed on it, two statements which both purport to be true of the contents of the packet. One says that what you inhale when you smoke *can* damage your health; the other says that what you inhale when you smoke is *bel air*, and 'good air' *cannot*, by definition, damage your health. I am expanding and interpreting the two statements to put them in formally contradictory form, but I don't think that my expansion is far from the truth.) Now, all students of philosophy know that if two statements are formally contradictory, then they cancel each other out. No meaning is 'produced'. Unless the buyer privileges either the Government's statement, or the meaning *Belair*, the formal effect of giving the name *Belair* to the cigarette is to cancel the Government's message. Of course, the meaning of the proposition implied by the name *Belair* is also cancelled. *Belair* remains as a name, and a set of connotations, that is all, though the cigarette manufacturer, like the Government, can try to get the buyer to privilege its statement against that of its opponent, in which case no cancelling of meaning occurs. But, apart from this, the effect of giving the cigarette the name *Belair* is to repulse and reduce the prior critical discourse of the Government.

Marcuse also refers to *telescoping* and *abridgement* of discourse as means by which rational thought with critical concepts is rendered difficult. He writes of this process of telescoping and abridgement that it 'cuts development of meaning by creating fixed images [which "militates against the development and expression of concepts" p. 95] which impose themselves with an overwhelming and petrified concreteness' (1964, 91; compare Barthes, 1972). Perhaps the best example of this process is the photo-journalism in which one is presented with the 'picture which sums it all up'. Of course, the picture is captioned to make sure that there is no misreading of it. But, very literally, meaning is reduced to an *image*. In political thinking, I think that this sort of photo-journalism encourages the reduction of structurally very complex situations to the level of exemplification of very general, a-historical and non-operational concepts, such as 'trouble', 'violence', 'fear', 'hunger', 'bewilderment', etc., all of which have their Faces. Such photo-journalism never improved anyone's understanding of the realities or complexities of political life. Its images fix understanding at the level of surface appearance.

Such practices as those discussed above can become important social phenomena because language, though the socially produced means of thought, is not socially controlled. Increasingly, control over the development of language and its use is held by State institutions, including mass media, and monopolistic private enterprise, as in journalism and advertising. Orwell's *1984* developed the possible consequences of the State's domination over language. The semiologists, who have studied the same kind of linguistic developments as those which interest Marcuse, have sometimes failed to appreciate the possibility and existence of class or other minority control over language, whilst recognizing that minority groups are responsible for the creation of sign systems and fixed combinations of signs in such fields as furniture and clothing. Even Barthes, on whose work Marcuse draws extensively, can write:

> In the linguistic model, nothing enters the language without having been tried in speech, but conversely no speech is possible ... if it is not drawn from the 'treasure' of the language.... But in most *other* semiological systems, the language is elaborated not by the 'speaking mass' but by a deciding group. In this sense, it can be held that in most semiological languages, the sign is really and truly 'arbitrary' since it is founded in artificial fashion by unilateral decision (1967, 31; my italic).[1]

But isn't the situation of 'most other semiological systems' also increasingly true of natural language? Is the language of politics really elaborated by the 'speaking mass'?

Beyond the question of vocabulary, and the effects on it of the way in which it is used, there is the question of how a given vocabulary is organized in the individual's mind, and how this in turn affects the possibilities of thought. What I mean by this can be illustrated by an example from Vygotsky's psychology. In his *Thought and Language*, Vygotsky points out that 'A child learns the word *flower*, and shortly afterwards the word *rose*; for a long time the concept "flower", though more widely applicable than "rose", cannot be said to be more general for the child. It does not include and subordinate "rose"— the two are interchangeable and juxtaposed. When "flower" becomes generalized, the relationship of "flower" and "rose", as well as of "flower" and other subordinate concepts, also changes in the child's mind. A system is taking shape' (1962, 92–3). Vygotsky has already indicated what he takes to be the significance of this development: 'To us it seems obvious that a concept can become subject to consciousness and deliberate control only when it is part of a system. If consciousness means generalization, generalization in turn means the formation of a superordinate concept that includes the given concept as a particular case' (1962, 92).[2] Two further points need to be made before the significance for political thinking of such phenomena can be indicated. First, that relations of superordination and subordination develop as a result of socialization and not as a result of some inner maturation process, proceeding independently of the particular social environment.

Vygotsky himself stresses the significance of formal instruction in school subjects, arguing that through school instruction concepts are learnt from the start in relations of superordination and subordination, and that this catalyses a similar development of the organization of concepts which the child has learnt 'spontaneously': 'It is our contention that the rudiments of systematization first enter the child's mind by way of his contact with scientific concepts and are then transferred to everyday concepts, changing their psychological structure from the top down' (p. 93). This also implies that there is nothing inevitable about the development of conceptual organization.

The second point to be made is that not all the words of a natural language are organizable into the 'trees' which can always be constructed for scientific words, and which—perhaps—makes them scientific. Lyons, who calls subordinate words 'hyponyms' (thus, 'scarlet', 'crimson', 'vermilion' are co-hyponyms of 'red' (1968, 454–5), writes that

> The main point to be made about the relation of hyponymy as it is found in natural languages is that it does not operate as comprehensively or as systematically there as it does in the various systems of scientific taxonomy . . . The vocabularies of natural languages tend to have many gaps, asymmetries and indeterminacies in them' (1968, 456).

—something which is explored at length in Wittgenstein's later writings (1958).

I think that these psychological and linguistic theses are relevant to the question of the possibility of different sorts of political thinking. I think that even if relevant political words are learnt, they need not be organized hierarchically or systematically, even in an adult's mind. In consequence, they can remain wholly or partly a-conceptual. If this is the case, it necessarily affects the possibility of understanding discourse which employs them as concepts. Lyons seems to make a similar point in a 'neutral' context, though it depends on how one reads the 'as for instance':

> It may be impossible to determine and perhaps also to know the meaning of one word without also knowing the meaning of others to which it is 'related'—as for instance, *cow* is to *animal* (1968, 409).

Let me now try to illustrate this line of argument with an example from the realm of political discourse.

Suppose that the concept of *anarchy* or *anarchism*, which would be involved in any proposition about the possibility or features of an anarchist society, is (partly) defined as being a *society without a government*. A verbal or conceptual tree[3] built up from the elements 'anarchy', 'society', 'government' and expanded to include the co-hyponyms of 'government', looks like this:

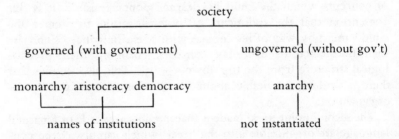

Within the hierarchy presented by the diagram, the higher up the tree you go, the greater the degree of abstraction, though all of the

concepts above the level of the names of institutions are abstract ones: they are concepts rather than complexes in Vygotsky's sense of 'complex', which is that a complex word is one for the application of which there is no finite set of necessary or sufficient defining characteristics: in Wittgenstein's terminology, the members of a complex possess no more than a *family resemblance* (1958, paragraphs 66, 67).

Now, I think that though the word 'society' is generally learnt, it is frequently not organized in a person's mind into the kind of tree given in the diagram; it can be and is learnt and retained a-conceptually. The understanding of 'government' which such a person would then have would not be one which related 'government' to 'society' but one where the concepts of types of government or the names of instantiations of governments were used to give it meaning. This would entail that 'government' was understood not as a concept, but as the family name of a collection of particulars. It would be understood as the name of a complex.[4]

Consider now what is required for 'anarchy' to be adequately understood. My theory is that it cannot be adequately understood except when organized within a tree which extends up to and including the level of 'society'. For, first, the concept of 'anarchy' cannot be understood by reference to its own instantiations, since there are none. And, second, the definition of 'anarchy' includes reference to both 'government' and 'society' and it cannot be understood on its own level as a simple *absence* of monarchy, aristocracy, etc. Monarchy, aristocracy, etc., are linguistic co-hyponyms, but I do not see how the concept of 'anarchy' can be produced by opposing these concepts to the word 'anarchy' unless there is already an implied reference to 'society'. In other words, the meaning of 'anarchy' cannot be generated or understood within an opposition to its co-hyponyms. It requires placing in a system which includes not only oppositional features, but superordination as well. If this is correct, my understanding (which may be inaccurate) of structuralist theories of meaning leads me to the conclusion that their account of the generation and understanding of meaning requires revision. For, as I understand such theories, their oppositions are made at only *one* level—indeed, the idea of *opposition* implies that of being on the same level (see Saussure, 1966).

But this point is an aside to my main object in this section, which is to suggest a theory of the following sort:

I am suggesting that adults can possess, and some do possess, a vocabulary in a particular area (I am using the case of political vocabulary) without having that vocabulary conceptually organized, with consequences similar to those which psychologists report for the non-conceptual organization of children's vocabularies. Not only would the existence of such non-organization explain failure to understand the meaning of terms, though those terms might be known, and thus explain failure to understand or generate the relevant sorts of discourse, but it would also explain such phenomena as insensitivity to contradiction which has frequently been remarked in adults for specific areas of discourse. Thus, in their case studies, Laing and Esterson remark the insensitivity of schizogenic parents to their own self-contradictions. Studies of the 'authoritarian personality' report the same thing (see Reich 1970, 1971) as do McKenzie and Silver in their study of working-class Conservatism (1969, especially 120, 121). In this last case in particular there are other possible explanations of apparent self-contradiction. Thus, limitations of vocabulary may lead a person to use contradiction as a means of conveying meaning for the explicit conveyance of which he lacks the necessary vocabulary. There is no self-contradiction in the bad sense when I say of a taste difficult to define 'It's sweet and yet it isn't.'

Classical cognitive-defect theories of schizophrenia also comment on insensitivity to contradiction in schizophrenics, and I think these studies are particularly valuable. (See Hanfmann and Kasanin, 1942, and Kasanin, 1944.) For whilst, as Eluned Price told me, these studies have largely been discredited as studies of phenomena specific to *schizophrenic* cognition (see, for example, Wason and Johnson Laird, 1972, chapter 18),[5] this discrediting takes the form of showing that what is allegedly related to schizophrenia is, in fact, related to level of formal education received. It was possible to think that features of schizophrenia were being described simply because most hospitalized schizophrenics have a low level of formal education. Theories about the 'schizophrenization' of culture thus turn out to have a firmer basis than simple analogy. For the features of 'schizophrenia' which originally prompted such analogies turn out to be non-specific to that state; they are features to be found in the thinking of a large proportion of the population.[6]

There may be objections to my procedure of using material from child psychology and psychopathology to understand sane, adult people, who are neither children nor schizophrenics. But there is no reason why they should not share characteristics with children and schizophrenics, and if the latter are better studied than the former (most psychological studies of 'normal adults' in fact use undergraduates as subjects), this is an added reason for using such studies as a jumping-off point. There may be theoretical objections to such a procedure, but this is different from a simple dislike of it, which can only be founded on a contempt for children and 'schizophrenics'. That is simply the chauvinism of the man in the street, defined as sane, adult, white, male and middle class. So I am not too worried by this dislike. I may well be wrong in thinking that some adults, as a result of their socialization, have important characteristics in common with children and schizophrenics. I am bound to think that the theory is at least worth testing.[7]

To return, then, to Vygotsky. In the report of an experiment, Vygotsky tries to show how children regard the name of an object as a property of that object, and thus lack a fully formed appreciation of the nature of symbolism: writers like Cassirer (1944) and Goldstein (1963) would say that the child lacks the *abstract attitude*.[8] To demonstrate his point, Vygotsky confronts the child with a situation in which the name of an object is arbitrarily changed: a dog is henceforth to be called a 'cow'. For most adults, I presume that such an arrangement would produce no substantial difficulties, and about the first thing a Philosophy student learns to recognize explicitly is the arbitrariness of the word-sign. I doubt that an average adult would respond to Vygotsky's questions as does the typical child, who, having been told that a dog is henceforth to be called a 'cow', responds to questions in the following way:

[Experimenter]—Does a cow have horns?
[Subject]　　　—Yes
[Experimenter]—But don't you remember that the cow is really a dog. Come now, does a dog have horns?
[Subject]　　　—Sure, if it's a cow, if it's called a cow, it has horns. That kind of dog has got to have little horns (1962, 129).

Even if this particular experiment was badly designed and conducted, I don't think it follows that the value of such an experiment is destroyed by the claim (made by objectors to the above argument) that the child is more intellectually sophisticated than the experimenter.[9]

I presume that most adults asked whether a dog, arbitrarily renamed 'cow', would have horns, would reply that it would not (Is that your reply?), but I also presume that it does not follow that they would get the answer right whatever the *kind* of word change involved. I think that the ability to perform this kind of intellectual operation

could be content-specific. And where the situation is a non-experi-
mental one, from which the motive either to please or displease an
experimenter is absent, I think that sane, adult people do sometimes
perform operations like those of the child in Vygotsky's experiment.
I suggest that in some areas, some adults do treat a word as the property of an object. Aaron Sloman remarked, in comments on draft
material for this chapter, that people can be conceptually agile in some
domains and strait-jacketed in others. I assume this is so. I shall illustrate the kind of phenomena which the assumption covers, and I shall
draw my examples from the realm of political discourse and understanding.

Consider the following case.[10] I come across a person who argues
in such a manner that it is clear that he believes that if something is
conventionally called a system of Justice, then it must have the property of being Just, again as conventionally defined. This entails such
consequences as that, confronted with empirical evidence that an
existing institution of Justice contravened in its practice the *conventional* norms of Justice (that is, it is unjust in its own terms), such
a person could not admit that such evidence *might be true*. The possibility of empirical evidence being relevant is ruled out *a priori*, and
this entails that for this person it is tautologically true that if something
is called a system of Justice, then it must be Just. This is not quite
the same kind of case as that where the practice of existing institutions,
whatever it may be, *defines* what is right, for I am not denying that
this person has a concept of Justice defined independently of practice.[11] I am claiming that this perosn cannot admit that the word 'Justice' could be erroneously applied. This seems to me analysable as a
case in which the arbitrariness of the word-sign 'Justice' is not recognized, that is, a case where the word-sign is treated as a property of
the object. Hence, any discussion which contrasts Reality with an independently defined Ideal is impossible, which means that any rational
discussion is impossible. Though this example, based on a single conversation, may seem extreme (and does leave many questions un-
answered), I think there is a widespread tendency to use political concepts in the above fashion. Marcuse sensed it and produced an anlysis
in terms of one-dimensional thought.

Take another example, a little easier to describe and substantiate
from experience. To me it seems that some people are unable to
understand, or argue in terms of propositions involving explicit
counter-factual conditionals, though again such inability need not be
across-the-board; it can be content-specific. What I mean is that

some people respond to arguments of the sort which begin 'Suppose you had...' with a straightforward 'But I didn't ...' It has been put to me that this *genre* of response does not show people's cognitive limitations, but rather their cognitive sophistication. They refuse to be drawn into the kind of hypothetical argument in which the most skilled in dialectical debate necessarily wins. Now, whilst I agree that some people use the response 'But I didn't ...' as a refusal, I don't accept that that this is always the case. My reasons are two-fold. First that one elicits the response 'But I didn't ...' even in circumstances where the respondent recognizes that it is in his interest to understand the hypothetical argument (as in direction giving: 'Imagine you're standing at the corner of Charing Cross Road and Oxford Street, with Centre Point on your right ...'). Second, that I find it inconsistent that people should be so intellectually sophisticated as my opponents' argument makes out, yet so frequently be taken for a ride by all sorts of con-men, from politicians upwards.

I have produced only two examples, but I am sure others can produce further instances of linguistic or logico-linguistic ways in which adults with little formal education and no experience of other relevant learning situations, can be inhibited or prevented from thinking certain thoughts and understanding certain sorts of discourse or argument. Such incapacities are content-specific and can be given a social explanation. The incapacities may not always be apparent, not least if the person consciously or unconsciously seeks to hide them. Thus, for example, when he does not understand an idea, he may say that it is 'Nonsense'. Roland Barthes has commented on this particular mode of response as a characteristic of petty-bourgeois thinking (Barthes, 1972, especially the essay *Blind and Dumb Criticism*, 34–5). Enoch Powell seems to employ this strategy of labelling as 'Nonsense' that which he does not understand (Wood, 1970, especially *The Enemy Within*, 104–12) though here it is difficult to distinguish the use of 'Nonsense' as an emotive synonym of 'False' from the use of 'Nonsense' to disguise lack of understanding.[12]

The reader could try to add his own examples and analyses to my list. Why is it, for example, that some people reply to Why? questions about causation with restatements of facts?

Theory

Part of my ignorance of physics consists in not knowing the substantive theories of physics. It is out of the question that I should re-invent such theories myself—at least, any but the most elementary ones. Quite aside from the material resources needed to set up and conduct experiments, one person does not have the time or intelligence to re-invent the product of centuries, if not millennia, of collective work. There is no practical alternative to reading other people's books, going to other people's lectures, and using apparatus under other people's supervision.

There are many theories of politics, both scientific and normative. Most people have never had any formal instruction in any of them, let alone the ones, like Marxism, which can help them understand and act upon their own political situation in the world. The *omission* of political education in *theory* from the curriculum of schools is more important, I think, than any substantive instruction they administer to their pupils, such as 'British Constitution', the ideology of which seems to consist in presenting the abstract formal description of institutions as a model of their actual functioning. Again, such political theories as the media present seem to me either to be of too high a level of abstractness, or to be trapped in the concrete example. It is the middle range of the theoretical concepts which is *missing*, and this quite aside from any overt *bias*. The abstractness of media concepts consists in the use of reified 'forces' such as 'progress', 'reaction', 'order', 'disorder', etc., as explanatory concepts; the concreteness of the media consists in the description of social reality at the level of isolated *events*. Of course, it is at the most abstract and most concrete levels that there is least disagreement (at least overtly so) and the resort to abstract and concrete may be the means whereby they discharge their obligation to be overtly unbiased. The middle range of concepts (which includes sociological concepts like 'class', 'status', etc.) is the area of greatest overt controversy and it is therefore *excluded*. (The exclusion of substantive *contents*, perhaps the most important way in which bias operates, is a different issue.)

Professional politicians are possibly even worse as sources of theoretical understanding of political reality. Their position depends on limiting understanding of politics and their own role within it. The fact that the speeches of very few politicians bear reprinting is some indication of the absence of theoretical (even informational) content from what they say. The reading public has nothing to learn from them, only about them: the Collected Speeches of Edward Heath or Harold Wilson could be used only to damn.

To the degree that people feel the need for explicit political theories, I think they are left very much to their own devices. The vocabulary of politics is determined externally, and certain ideologies of voting are propagated, but for the rest, politics, far from being the field *par excellence* of deliberately propagated ideology, is left to a great degree to be occupied by *spontaneous ideologies*.

These spontaneous ideologies reflect closely the immediate circumstances of daily life and do not transcend them; they take appearance for reality and concrete incident for theory. They reify the existing order of things. Thus, racism and working-class conservatism. Reification involves at least three processes absent from radical and revolutionary theories. First, there is no theoretical recognition of the historical character of the present social order. Even if there is an awareness of the historical emergence of the present system, that system is seen as the culminating goal of the historical process beyond which no substantial change is possible. Second, there is no conscious awareness of the dependence of social change on human action, whether collective or individual. This is true of religious conceptions in which 'God has his plan', of technocratic conceptions in which technology has its own immanent plan, and in deference views in which 'You've got to have the people with money'—where a contingent feature of society, that wealth is the dominant source of power, is reified into a necessary feature of social existence. Third, the needs, wants or interests which might stimulate action to change the social order are repressed and sublimated. Wilhelm Reich theorizes in detail about the mechanisms by which this is accomplished (1970, 1971).

The argument of this chapter has been that many people are linguistically inhibited from thinking theoretically about politics, and if this is correct it helps explain the weakness of spontaneous ideologies. For essential to theory (which is what such ideologies aspire to) is the employment of elaborate causal and functional concepts and the corresponding vocabulary. In my teaching, I noticed that when asked for explanations of social phenomena, apprentices often redescribed the phenomena or restated the question minus the interrogative (e.g., Why is there a housing shortage? There aren't enough houses. Compare Halliday, 1969, 35). There was, at least, a lack of readiness to volunteer causal explanations, though no lack of readiness to offer answers. In terms of theory, I have read and been influenced by the work of Basil Bernstein, but I do not think that my arguments depend for their validity on acceptance of his theory of restricted and elaborated linguistic *codes*. For Bernstein, it is a defining feature of a restricted code, to which the lower working class (at least) is allegedly confined that it lacks 'elaborate causal conceptions' (1971, 47). I agree that elaborate causal conceptions are lacking, but doubt that the lack is necessarily or empirically systematic enough to merit the use of the concept of 'code'.

If there is such a thing as a restricted code, lacking in elaborate causal concepts, then I think its existence would have to be explained by reference to the fact that some people think they have no *use* for elaborate causal conceptions. They may have reconciled themselves, for example, to their real exclusion from politics (see section following). Such privatization would explain the use of a restricted code, as Bernstein himself indicates (1971, 147), though I would expect a dialectical relationship between code and circumstances: that is to say, that whilst the circumstances produce the code, the code strengthens the grip of circumstances.

Practice

> I don't think explanations are needed of people's conceptual limitations. What is needed is an explanation of how such limitations are ever broken out of. Aaron Sloman, in remarks on draft material for this book. (Compare Wertheimer, 1961.)

If I were to make the attempt to learn physics, I should need a motive (and a pretty strong one) if I were to make any progress in the subject. I might be driven by ambition, pure or idle curiosity, or necessity. It is unlikely that I shall ever be strongly enough 'motivated' to learn physics.

Could the relation of people to the understanding of politics be similar? A motive is needed equally for someone to set out to understand politics, but it would seem, at first glance, that such a motive is always and universally present. For the life of every person is inescapably a political life, and chances of being happy and free depend in direct and important ways on the form of society within which a person lives. Failure to 'recognize' such facts is precisely what constitutes the psychological side of real alienation and political exclusion (see my 1973b).

Because of real and psychological alienation, the ever-present motive for understanding politics does not 'surface' in the form of an interest in politics, whilst alienation does surface in the 'flight'[13] from politics into 'private' modes of existence, doomed to defeat because based on belief in a non-existent possibility of privacy. Rather than challenge a real state of affairs, or the psychological states which it generates, people try to escape them both. Perhaps they can conceive of no other way out. Certainly, their attempted solutions only compound their powerlessness and sense of powerlessness; but why might they not be able to conceive of any other way out?

On the one hand, I am sure that some people make a rational calculation and conclude that change is practically impossible. On the other, I am sure—as indicated in previous sections—that there are people who can't or don't envisage radically different situations, let alone believe that it is possible to bring them about. The non-existence of fully acceptable alternatives elsewhere in the world is a potent factor in confirming both these perspectives, which is why it is far from irrelevent for left-wing organizations to devote a great deal of intellectual effort to analysing the structure of the Soviet Union, China, Cuba, etc.

Again, it is not as if the work or the family situation provides alternative experience which might be applied critically to the political realm from the point of view of changing it. If anything, work and family are less democratic situations than is politics, though, interestingly, the family situation at least produces reactions in children structurally very similar to the reactions of adults to the political situation in which they find themselves. For example, in their studies of the families of schizophrenics (many of the characteristics of which must be regarded as typical rather than deviant, at least of practice if not of ideological norms), Laing and Esterson (1970) show how children respond to denial or prohibition of their practice, or invalidation or negation of their own self-definitions, by *withdrawal* (which becomes catatonia in the clinical stage). When there is no way out through the door, or there seems no way out, or where they lack the means to fight back (including the cognitive means), children may withdraw as the only alternative to complete submission. It resembles political apathy or privatization in being a fugitive practice in response to a denial of the *need* for self-determination.[14]

Last but not least, changing the world demands a great deal of time, effort, strength and courage. Serious efforts to change society frequently encounter severe repression. Who'd be a revolutionary?

The powerful, over-determined character of the obstacles to political action and knowledge does illustrate the meaning and realism of the Marxist perspective which emphasizes not an abstract political-educational effort as that which generates a political movement, but, rather, the force of economic circumstances, and the needs and interests which economic developments simultaneously generate and frustrate. But if this is so, then the greatest of the obstacles to political action would then appear to be those practices which encourage people to accept frustration, or make them fearful of fighting for their needs, or lead them to repress their self-knowledge of their own frustrations. In chapter I, section 6,* I discussed and criticized the established assumption that men *will* act to satisfy their needs and further their interests. The most difficult problem facing radicals and revolutionaries is that where men do not or will not act to satisfy their needs, where they accept frustration or repress their knowledge of it.[15]

This is why I think the writings of Wilhelm Reich deserve such careful study, and also why I think that any political movement today must itself be a source of satisfaction to its members and not purely a sacrifice. There should be nothing 'religious' about a political movement.[16] Activities like theatre, film and music should be neither decorative features of a political movement or narrowly instrumental. For in them people may come to know their own desires and become willing to act collectively to satisfy them.[17]

Conclusions

I have compared politics to physics, but I do not wish to encourage the scientization of politics in the sense that that phrase is understood by writers like Habermas. That is, I do not wish to regard politics as a sphere in which exclusively instrumental problems arise; nor do I wish that political control should be vested in 'experts'. On the other hand, I do believe that theory is needed to understand what is going on in political society, and I come reluctantly to the conclusion that people will always remain unequal in the level of their theoretical sophistication, and that, in consequence, there will be theoretical leaders. But they need not be leaders in everything else as well: and if they claim to be, and enforce their claim, the effects are often enough disastrous. Leaders can also be subject to greater control and enjoy less permanence than they now do.[18] Yet it still remains true, I think, that people cannot spontaneously generate the range and depth of political knowledge required for them to function effectively as political agents. In this sense, I think my heuristic analogy between physics and politics is not so misleading, and I have to come down, against some of the anarchists, on the side of Lenin.

My ignorance of physics is historically explicable and of no importance. Comparable ignorance about politics is common, explicable and important. I think that the theories I have sketched in this chapter

* Not included in this extract.

are relevant to political activists in their daily work, and that the effort to confirm or refute them would be worthwhile. This book would more than have achieved its purpose if some of its remarks were found useful by those engaged in the nitty-gritty work of achieving radical social change.

Section IV

Meaning and interpretation

In this section of the Reader we want to offer some work which raises issues important to most kinds of human communication, though these issues have not always received the attention we think they deserve.

The attempt to provide an adequate account of social meaning, that is to say meaning seen as the product of cultural and social activity, has long been a concern in Humanities inquiry both in the Arts and the Social Sciences. The growth of Linguistics research in the last twenty years or so has fed new complications and new possibilities into such study.

One of the main difficulties in attempting to chart and explain the characteristics of social and cultural meaning is that, in comparison with many other dimensions of human action, meanings are often very difficult to identify and to study in a way which is both systematic and which relates them to other social factors.

For instance, a sociologist wanting to conduct research on the relation, amongst undergraduates living at home, between examination success and library use, is at least working with factors having a fair degree of accessibility as potential data. That is not to argue that such a project wouldn't require some critical sensitivity to the problems of categories and definitions. But if we compare it with, say, an attempt to investigate students' attitudes towards academic work through an analysis of tape-recordings made of conversations in bars, refectories and common-rooms, then we can see the special difficulties which a direct attention to questions of meaning involves.

How are we to allow for the fact that joking, irony and a variety of social conventions (including, perhaps, some of a rather exclusive kind) will often make the relation between what is said and what is meant a very complex one indeed? Moreover, what guarantee have we that the way in which we choose to understand a remark is the way in which it was understood by its intended audience? And if the addressees seemed to react differently to a remark to what extent might this be due to their having different *responses* to what was meant and to what extent might it be attributable to their having different *interpretations* of what was meant?

Such an example raises the general question of interpretation and with it the problem that because interpretation is an *activity* the interpreter (reader, viewer, listener) is always involved in the production of the meanings which he or she wishes to 'receive' and perhaps to analyse.

In literary criticism, where a personal response and an individualized reading are encouraged, at least as the essential grounding for anything else, interpretation is often regarded as more of a celebrated first principle than a block to knowledge.

However, in the general area of Social Studies, what use is an account of social behaviour which is subjectively dependent on the personal set of interpretative frameworks with which the observer happens to 'read the social world'? If coming to conclusions about the meaning of literary texts is a subtle and delicate matter which can come uncomfortably close to being a 'matter of taste', then how much more difficult might it be to read the 'texts' of social life?

If this latter phrase seems an outlandish misapplication, it is worth noting that at least one distinguished communications researcher in America (Carey, 1977) has recently argued that

> A cultural science of communication, then, views human behaviour, or more accurately human action, as a text. Our task is to construct a 'reading' of the text.

In Britain an area of work known as Cultural Studies, developing out of Literary Studies, has placed a similar emphasis on the investigation of social processes through a close analysis of expressive forms and behaviours. We shall suggest later some reading you might do in order to develop your own thinking and discussion in this area, but an introduction to the particular extracts and essays we have chosen to reproduce here might now be the best way of aiding your initial engagement with the arguments.

William Empson is a literary critic with a particularly keen interest in the complexities of language—one of his later works is entitled *The structure of complex words*. What perhaps helps to distinguish literature as an area of language use is the high degree of carefully wrought subtlety and expressive power which a lot of it displays. As a deliberate employment of language to stimulate imaginative activity in the reader and to give pleasure, it prompts us to ask questions of a very interesting kind about communicative form.

In the work from which our first extract is taken, Empson is concerned with the idea of 'ambiguity', that is to say the way in which certain words, either through their specific contexts of use or their own accumulated semantic richness, can generate in our minds more than one meaning, indeed can generate a number of very different and even conflicting meanings. This property of language, whilst no doubt something of a nuisance to the writers of legal documents and handbooks, can be put to good use by a writer intent on provoking in his reader a complex, associative mental activity centred upon the ideas, emotions or descriptions which he has written down.

Poetry, particularly the short poem or lyric, has a relative brevity and density of word organization which makes it perhaps the finest literary form for this type of closely worked, often difficult but also often very rewarding language-game in which the reader's mind is sometimes strenuously exercised in the act of reading.

In the extract, Empson restricts himself to a discussion of the latter half of a nineteenth-century lyric poem notable for its unusual and powerful verbal effects. He works from his own response, his own 'realization' of the poem, to an analysis of the multiple meanings generated by particular words.

The second extract is also taken from the work of a literary critic and also concerns itself with ambiguity of meaning, although this time the instances are not taken from literature.

Roland Barthes is perhaps the most well known and widely quoted theorist and practitioner of Semiology—the study of signs and sign systems which we have referred to earlier in this Reader as a controversial and quite recent development in the study of social meaning. Barthes's long-established interest in the cultural complexities of signification and representation has produced a great deal of work which any communications student will find of interest regardless of whether or not the perspectives of semiological analysis are found to be acceptable.

In the pieces reprinted here Barthes is writing in a more deliberately entertaining vein than that which he adopts in his major academic papers yet his characteristic concern with the patterned complexity of social meaning is clearly evidenced. The plotting of how cultural meanings are produced within a cultural 'language system' (the extent, therefore, to which they are *positional*; that is, related to a position within a system which includes the 'cultural set' of possible meanings) is central to all his work.

Barthes's approach, one he shares with many researchers in British Cultural Studies on whom he was a major influence, is to describe communicative activity in terms of its being made up of symptoms or clues which are traceable back to general aspects of social structure and social belief. In both the pieces we have chosen Barthes directs our attention to 'performances', social activities designed to entertain audiences and activities which might therefore be viewed as a form of play. One might describe much of Barthes's work as an attempt to chart the rules and conventions of structured play. In these pieces, Barthes discusses audience interpretations and speculates upon the processes of meaning which link the forms of entertainment to the forms of social behaviour of particular societies.

Our third extract comes from the work of Umberto Eco who, like Barthes, is a semiologist of international reputation. In his recent work he has gone further than Barthes in the quest for a comprehensive theory of coding and of sign production. There are, however, many linguisticians and sociologists who find such detailed typologies of codes and subcodes as those offered by Eco to be impossibly abstract and informed by too many assumptions about the sorts of regularity and predictability which one can expect from cultural meaning-systems and what Eco has termed 'the logic of cultures'.

We include an early piece by Eco in which he discusses the 'codes' of television. The paper is useful because it contains a lucid account of what his particular semiotic project is all about and because, although it moves towards an abstract classificatory system, it does offer examples of communicative behaviour together with Eco's comments on them.

Eco's work, like Barthes's has been influential in Britain, where a number of research papers have developed his rather general references to the difficult notion of 'ideology' far more thoroughly within the semiological frameworks he has suggested. In this connection, it is interesting to note that Eco emphasizes the need for audience research to find out just how the audiences of mass communication actually interpret media performances. On the whole, researchers in Cultural Studies have tended not to engage with direct audience surveys of any kind but have instead sought to *infer* audience interpretations from a combination of textual analysis and a typology of audience response drawn up in terms of social class and political affiliation but un-supported by empirical data of any kind. There are signs that such an approach is now giving way to a more direct study of audiences and you will find more about this in Section Five of the Reader.

The last two extracts are taken from the work of the American sociologist Erving Goffman. Goffman has been mainly concerned with personal interaction and his research connects fully with the studies of interpretation, cultural meaning and performance discussed earlier. It is his skill as a keen observer and recorder of behaviour that distinguishes Goffman's work. He often provides accounts which have an interesting resemblance to the craft of the novelist, so fascinated is he with the rich particularity of social conduct. This, together with a dryness of wit and an apparent unwillingness to link his accounts and his inventories of the repertoires of human behaviour to any notion of social structure or patterns of belief, has often brought him criticism.

The first extract needs no comment since it is itself an introductory discussion. The second extract shows Goffman turning his attention to the specialized aesthetic conventions of the radio play—a form of 'transcription practice' which allows him to make some very useful and provocative points having a relevance for more general questions of performance, convention, realized meaning and selective perception in human communication.

Further reading

We list below a brief selection of books which engage with the sorts of questions raised in this section, frequently doing so in the context of specific inquiries.

Barthes, Roland 1957: *Mythologies*. Paris: Editions du Seuil. English translation (Annette Lavers) London: Jonathan Cape 1972. Paladin Books edition 1973.
An engaging and witty collection of short essays on aspects of contemporary French culture and daily life in which substantive sociological commentary is mixed with a concern for analysing cultural meaning-systems. The last essay, 'Myth Today', was one of the most influential early discussions of Semiology, developing the insights of the Swiss linguistician Ferdinand De Saussure.
Berger, John 1972: *Ways of seeing*. Harmondsworth: Penguin Books.
A widely praised and superbly illustrated discussion of the historical and cultural contexts of perception in relation to painting and photography.

Goffman, Erving 1959: *The presentation of self in everyday life.* New York: Doubleday Anchor. Harmondsworth: Penguin Books 1969.
An inquiry into the meanings of primary social behaviour. Working with notions of 'role', 'performance' and the complexities of social 'selfhood', Goffman conducts a finely detailed discussion of the conventions and symbolic organization at work in human interaction. A very readable and important book.

Goffman, Erving 1974: *Frame analysis.* New York: Harper & Row. Harmondsworth: Penguin Books 1975.
Subtitled 'An Essay on the Organization of Experience' this book discusses many different forms of social experience in an attempt to examine the frameworks with which people make sense of events. There is a heavy reliance on material found in newspapers but the penetration of the author's analysis and his engagement with the subtleties of social meaning in the making give the book the status of a classic for students of communication.

Hall, Stuart and Jefferson, Tony (eds) 1976: *Resistance through rituals.* London: Hutchinson.
A collection of theoretical papers and social research projects which looks at the development of youth subcultures in post-war Britain. Very useful on questions of meaning and interpretation in relation to ethnographic inquiry, and concerned to trace the way in which mass communications contribute to subcultural styles and symbolic organization. The book develops a Marxist approach to social change and generational style.

Baggaley, J. and Duck, S. 1976: *Dynamics of television.* Farnborough: Saxon House.
The authors base their discussion of television processes on a series of experiments carried out using CCTV equipment. The question of image interpretation and its relation both to audience understanding and producer intentions is central to the research. Findings are discussed alongside the theories and propositions of a wide variety of other media research projects, including those involving the semiological analysis of texts.

Nichols, Bill (ed.) 1976: *Movies and methods: an anthology.* Berkeley: University of California Press.
One of the most useful collections of work in film studies available. Nichols has put together reprinted material from many sources, much of it concerned with film and photographic imagery and the history of cinematic forms. An excellent volume for the student of communication who is beginning to inquire into the aesthetic

and social distinctiveness of film and television as ways of producing meanings.

Smith, A. C. H. 1975: *Paper voices*. London: Chatto & Windus.

An interesting research project which inquires into social change in Britain between 1935 and 1965 by a detailed analysis of popular newspapers. The early section on problems of method is very useful but the book as a whole is an important achievement (though one heavily text-based) in the analysis of mass communications as a constituent of social and public meanings.

15

Analysis of the Gerard Manley Hopkins poem 'Spring and Fall'
William Empson

From Empson, William 1930: *Seven types of ambiguity*. London: Chatto & Windus.
Extract taken from Penguin Books edn 1973, 148–9.

Margaret, are you grieving
Over Goldengrove unleafing?
Leaves, like the things of man, you
With your fresh thoughts care for, can you?
Ah, as the heart grows older
It will come to such sights colder
By and by, nor spare a sigh
Though world of wanwood leafmeal lie;
And yet you will weep and know why.
Now no matter, child, the name.
Sorrow's springs àre the same.
Nor mouth had, no, nor mind express'd,
What heart heard of, ghost guess'd:
It is the blight man was born for,
It is Margaret you mourn for.

Will weep may mean: 'insist upon weeping, now or later', or 'shall
weep in the future'. *Know* in either case may follow *will*, like *weep*,
'you insist upon knowing, or you shall know,' or may mean: 'you
already know why you weep, why you shall weep, or why you insist
upon weeping', or thirdly, may be imperative, 'listen and I shall tell
you why you weep, or shall weep, or shall insist upon weeping, or
insist upon weeping already'. Mr Richards, from whom I copy this
(*Practical Criticism*, p. 83), considers that the ambiguity of *will* is removed by the accent which Hopkins placed upon it; it seems to me
rather that it is intensified. Certainly, with the accent on *weep* and
and, *will* can only be the auxiliary verb, and with the accent on *will*
its main meaning is 'insist upon'. But the future meaning also can be
imposed upon this latter way of reading the line if it is the tense which
is being stressed, if it insists on the contrast between the two sorts of
weeping, or, including *know* with *weep*, between the two sorts of

knowledge. Now it is useful that the tense should be stressed at this crucial point, because it is these two contrasts and their unity which make the point of the poem.

It seems difficult to enjoy the accent on *are*, which the poet has inserted; I take it to mean: 'Sorrow's springs, always the same, independent of our attitude to them and of our degree of consciousness of them, exist,' permanently and as it were absolutely.

The two sorts of knowledge, intuitive and intellectual, form ambiguities again in the next couplet; this may help to show they are really there in the line about *will*. *Mouth* and *mind* may belong to *Margaret* or somebody else; *what heart heard of* goes both forwards and backwards; and *ghost*, which in its grammatical position means both the profundities of the unconsciousness and the essentially conscious spirit, brings to mind both immortality and a dolorous haunting of the grave. 'Nobody else's mouth had told her, nobody else's mind had hinted to her, about the fact of mortality, which yet her own imagination had already invented, which her own spirit could foresee.' 'Her mouth had never mentioned death; she had never stated the idea to herself so as to be conscious of it; but death, since it was a part of her body, since it was natural to her organs, was known at sight as a portent by the obscure depths of her mind.' My point is not so much that these two are mixed up as that the poet has shown precisely by insisting that they were *the same*, that he knew they were distinguishable.

16

Striptease
Roland Barthes

From Barthes, Roland 1957: *Mythologies*. Paris: Editions du Seuil. Extract taken from Paladin books edition. Translated by Annette Lavers. London: Granada Publishing 1973, 84–7.

Striptease—at least Parisian striptease—is based on a contradiction: Woman is desexualized at the very moment when she is stripped naked. We may therefore say that we are dealing in a sense with a spectacle based on fear, or rather on the pretence of fear, as if eroticism here went no further than a sort of delicious terror, whose ritual signs have only to be announced to evoke at once the idea of sex and its conjuration.

It is only the time taken in shedding clothes which makes voyeurs of the public; but here, as in any mystifying spectacle, the decor, the props and the stereotypes intervene to contradict the initially provocative intention and eventually bury it in insignificance: evil is *advertised* the better to impede and exorcize it. French striptease seems to stem from what I have earlier called 'Operation Margarine', a mystifying device which consists in inoculating the public with a touch of evil, the better to plunge it afterwards into a permanently immune Moral Good: a few particles of eroticism, highlighted by the very situation on which the show is based, are in fact absorbed in a reassuring ritual which negates the flesh as surely as the vaccine or the taboo circumscribe and control the illness or the crime.

There will therefore be in striptease a whole series of coverings placed upon the body of the woman in proportion as she pretends to strip it bare. Exoticism is the first of these barriers, for it is always of a petrified kind which transports the body into the world of legend or romance: a Chinese woman equipped with an opium pipe (the indispensable symbol of 'Sininess'), an undulating vamp with a gigantic cigarette-holder, a Venetian decor complete with gondola, a dress with panniers and a singer of serenades: all aim at establishing the woman *right from the start* as an object in disguise. The end of the striptease is then no longer to drag unto the light a hidden depth, but to signify, through the shedding of an incongruous and artificial clothing, nakedness as a *natural* vesture of woman, which amounts in the end to regaining a perfectly chaste state of the flesh.

The classic props of the music-hall, which are invariably rounded up here, constantly make the unveiled body more remote, and force it back into the all-pervading ease of a well-known rite: the furs, the fans, the gloves, the feathers, the fishnet stockings, in short the whole spectrum of adornment, constantly makes the living body return to the category of luxurious objects which surround man with a magical decor. Covered with feathers or gloved, the woman identifies herself here as a stereotyped element of music-hall, and to shed objects as ritualistic as these is no longer a part of a further, genuine undressing. Feathers, furs and gloves go on pervading the woman with their magical virtue even once removed, and give her something like the enveloping memory of a luxurious shell, for it is a self-evident law that the whole of striptease is given in the very nature of the initial garment: if the latter is improbable, as in the case of the Chinese woman or the woman in furs, the nakedness which follows remains itself unreal, smooth and enclosed like a beautiful slippery object, withdrawn by its very extravagance from human use: this is the underlying significance of the G-string covered with diamonds or sequins which is the very end of striptease. This ultimate triangle, by its pure and geometrical shape, by its hard and shiny material, bars the way to the sexual parts like a sword of purity, and definitively drives the woman back into a mineral world, the (precious) stone being here the irrefutable symbol of the absolute object, that which serves no purpose.

Contrary to the common prejudice, the dance which accompanies the striptease from beginning to end is in no way an erotic element. It is probably quite the reverse: the faintly rhythmical undulation in this case exorcizes the fear of immobility. Not only does it give to the show the alibi of Art (the dances in strip-shows are always 'artistic'), but above all it constitutes the last barrier, and the most efficient of all: the dance, consisting of ritual gestures which have been seen a thousand times, acts on movements as a cosmetic, it hides nudity, and smothers the spectacle under a glaze of superfluous yet essential gestures, for the act of becoming bare is here relegated to the rank of parasitical operations carried out in an improbable background. Thus we see the professionals of striptease wrap themselves in the miraculous ease which constantly clothes them, makes them remote, gives them the icy indifference of skilful practitioners, haughtily taking refuge in the sureness of their technique: their science clothes them like a garment.

All this, this meticulous exorcism of sex, can be verified *a contrario* in the 'popular contests' (*sic*) of amateur striptease: there, 'beginners' undress in front of a few hundred spectators without resorting or resorting very clumsily to magic, which unquestionably restores to the spectacle its erotic power. Here we find at the beginning far fewer Chinese or Spanish women, no feathers or furs (sensible suits, ordinary coats), few disguises as a starting point—gauche steps, unsatisfactory dancing, girls constantly threatened by immobility, and above all by a 'technical' awkwardness (the resistance of briefs, dress or bra) which gives to the gestures of unveiling an unexpected importance, denying the woman the albi of art and the refuge of being an object, imprisoning her in a condition of weakness and timorousness.

And yet, at the *Moulin Rouge*, we see hints of another kind of exorcism, probably typically French, and one which in actual fact tends less to nullify eroticism than to tame it: the compère tries to give striptease a reassuring petit-bourgeois status. To start with, striptease is a *sport*: there is a Striptease Club, which organizes healthy contests whose winners come out crowned and rewarded with edifying prizes (a subscription to physical training lessons), a novel (which can only be Robbe-Grillet's *Voyeur*), or useful prizes (a pair of nylons, five thousand francs). Then, striptease is identified with a *career* (beginners, semi-professionals, professionals), that is, to the honourable practice of a specialization (strippers are skilled workers). One can even give them the magical alibi of work: *vocation*; one girl is, say, '*doing well*' or '*well on the way to fulfilling her promise*', or on the contrary '*taking her first steps*' on the arduous path of striptease. Finally and above all, the competitors are socially situated: one is a salesgirl, another a secretary (there are many secretaries in the Striptease Club). Striptease here is made to rejoin the world of the public, is made familiar and bourgeois, as if the French, unlike the American public (at least according to what one hears), following an irresistible tendency of their social status, could not conceive eroticism except as a household property, sanctioned by the alibi of weekly sport much more than by that of a magical spectacle: and this is how, in France, striptease is nationalized.

17

The poor and the proletariat
Roland Barthes

From Barthes, Roland 1957: *Mythologies*. Paris: Editions du Seuil. Extract taken from Paladin Books edition. Translated by Annette Lavers. London: Granada Publishing 1973, 39–40.

Charlie Chaplin's latest gag has been to transfer half of his Soviet prize into the funds of the Abbé Pierre. At bottom, this amounts to establishing an identity between the nature of the poor man and that of the proletarian. Chaplin has always seen the proletarian under the guise of the poor man: hence the broadly human force of his representations but also their political ambiguity. This is quite evident in this admirable film, *Modern Times*, in which he repeatedly approaches the proletarian theme, but never endorses it politically. What he presents us with is the proletarian still blind and mystified, defined by the immediate character of his needs, and his total alienation at the hands of his masters (the employers and the police).

For Chaplin, the proletarian is still the man who is hungry; the representations of hunger are always epic with him: excessive size of the sandwiches, rivers of milk, fruit which one tosses aside hardly touched. Ironically, the food-dispensing machine (which is part of the employers' world) delivers only fragmented and obviously flavourless nutriment. Ensnared in his starvation, Chaplin-Man is always just below political awareness. A strike is a catastrophe for him because it threatens a man truly blinded by his hunger; his man achieves an awareness of the working-class condition only when the poor man and the proletarian coincide under the gaze (and the blows) of the police. Historically, Man according to Chaplin roughly corresponds to the worker of the French Restoration, rebelling against the machines, at a loss before strikes, fascinated by the problem of bread-winning (in the literal sense of the word), but as yet unable to reach a knowledge of political causes and an insistence on a collective strategy.

But it is precisely because Chaplin portrays a kind of primitive proletarian, still outside Revolution, that the representative force of the latter is immense. No socialist work has yet suceeded in expressing the humiliated condition of the worker with so much violence and generosity. Brecht alone, perhaps, has glimpsed the necessity, for socialist art, of always taking Man on the eve of Revolution, that is to say, alone, still blind, on the point of having his eyes opened to the revolutionary light by the 'natural' excess of his wretchedness. Other works, in showing the worker already engaged in a conscious fight, subsumed under the Cause and the Party, give an account of a political reality which is necessary, but lacks aesthetic force.

Now Chaplin, in conformity with Brecht's idea, shows the public its blindness by presenting at the same time a man who is blind and what is in front of him. To see someone who does not see is the best way to be intensely aware of *what* he does not see: thus, at a Punch and Judy show, it is the children who announce to Punch what he pretends not to see. For instance, Charlie Chaplin is in a cell, pampered by the warders, and lives there according to the ideal of the American petit-bourgeois: with legs crossed, he reads the paper under a portrait of Lincoln: but his delightfully self-satisfied posture discredits this ideal completely, so that it is no longer possible for anyone to take refuge in it without noticing the new alienation which it contains. The slightest ensnarements are thus made harmless, and the man who is poor is repeatedly cut off from temptation. All told, it is perhaps because of this that Chaplin-Man triumphs over everything: because he escapes from everything, eschews any kind of sleeping partner, and never invests in man anything but man himself. His anarchy, politically open to discussion, perhaps represents the most efficient form of revolution in the realm of art.

18

Towards a semiotic inquiry into the television message
Umberto Eco

From Eco, Umberto 1965: Towards a semiotic inquiry into the television message. Translated from the Italian by Paola Splendore. Reprinted in *Working Papers in Cultural Studies* 3, Autumn 1972. Birmingham: University Centre for Contemporary Cultural Studies, 103–21.

The text which follows was a paper given at 'The Study Group for the setting-up of an interdisciplinary research model on the television audience relationship', held in Perugia by the Italian Centre for Mass Communication Studies of Perugia and by the Department of Ethnology and Cultural Anthropology of the University of Perugia (23–24 October 1965). The text was part of an 'outline draft' proposed by the author, by Paolo Fabbri, Pierpaolo Giglioli, Franco Lumachi, Tullio Seppilli and Gilberto Tinacci-Mannelli. The text owes much to their contributions.

This research proposal first appeared—as we have already said—in 1965. Since then, the author has developed more fully his perspective on methodology in La Struttura Assente, Milano Bompiani, 1968 (cf. the revised edition La Structure Absente, Paris, Mercure de France, 1972, and the forthcoming The Semiotic Threshold, The Hague, Mouton).

I Introduction

To understand the extent of the influence of the television message on the audience, it is not enough to carry out a market-research survey on the preferences of the viewers.

What we consider urgent is to understand, not: (*a*) what the audience likes (a piece of research which would no doubt be very useful, but totally inadequate as guidelines for an organization which is concerned with the promotion of culture rather than with commercial aims); but rather (*b*) *what in fact the audience gets*, both through the programmes it likes and through those it dislikes.

Issue (*b*) implies that a given television programme is analysed as a message in relation to which we single out: (1) the intentions of the sender; (2) the objective structure of the message; (3) the reactions of the addressee to items 1 and 2.

It is clear that such research is concerned with the television outputs as *a system of signs*. As is true of every system of signs, signs and their correlations are to be seen in relation to a *sender* and an *addressee*; based on a *code* supposed to be common to both; emitted in a *context* of communication which determines the meaning of the three previous terms.

As we shall see, research on the television outputs as a system of signs does not have as its sole object the clarification of the formal aspects of the process of communication. Some definitions which follow will help us to understand how, when considering the various levels of a message, the so-called *content levels* must also be brought into consideration. In other words, *a system of signs is not only a system of sign vehicles but also a system of meanings*.

We emphasize however that we do not intend to restrict all potential research on television programmes to semiotic research. If, as we shall see, the analysis of the public comes in necessarily as a second 'checking' phase of the semiotic research, and the two are closely linked, none the less there exist enormous areas for different kinds of sociological research (for example the real influence of television on the public behaviour of a community).

Semiotic research is therefore only one aspect of research: but it is essential for answering a question which, in plain words, could be put this way: 'When I send a message, what do different individuals in different environments actually receive? Do they receive the same message? A similar one? A totally different one?'

Questions of this kind are common to all research in human communication; but they are particularly pressing in the field of mass communication.

In the past, the author of a communicative act, such as for instance the artist of the palace of Knossos in Crete, produced a message (for example the coloured stucco relief of the Prince of the Lilies) for a well-defined community of receivers. Such a community would have had the same reading code as the artist: it knew for instance that the stick held in the left hand stood for a sceptre, that the flowers which appeared on the necklace, on the diadem and in the background were lilies; that the yellow-brown colour of the face meant youth; and so forth. The fact that this work could be looked at in a completely different way by the Achaean conquerors, who had different attributes to express royalty, was purely accidental to the communication itself. It was an *aberrant decoding* which the artist would never have thought of.

There were different kinds of such aberrant decodings:

(a) first of all for foreign people *who didn't know that particular code* (as is the case for us with the Etruscan language);

(b) for future generations, or people from a different culture who would superimpose a different code on the message (this is what happened in the first centuries of Christianity, and even after, when a pagan image was interpreted as a holy one; the same thing would happen today to an Oriental who knew nothing about Christian iconography and so could mistake an image of St Paul for a warrior, since by convention he carries a sword);

(c) for different hermeneutic traditions (the romantic interpretation of a sonnet of the Stilnovo school which would understand as erotic images what the poet conceived of as philosophical allegories);

(d) for different cultural traditions, which understand the message as if it were based on their code rather than on that in which it was originally cast (thus the sixteenth-century scholar could take as a mistake in perspective the picture by a primitive conforming to the conventions of 'herring-bone' perspective rather than to Brunelleschi's rules).

Things are completely different when we consider a message trans-decoding was the unexpected exception, not the rule. It was the task of philologists in the later, and more sharply critical, epochs, more discerning of historical and ethnological differences, to guarantee the correct decoding.

Things are completely different when we consider a message transmitted to an undifferentiated mass of receivers and channelled through the mass media. In this case the transmitter of the message works within a communicative code which he knows *a priori* is not shared by all the receivers. We need only read a book like *New Lives for Old* by Margaret Mead[1] to observe how the natives of the island of Manus (Melanesia) would interpret the American films shown to them by the occupation troops. These stories of American characters, situated in a different ethical, social and psychological context, were seen in the light of the natives' own frame of reference; the consequence of all this was the birth of new type ethics which was no longer either native or western.

An example of such a situation can be given by the pun well known to schoolchildren: /I Vitelli dei romani sono belli/. If we refer the sentence to the Italian language code, it means: 'The Roman calves are beautiful'; if we refer it to the Latin language code, it means: 'Go, Vitellus, to the war cry of the Roman god.'

This is an extreme example of something which occurs quite

normally in most transmissions in the field of the mass media. The aberrant decoding (which was a mere accident with regard to the message which the Renaissance painter actually addressed to his patron and his fellow-citizens, living in an identical cultural context) *is the rule in the mass media.*

II Phases of the research

1 (*a*) The research will therefore, first of all, define terms such as 'code', 'message', 'levels of meaning'; (*b*) it will then make a distinction between the codes of the transmitting organization and the codes of the specific technical operators (producers-authors working within the organization); analyse some messages, establishing the codes they refer to and all the references the addressees are supposed to have. This constitutes the first phase of the semiotic analysis of the message.

2 In a second phase it will have to check, by means of field research, how the messages, previously analysed, have in fact been received in selected sample situations—and this constitutes the main contribution to research in this field.

3 Thirdly, all the data on how they were received having been collected, these will have to be compared to the analysis previously carried out on the messages themselves to see: (*a*) if all the different cases of reception were justified; (*b*) if some receptions had shown levels of meaning in the message which had escaped notice of both our analysis and the sender; (*c*) if some receptions proved that given messages could be interpreted totally differently from what was intended for the communication, though none the less consistently; (*d*) if, in given situations, the users project freely on the message, whatever it is, the meanings they would want to find there. And so forth.

The research could lead to conclusions of different kinds. We could discover that certain messages, supposed to be especially full and penetrating for a given meaning, prove to be the least communicative.

We could discover that the community of the users has such freedom in decoding as to make the influencing power of the organization much weaker than one could have thought. Or just the opposite.

We might have to conclude that those political or cultural organizations which work towards modifying the attitudes of the sending organization, should instead concentrate on the receiving end (audience education) because this is where the battle of the meanings, of the freedom of the passivity of reception, etc., actually takes place.

We could discover that the redundancy load necessary for the un-equivocal reception of a message is such that it is totally useless to carry on political or cultural struggles to put middle-length messages into programmes, while it would be better to bring a wide range of pressures to bear for the production of a few messages with a high redundancy load and, of necessity, greater length.

This research therefore develops out of the belief that what the researcher sees on the video is not necessarily what the common viewer sees. And that there is a gap between the image which appears on the video—as it has been conceived by the transmitting organiza-tion—and the images received by the viewers in many and different situations, a gap which can be filled (or possibly enlarged) only through a deeper knowledge of the mechanisms of communication.

This research derives from the persuasion that the problem of com-munication is an ideological problem and not merely a technical matter.

The pages which follow are concerned with the phase of semiotic research referred to as phase 1 [(*a*) and (*b*)] of the research as a whole. As can easily be understood, phase 2 (audience research) requires the practical application of the theoretical propositions of phase 1, that is of some sociological field work. Only after this will it be possible to pass on to phase 3 where possibly we'll arrive at some theoretical conclusions.

III Preliminary definitions

The message

We are not concerned here with the television message as an ideal con-tent of communication, an appeal, or a group of abstract meanings.

First of all a message is a *sign object* in which the first impact is made up of sign vehicles as relations among luminous impulses on the video. The relations among these impulses could cover the whole idea of message from the purely quantitative point of view of a 'theory of information'. On the contrary, from the point of view of a 'theory of communication', the message is the objective complex of sign vehicles built on the basis of one or more codes to transmit certain meanings, and interpreted and interpretable on the basis of the same or other codes.

A message can have different *levels of meaning*: a road sign showing a child held by the hand by one of his parents, means, first of all to the layman, 'child accompanied by a parent'; but to the road user who knows a certain 'code', it means: 'with care, schoolchildren'. The same sign copied or put on canvas by a pop artist, automatically acquires more levels of meaning.

It is possible to decode each level of meaning, referring it to a specific reference table. So far we have been referring to these reference tables by the generic name of 'code'. We'll try now to define this concept better and to analyse it.

The code

By code we mean a system of communicative conventions *paradigmatically* coupling term to term, a series of sign-vehicles to a series of semantic units (or 'meanings'), and establishing the structural organization of both systems: each of them being governed by combinatorial rules, establishing the way in which the elements (sign-vehicles and semantic units) are syntagmatically concatenated.

We mean by code, for instance, a verbal language such as English, Italian or German; visual systems, such as traffic signals, road signals, card games, etc.; and so on. Verbal languages or road-signal languages are mixed and complex codes, in so far as they: (*a*) entail two planes, the plane of expression (sign-vehicles) and the plane of content (semantic units); and (*b*) they allow either a paradigmatic or selective choice or a syntagmatic (combinatorial) enchainment.

Musical codes (if we assume that music does not carry any meaning—which remains to be demonstrated) have only (*a*) an expression plane which allows both the paradigmatic and syntagmatic possibility. So they are complex but not mixed.

Morse code has both the expression and the content plane, but allows only a paradigmatic possibility, in so far as its dots and dashes, expressing the letter of the alphabet, are to be combined according to the combinatorial rules of the verbal and written language. So it is mixed, but only paradigmatic or selective; whereas the traffic-lights code is mixed and complex because it prescribes combinatorial rules between elements endowed with meaning.

After these definitions, let us restrict the concept of code to the basic conventional systems; it is in fact with these elements that it is possible to then work out 'secondary codes' or 'subcodes', more or less systematized, which furnish new *lexical* elements or give a different connotation to lexical elements contained in the basic code.

The word /disegno/ (design) and the word /leggi/ (law) have definite meanings in Italian: but the combination /disegno di leggi/ (design for a law; bill)—which is a metaphor in itself—is not understandable by making reference to the meanings of the two nouns; to be understood it must be referred to a specialized jargon which gives to this syntagm a specific meaning. This jargon, which works in relation to the language-code, becomes then a specific subcode. A listener can have the code but not the subcode. A recent inquiry carried out by the RAI [*RADIO TELEVISIONE ITALIANA* (Italian Radio-Television State Network)] on the reception of the news has brought to light a situation of this kind.

In the reception of a message, the singling out of the right code and lexicon is made easier through the *communication context* in which the message is sent. The context, 'parliamentary news' makes easier the singling out of the right lexicon to decode the syntagm 'design for a law'.

We must emphasize that the concepts of code and subcode do not make reference only to linguistic conventions but to every possible field of conventional references: the conventions at the basis of gastronomic choices (conventions of palate-taste) form a code, more or less systematized, which can vary in every culture.

The statement /Pork steaks are good and nourishing, so they must be eaten, provided they belong to us/, uttered in the context of the present western culture, has one meaning if interpreted according to the English language code; and if it is then referred to: (*a*) the most accepted system of medical–sanitary–dietetic rules; (*b*) the system of social rules known as the 'criminal code'. If it is uttered in the context of a Muslim country, where pork is considered impure and is forbidden, the statement, even if it did not mean something different, would nevertheless be interpreted as an instigation to crime rather than an obvious statement. Its semantic-syntactic dimension would not change, but its *pragmatic dimension* would.

The various codes and subcodes, on which the various levels of meaning of a given message are based, can be differentially systematic and flexible. The conventional system of palate-taste is rather rigid (you can't mix sugar and salt). The conventional system of aesthetic-erotic taste is more flexible: two different feminine ideals such as Audrey Hepburn and Jayne Mansfield can be both equally desirable and beautiful, by convention.

The use of a subcode generally transforms the process of *denotation* into a process of *connotation*. The expression /winged-boy/, in a poetic-erotic context, must be referred to a mythological reference table (mythological subcode), where it not only *denotes* a winged child but *connotes* 'Eros'. The context, without the form of the message being altered, requires for its decoding the use of a supplementary lexicon which gives the message another level of significance. The man without the mythological lexicon, or who doesn't understand from the context that he needs it, will interpret the message as the indication of a paradoxical situation. Or he might use the wrong subcode (the Biblical one, for example) and decode the message in an aberrant way, as if it were a seraph. (We would like to make clear that such examples are not theoretical, but have their exact equivalents in the reception of television messages.)

Having given these definitions, let's try and single out a series of codes and subcodes which occur in the production and in the interpretation of a television message and on which different levels of meaning of the messages are based.

IV The system of codes and subcodes which occur in the definition of a television message

The television message, in as much as it is formed of images, musical sounds or noises, and verbal emissions, can be considered as based on three basic codes from which then derive dependent subcodes:

1. *The Iconic Code*, which includes also:
   A. iconologic subcode
   B. aesthetic subcode
   C. erotic subcode
   (these three at the level of selection of the images)
   D. montage subcode
   (at the level of combination of the images)
2. *The Linguistic Code*, which includes also:
   A. emotional subcodes
   B. syntagms with an acquired stylistic value
   C. syntagms with a conventional value

Let us now describe in detail these various codes and subcodes.

1 *The Iconic Code*

This is based on the processes of visual perception (which are in turn based on a code if perception is, as we here assume, not the photographic recording of a preconstructed presumed reality, but an interaction between the stimuli of a given field and the perceptual schemes, learned and imposed by the subject).

Once it has been perceived on the video, according to the usual perceptual process, a shape can be taken either as *denoting itself* (and this is the case of a circular or triangular shape; of a black line against a white background, etc.) or as *denoting another shape* which the receiver recognizes as an element of his physical and cultural reality (a tree, a letter of the alphabet). To this second type of denotation we can refer back the first, inasmuch as the perception on the video of a circular shape can be understood as the denotation of a shape of a 'circle'. In this sense the code is always *figurative* or *iconic*; I perceive certain shapes on the video as images of other already known shapes, if the first ones have structural elements similar to the second ones, and if these are enough to be considered their 'reduced model'. It can happen that the receiver sees on the video images of unknown realities (a native who sees for the first time the image of an aircraft). In this case he will perceive the image not on the basis of the figurative code, but on the basis of the common perceptual code, as a form in itself which denotes itself and no more (in the same way in which the same native, hearing the English word /house/ and not having the code to decipher it, takes it merely in the form of sound). You can on the contrary have the case that the receiver, perceiving a form without a meaning, and guessing from the context that it should have one, is able to deduce the code from the message itself. Thus, if I see the image of a strange unknown piece of machinery, I understand that it is the sign-vehicle of something, and I include this something in the framework of my knowledge; from that moment onwards I apply the correspondence expected from the code. As the iconic sign has many peculiarities in common with the object it denotes (unlike the linguistic sign which is conventional), communication through images proves more valid and immediate than that through words because it allows the receiver to refer at once to the unknown referent. Such a process can only take place if the whole context of images helps me to fill the gap: I can recognize the image of a chain of molecules if the context of the other images, or a verbal hint, do not help me to decode it (in this case decoding becomes more like cryptoanalysis, as in reading messages in an unknown code).

Let us leave out of the discussion the possible existence of a code of the collective subconscious. If it exists, inasmuch as it is subconscious, it escapes the characteristics of conventionality typical of any code. We are interested in it only if it comes out empirically at the level of the decoding analysis (the receivers experience certain forms as a stimulus sufficient for a series of projections, identifications, etc.). It will be studied under a different aspect when considering item 1.A (iconological subcode).

A. *The iconological subcode*

Certain images connote something else by tradition. A little old man bent and smiling, and a happy child running towards him with outstretched arms, *connotes* a 'grandfather'. A flag perceived as white, red and green (or guessed as such in a black and white context, with for example a 'bersagliere' near it) denotes 'Italian flag' according to a specific international subcode, and in some contexts it could denote 'Italian spirit'. A geometrical form which reproduces a Greek temple on a reduced scale can connote 'harmonious beauty, Hellenism'.

Certain images can be included in this section, which by convention connote something on the basis of unconscious tendencies which have in turn determined the iconological choice: for example, the image of water connotes 'tranquillity' by convention. But in the process of connotation there intervene also unconscious elements which the iconological tradition has accepted and legitimated at the cultural level (in such cases the image could work at the unconscious level even for those who would not be aware of its conventional connotation).

B. *The aesthetic subcode*

Determined by the tradition of taste. A certain representation is 'beautiful' by tradition. A certain *topos* acquires a certain meaning according to aesthetic conventions (for example the end-shot of a lone man walking off down a road into the distance, seen after Chaplin, has a definite connotation).

C. *The erotic subcode*

Brigitte Bardot is beautiful and desirable. A fat woman is not. These two value judgements are based upon conventions, that is upon a historical-sociological sedimentation of taste, accepted by the whole community. This subcode can mingle under many of its aspects with the aesthetic code: a certain type of woman is ridiculous if considered in terms of a comic tradition. A man wearing a black patch on one eye becomes erotically interesting if considered in the iconological subcode which connotes him as a 'pirate', and in an aesthetic subcode which connotes the pirate as 'romantic'.

D. *The montage subcode*

Whereas the preceding subcodes offered a paradigm of available images, this one provides a series of ready-made syntagms. It sets combinatory rules for the images in accordance with the cinematographic and television rules, both in the composition of the shots and in their sequence. The native who is not used to film language will not understand the fact that the person who appears in a reverse shot is the same as the person he has seen before. In the same way he will not understand the connecting function of a 'fondu'. For example, with the help of the montage subcode, it is possible to understand by means of a succession of isolated shots the *meeting* between a child and an old man, while with the help of the iconological subcode it is possible to understand the *grandfather–grandchild relationship*.

2 *The Linguistic Code*

This is the code of the language which is used. All the verbal formulations of a transmission make reference to it. It may not be known in its available totality and its combinatorial complexity. Certain rural communities may have it in a reduced form. Its subcodes are:

A. *Specialized jargons*

(an enormous range, which includes scientific, political, legal, professional, etc., jargons). The above-mentioned RAI inquiry on the reception and comprehension of the news referred to this level of messages. They are mostly lexical patrimonies.

B. *Stylistic syntagms*

They are equivalent to the aesthetic subcodes at the level of the iconic code. They connote social class, artistic attitude, etc. They include the figures of speech. The various emotional connotations (irony, fear, suspicion, etc.) must make reference to them. One ascertains in relation to them whether a message offends the basic linguistic code, by mistake or intentionally. Other typological connotations related to the linguistic style are included in this code.

3 *The Sound Code*

This includes all the sounds of the musical range and the combinatory rules of the tonal grammar; it includes the noises as well, inasmuch as they are distinct from the sounds and relatable iconically to already known noises. Whereas sounds denote only themselves (they have no semantic weight) noises can have imitative value (imitation of already known noises). Timbres can also have imitative value (bell timbre, drum timbre). In this case noises and timbres are sound images which denote noises and timbres already heard in reality.

A. *Emotional subcodes*
(for example, 'thriller' music is such by convention).

B. *Stylistic syntagms*
there is a musical typology in accordance with which a melody is 'country', 'classic', 'wild', etc. Also different types of connotations occur, often with either an emotional or an ideological value. Music linked to definite ideologies.

C. *Syntagms with a conventional value*
'Attention!', 'To the mess', 'Charge!' Silence. The Drums. They have acquired other connotative values: the charge as 'fatherland, war, valour, etc.'.

The framework of cultural reference

Codes and subcodes are applied to the message in the light of a general framework of cultural references, which constitutes the receiver's patrimony of knowledge: his ideological, ethical, religious standpoints, his psychological attitudes, his tastes, his value systems, etc.

Likewise, the transmitting organization and the technical interpreter codify the message on the basis of their own framework of cultural reference: they select the meanings they want to communicate, why, for whom, and how they should be arranged by means of the different levels of the message.

In this way, both the organization and the technical interpreter take for granted in the receiver a framework of cultural references. They can believe it to be similar to their own, or different; and in this case they will adjust the message according to the gap, or even try to fill it up, stimulating by means of the message a modification of the receiver's framework of cultural references.

This framework, which we could call ideology (using the word in its broadest sense), constitutes a system of assumptions and expectations which interacts with the message and determines the selection of the codes with which to read it.

For example the statement /he is a rebel/ is immediately understood in its denotation value in the light of the language code; but it will acquire, in the first place, a specific connotation if it is uttered in a communication context which relates it to a child or to an irregular fighter—or to someone who challenges the established order; secondly, it acquires more connotations if, in the case of the child, either the ideology of the sender or that of the addressee provides an authoritarian or a liberal pedagogy; or if, in the second case, the ideology of the sender or that of the addressee considers as positive either conforming to the established order or else resisting power.

Likewise, the iconological topos /negro beaten up by white man/ connotes normally 'colonialism', while the topos /black man rapes white woman/ connotes 'racism'; but the two messages can only appear repulsive or thrilling when related to the ideological framework either of the emitter or of the receiver, and only then connote 'a praiseworthy act' or 'a shameful act'. It can happen that a message supposed to connote a 'shameful act' is received as connoting a 'praiseworthy act'.

The cultural reference framework allows us, therefore, to single out the codes and subcodes. A boy wearing a 'blouson noir' can connote 'an antisocial person' in one iconological subcode, 'an unconventional hero' in another. The choice of criterion is always guided by the ideological framework.

We have then an *ideological* system (system of meanings pre-existent to the message) interacting with a system of *rhetorical* devices (codes and subcodes) which regulates the relationship of sign-vehicles to meanings in the message. These elements together can be defined as a *significance system*.

The semiological analysis of the message must therefore delineate the 'significance system' which the message as a whole connotes, and provides the definition of:

(a) the significance system of the transmitting organization and the significance system that it assumes in the addressee;

(b) the significance system of the technical interpreter (which can be different from that of the organization) and the significance system that he assumes in the addressee.

What the semiotic analysis cannot define is the actual system of every single addressee. This can only be discovered through field research on the audience.

Thus the semiotic inquiry is only one aspect of research into the process of communication. It can make clear the intentions of the emitter, but not the way the message has been received.

V The message

In the finished message, codes and subcodes interact with the receiver's framework of reference and make the different kinds of meaning reverberate one upon another. Inasmuch as the message, at the level of the sign-vehicles and meanings, proves to be harmoniously composed and appropriate at all other levels, it acquires artistic quality and comes to have an aesthetic function.

The aesthetic function of a message occurs when the message makes evident, first of all, its own structure as its primary meaning; in other words it is *self-focusing* (that is, when it is organized not only to communicate something but it is 'formed to form').

In the course of the semiotic inquiry one will therefore distinguish:

(a) messages with an aesthetic quality, where the sign-vehicles and the meanings are closely related to each other;

(b) 'non-articulated' messages which enable the message to be analysed separately at each level;

(c) messages which are supposed to perform a function different from the aesthetic function (according to the following table) and which therefore appear coordinated enough for that purpose, but are not self-focusing.

Likewise, in the course of the analysis of the audience one will distinguish:

(a) types of reception in which the message is considered as a purely aesthetic object and is understood to have been so intended;

(b) types of reception in which the message is considered as performing other functions and is understood to have been so intended.

Accepting this, let us examine the six different functions of a message proposed by Roman Jakobson. These functions seldom appear separately; generally they all exist at one time in one message but with one predominating:

1. *Referential function*

The message 'points to' something. It occurs in all the normal processes of denotation and connotation, even if the intended reference tends to restrict to the minimum the semantic field which exists around a sign and to focus the receiver's attention on one single referent.

2. *Emotive function*
The message tends to stimulate emotions (association of ideas, projections, identifications, etc.).

3. *Imperative function*
The message aims to command something, to persuade to an action.

4. *Phatic function, or contact function*
The message aims at establishing a psychological contact with the receiver (the most common form is the expression of greeting).

5. *Metalinguistic function*
The message speaks about another message or about itself.

6. *Aesthetic function*
The message, even if it performs other functions, aims primarily to be considered as such, as a system harmonious at all levels and for all functions.

Each time these different functions are performed, different levels of meaning are stressed. An advertising message can denote 'man, woman, children around a table with a saucepan and a box of X cubes', secondly it can connote 'happiness and serenity'—and in this it performs the *reference, emotional, and imperative functions together* (it could also perform an *aesthetic* function). As a matter of fact, it is very likely for the addressee to interpret it in the light of the first three functions and to leave the fourth one out of consideration. But a more guarded and sensitive addressee could be not persuaded that he must buy X cubes and yet appreciate the technical perfection of the shot and of the characterization.

The structure of the message

Performing some functions and involving various levels of meaning, the various messages structure themselves in different ways (from a maximum of coherence to a maximum of disarticulation), bringing about a communication dialectic between *probability* and *improbability* (that is between *the obvious* and *the new*—and ultimately, in a more technical phraseology, between *meaning* and *information*).

The more a message *conforms* to the rules of the significance system which it is based on, the more probable and obvious it is.

The more a message *contravenes* the rules of the significance system which it is based on, the more improbable and new it becomes.

An obvious message communicates a definite meaning which everybody can understand (it communicates what I already know).

An improbable message communicates a load of information (what I do not yet know) which, beyond certain bounds of improbability, becomes mere disorder and 'noise'.

In the message therefore it is necessary to establish a *dialectic between the obvious and the new*.

The message can prove obvious or improbable either in relation to the codes and subcodes which it is based on, or in relation to the receiver's framework of cultural references.

A message like /I say you must love your mother/ conforms both to the rules of the English language code, and to the ethical rules of the reference table of most of the addressees. A message like /I say you must hate your mother/ conforms to the rules of the English language code, but contravenes the ethical dictates of the cultural framework of the addressees and in this it carries a high rate of information with it. As everybody can see, the information, or the improbability, is connected to an element of unexpectedness which upsets the system of expectations of the addressees. The message can simply upset the system of linguistic expectations (in relation to the language code and the stylistic code). If you advertise: /Me like soops! (in a sort of Dog-patch dialect) instead of/I prefer this brand of canned soup .../ you violate the system of linguistic expectations. You do not violate the system of ideological expectations, because the addressee expects during a commercial, that the products will be praised. Thus a message like /Me hate soop!/ would be very improbable both in relation to the ideological and to the linguistic framework.

It is useful to note how a message like this has proved informative only the first time it has been received; afterwards an element of repetition has come into it, rendering it obvious. This repetitive element is a sort of *redundance* which is concerned with the iteration over time. The most common form of redundance, on the contrary, acts within a single message, and is used to wrap up the meaning in repetitions so as to make it more and more acceptable. For example: /I say that this brand of canned soup is really good, that is palatable and nutritious/. The message is new and improbable as long as it is based on a minimum of redundance. However, a high rate of improbability runs the risk of not being received and therefore the message must be tempered in small degree with conventionalities, common-places, and must be reiterated through a redundance form over time.

One of the problems in message-coding is the balance between the obvious and the new. How few conventionalities are necessary to communicate a piece of information (as a new thing?): this is a prob-lem which both the semiological analysis of the message and the audience survey must come to terms with. Only field surveys of the public will establish whether there is a good enough balance in the television message.

The problem of the relationship between the new and the obvious is only formal inasmuch as probability and improbability are values which leave out of consideration what is actually communicated and are concerned with the formal structuring of the message. But because they are values which are concerned also with the cultural framework, their efficacy goes beyond the technical aspects of the communication sphere and reaches the more comprehensive sphere of the television communication as ideological matter.

An element of information, in so far as it goes against the accepted rules of a general system of significance, puts the addressee in a state of autonomy, enables him to make an effort of interpretation and obliges him to reconsider his codes and reference tables. Even a piece of political news (which in so far as it is unexpected, is 'informative') such as /The President of the USA has visited Moscow/ obliges the addressee to modify his own experience of American foreign policy. A complex message, such as the TV serial *The captain's daughter*, if it presents in a completely new way the character of the rebel Cossack, obliges the receiver (whose cultural framework would persuade him that he who rebels against power is wicked) to modify his own system of ethico-psychological expectations. Information and the improb-able are therefore creative, in different degrees. Commonplaces, con-ventionalities, probabilities, on the contrary, work to confirm the reference tables and codes of the receiver.

VI Conclusions

What is the redundance load below which the 'new' cannot be re-ceived, and beyond which it shades into the 'obvious'?

How much does 'novelty' at the level of the sign-vehicles imply 'novelty' at the level of the meanings? How much can a message, highly conventional in its conformity to the codes, channel new meanings, able to modify the reference tables of the receivers?

To these and other problems semiotic analysis can provide answers, working out a wider typology of codes and of reference tables: analysing certain messages and delineating their levels and communication structure, in terms of a dialectic between probability and improbability, at the level of the codes as well as of the reference tables. It will be the task of audience research to establish how wide is the gap between the intentions of the emitter and the interpretation of the addressee. Only at this point will it be possible for us to understand something of the homogeneity of the significance systems of the emitter and of the addressee and therefore something about the real communication effectiveness of the television message in a given social context.

This higher awareness can be of concern to those who have the problem of sender, as well as to those who have an interest in the addressees as a community to be organized and made conscious.

Should this awareness be lacking, the television message will remain an abstract hypothesis of communication, the intention of which one could perhaps guess, but never know in the final reality. In this case the political and cultural operations carried out *on* (or *against*) the organization and on the user would also remain abstract.

Post-Scriptum 1972

This Report was presented at a time when Italian Radiotelevision's 'Servizio Opinioni' (Audience Survey)—and, indeed, sociological research in general—were more concerned with a sort of Trendex-like polls which aimed to test how many people followed and appreciated a given programme. In the last few years, however (partly as a consequence of the impact of our Report), RAI has begun to test, in a more complex way, not only what the audience likes, but what it understands, comparing the message transmitted with the message received. At present, I am directing a research programme, sponsored by the *Servizio Programmi Sperimentali* of the RAI which will try to discover how much the temporal structure of the discourse of a television programme (presence or absence of flashbacks, high or low stress in causal connections, etc.) determines the 'fit' between the emitted and the received message. In my *La Struttura Assente*[2] I proposed, also, the possibility of a 'semiotic guerilla warfare'; the gap between the transmitted and the received message is not only an aberration, which needs to be reduced—it also can be developed so as to broaden the receiver's freedom. In political activity it is not indispensable to change a given message: it would be enough (or, perhaps better) to change the attitude of the audience, so as to induce a different decoding of the message—or in order to isolate the intentions of the transmitter and thus to criticize them. In this sense, semiotics becomes not only a cognitive discipline, which enables us to understand how communication works, but also a pragmatic activity, intended to transform communication processes. Methodologically speaking, the project imposes another reading of (from the semiotic point of view) the sociological hypothesis put forward by Merton and Lazarsfeld[3] about the function of group leaders and the face-to-face reinforcement of the mass media message. U.E.

19

Introduction to the presentation of self in everyday life
Erving Goffman

From Goffman, Erving 1959: *The presentation of self in everyday life*. New York: Double-day Anchor. Extract taken from Penguin books edition: Harmondsworth 1969, 14–27.

When an individual enters the presence of others, they commonly seek to acquire information about him or to bring into play information about him already possessed. They will be interested in his general socio-economic status, his conception of self, his attitude towards them, his competence, his trustworthiness, etc. Although some of this information seems to be sought almost as an end in itself, there are usually quite practical reasons for acquiring it. Information about the individual helps to define the situation, enabling others to know in advance what he will expect of them and what they may expect of him. Informed in these ways, the others will know how best to act in order to call forth a desired response from him.

For those present, many sources of information become accessible and many carriers (or 'sign-vehicles') become available for conveying this information. If unacquainted with the individual, observers can glean clues from his conduct and appearance which allow them to apply their previous experience with individuals roughly similar to the one before them or, more important, to apply untested stereotypes to him. They can also assume from past experience that only individuals of a particular kind are likely to be found in a given social setting. They can rely on what the individual says about himself or on documentary evidence he provides as to who and what he is. If they know, or know of, the individual by virtue of experience prior to the inter-action, they can rely on assumptions as to the persistence and generality of psychological traits as a means of predicting his present and future behaviour.

However, during the period in which the individual is in the immediate presence of the others, few events may occur which directly provide the others with the conclusive information they will need if they are to direct wisely their own activity. Many crucial facts lie beyond the time and place of interaction or lie concealed within it. For example, the 'true' or 'real' attitudes, beliefs, and emotions of the individual can be ascertained only indirectly, through his avowals or through what appears to be involuntary expressive behaviour. Similarly, if the individual offers the others a product or service, they will often find that during the interaction there will be no time and place immediately available for eating the pudding that the proof can be found in. They will be forced to accept some events as conventional or natural signs of something not directly available to the senses. In Ichheiser's terms,[1] the individual will have to act so that he intentionally or unintentionally *expresses* himself, and the others will in turn have to be *impressed* in some way by him.

The expressiveness of the individual (and therefore his capacity to give impressions) appears to involve two radically different kinds of sign activity: the expression that he *gives*, and the expression that he *gives off*. The first involves verbal symbols or their substitutes which he uses admittedly and solely to convey the information that he and the others are known to attach to these symbols. This is communication in the traditional and narrow sense. The second involves a wide range of action that others can treat as symptomatic of the actor, the expectation being that the action was performed for reasons other than the information conveyed in this way. As we shall have to see, this distinction has an only initial validity. The individual does of course intentionally convey misinformation by means of both of these types of communication, the first involving deceit, the second feigning.

Taking communication in both its narrow and broad sense, one finds that when the individual is in the immediate presence of others, his activity will have a promissory character. The others are likely to find that they must accept the individual on faith, offering him a just return while he is present before them in exchange for something whose true value will not be established until after he has left their presence. (Of course, the others also live by inference in their dealings with the physical world, but it is only in the world of social interaction that the objects about which they make inferences will purposely facilitate and higher this inferential process.) The security that they justifiably feel in making inferences about the individual will vary, of course, depending on such factors as the amount of information they already possess about him, but no amount of such past evidence can entirely obviate the necessity of acting on the basis of inferences. As William I. Thomas suggested:

It is also highly important for us to realize that we do not as a matter of fact lead our lives, make our decisions, and reach our goals in everyday life either statistically or scientifically. We live by inference. I am, let us say, your guest. You do not know, you cannot determine scientifically, that I will not steal your money or your spoons. But inferentially I will not, and inferentially you have me as a guest.[2]

Let us now turn from the others to the point of view of the individual who presents himself before them. He may wish them to think highly of him, or to think that he thinks highly of them, or to perceive how in fact he feels towards them, or to obtain no clear-cut impression; he may wish to ensure sufficient harmony so that the interaction can be sustained, or to defraud, get rid of, confuse, mislead, antagonize, or insult them. Regardless of the particular objective which the individual has in mind and of his motive for having his objective, it will be in his interests to control the conduct of the others, especially their responsive treatment of him.[3] This control is achieved largely by influencing the definition of the situation which the others come to formulate, and he can influence this definition by expressing himself in such a way as to give them the kind of impression that will lead them to act voluntarily in accordance with his own plan. Thus, when an individual appears in the presence of others, there will usually be some reason for him to mobilize his activity so that it will convey an impression to others which it is in his interests to convey. Since a girl's dormitory mates will glean evidence of her popularity from the calls she receives on the phone, we can suspect that some girls will arrange for calls to be made, and Willard Waller's finding can be anticipated:

> It has been reported by many observers that a girl who is called to the telephone in the dormitories will often allow herself to be called several times, in order to give all the other girls ample opportunity to hear her paged.[4]

Of the two kinds of communication—expressions given and expressions given off—this report will be primarily concerned with the latter, with the more theatrical and contextual kind, the non-verbal, presumably unintentional kind, whether this communication be purposely engineered or not. As an example of what we must try to examine, I would like to cite at length a novelistic incident in which Preedy, a vacationing Englishman, makes his first appearance on the beach of his summer hotel in Spain:

> But in any case he took care to avoid catching anyone's eye. First of all, he had to make it clear to those potential companions of his holiday that they were of no concern to him whatsoever. He stared through

them, round them, over them—eyes lost in space. The beach might have been empty. If by chance a ball was thrown his way, he looked surprised; then let a smile of amusement lighten his face (Kindly Preedy), looked round dazed to see that there *were* people on the beach, tossed it back with a smile to himself and not a smile *at* the people, and then resumed carelessly his nonchalant survey of space.

But it was time to institute a little parade, the parade of the Ideal Preedy. By devious handlings he gave any who wanted to look a chance to see the title of his book—a Spanish translation of Homer, classic thus, but not daring, cosmopolitan too—and then gathered together his beach-wrap and bag into a neat sand-resistant pile (Methodical and Sensible Preedy), rose slowly to stretch at ease his huge frame (Big-Cat Preedy), and tossed aside his sandals (Carefree Preedy, after all).

The marriage of Preedy and the sea! There were alternative rituals. The first involved the stroll that turns into a run and a dive straight into the water, thereafter smoothing into a strong splashless crawl towards the horizon. But of course not really to the horizon. Quite suddenly he would turn on his back and thrash great white splashes with his legs, somehow thus showing that he could have swum further had he wanted to, and then would stand up a quarter out of water for all to see who it was.

The alternative course was simpler, it avoided the cold-water shock and it avoided the risk of appearing too high-spirited. The point was to appear to be so used to the sea, the Mediterranean, and this particular beach, that one might as well be in the sea as out of it. It involved a slow stroll down and into the edge of the water—not even noticing his toes were wet, land and water all the same to *him*!—with his eyes up at the sky gravely surveying portents, invisible to others, of the weather (Local Fisherman Preedy).[5]

The novelist means us to see that Preedy is improperly concerned with the extensive impressions he feels his sheer bodily action is giving off to those around him. We can malign Preedy further by assuming that he has acted merely in order to give a particular impression, that this is a false impression, and that the others present receive either no impression at all, or, worse still, the impression that Preedy is affectedly trying to cause them to receive this particular impression. But the important point for us here is that the kind of impression Preedy thinks he is making is in fact the kind of impression that the others correctly and incorrectly glean from someone in their midst.

I have said that when an individual appears before others his actions will influence the definition of the situation which they come to have. Sometimes the individual will act in a thoroughly calculating manner, expressing himself in a given way solely in order to give the kind of impression to others that is likely to evoke from them a specific response he is concerned to obtain. Sometimes the individual will be calculating in his activity but be relatively unaware that this is the case. Sometimes he will intentionally and consciously express himself in a particular way, but chiefly because the tradition of his group or social status require this kind of expression and not because of any particular response (other than vague acceptance or approval) that is likely to be evoked from those impressed by the expression. Sometimes the traditions of an individual's role will lead him to give a well-designed impression of a particular kind and yet he may be neither consciously nor unconsciously disposed to create such an impression. The others, in their turn, may be suitably impressed by the individual's efforts to convey something, or may misunderstand the situation and come to conclusions that are warranted neither by the individual's intent nor by the facts. In any case, in so far as the others act *as if* the individual had conveyed a particular impression, we may take a functional or pragmatic view and say that the individual has 'effectively' projected a given definition of the situation and 'effectively' fostered the understanding that a given state of affairs obtains.

There is one aspect of the others' response that bears special comment here. Knowing that the individual is likely to present himself in a light that is favourable to him, the others may divide what they witness into two parts: a part that is relatively easy for the individual to manipulate at will, being chiefly his verbal assertions, and a part in regard to which he seems to have little concern or control, being chiefly derived from the expressions he gives off. The others may then use what are considered to be the ungovernable aspects of his expressive behaviour as a check upon the validity of what is conveyed by the governable aspects. In this a fundamental asymmetry is demonstrated in the communication process, the individual presumably being aware of only one stream of his communication, the witnesses of this stream and one other. For example, in Shetland Isle one crofter's wife, in serving native dishes to a visitor from the mainland of Britain, would listen with a polite smile to his polite claims of liking what he was eating; at the same time she would take note of the rapidity with which the visitor lifted his fork or spoon to his mouth, the eagerness with which he passed food into his mouth, and the gusto expressed in chewing the food, using these signs as a check on the stated feelings of the eater. The same woman, in order to discover what one acquaintance (A) 'actually' thought of another acquaintance (B), would wait until B was in the presence of A but engaged in conversation with still another person (C). She would then covertly examine the facial expressions of A as he regarded B in conversation with C. Not being in conversation with B, and not being directly observed by him, A would sometimes relax usual constraints and tactful deceptions, and freely express what he was 'actually' feeling about B. This Shetlander, in short, would observe the unobserved observer.

Now given the fact that others are likely to check up on the more controllable aspects of behaviour by means of the less controllable, one can expect that sometimes the individual will try to exploit this very possibility, guiding the impression he makes through behaviour felt to be reliably informing.[6] For example, in gaining admission to a tight social circle, the participant observer may not only wear an accepting look while listening to an informant, but may also be careful to wear the same look when observing the informant talking to others; observers of the observer will then not as easily discover where he actually stands. A specific illustration may be cited from Shetland Isle. When a neighbour dropped in to have a cup of tea, he would ordinarily wear at least a hint of an expectant warm smile as he passed through the door into the cottage. Since lack of physical obstructions outside the cottage and lack of light within it usually made it possible to observe the visitor unobserved as he approached the house, islanders sometimes took pleasure in watching the visitor drop whatever expression he was manifesting and replace it with a sociable one just before reaching the door. However, some visitors, in appreciating that this examination was occurring, would blindly adopt a social face a long distance from the house, thus ensuring the projection of a constant image.

This kind of control upon the part of the individual reinstates the symmetry of the communication process, and sets the stage for a kind of information game—a potentially infinite cycle of concealment, discovery, false revelation, and rediscovery. It should be added that since the others are likely to be relatively unsuspicious of the presumably unguided aspect of the individual's conduct, he can gain much by controlling it. The others of course may sense that the individual is manipulating the presumably spontaneous aspects of his behaviour, and seek in this very act of manipulation some shading of conduct that the individual has not managed to control. This again provides a check upon the individual's behaviour, this time his presumably uncalculated behaviour, thus re-establishing the asymmetry of the communication process. Here I would like only to add the suggestion that the arts of piercing an individual's effort at calculated unintentionality seem better developed than our capacity to manipulate our own behaviour, so that regardless of how many steps have occurred in the information game, the witness is likely to have the advantage over the actor, and the initial asymmetry of the communication process is likely to be retained.

When we allow that the individual projects a definition of the situation when he appears before others, we must also see that the others, however passive their role may seem to be, will themselves effectively project a definition of the situation by virtue of their response to the individual and by virtue of any lines of action they initiate to him. Ordinarily the definitions of the situation projected by the several different participants are sufficiently attuned to one another, so that open contradiction will not occur. I do not mean that there will be the kind of consensus that arises when each individual present candidly expresses what he really feels and honestly agrees with the expressed feelings of the others present. This kind of harmony is an optimistic ideal and in any case not necessary for the smooth working of society. Rather, each participant is expected to suppress his immediate heartfelt feelings, conveying a view of the situation which he feels the others will be able to find at least temporarily acceptable. The maintenance of this surface of agreement, this veneer of consensus, is facilitated by each participant concealing his own wants behind statements which assert values to which everyone present feels obliged to give lip service. Further, there is usually a kind of division of definitional labour. Each participant is allowed to establish the tentative official rule regarding matters which are vital to him but not immediately important to others, e.g. the rationalizations and justifications by which he accounts for his past activity. In exchange for this courtesy he remains silent or noncommittal on matters important to others but not immediately important to him. We have then a kind of interactional *modus vivendi*. Together the participants contribute to a single overall definition of the situation which involves not so much a real agreement as to what exists but rather a real agreement as to whose claims concerning what issues will be temporarily honoured. Real agreement will also exist concerning the desirability of avoiding an open conflict of definitions of the situation.[7] I will refer to this level of agreement as a 'working consensus'. It is to be understood that the working consensus established in one interaction setting will be quite different in content from the working consensus established in a different type of setting. Thus, between two friends at lunch, a reciprocal show of affection, respect, and concern for the other is maintained. In service occupations, on the other hand, the specialist often maintains an image of disinterested involvement in the problem of the client, while the client responds with a show of respect for the competence and integrity of the specialist. Regardless of such differences in content, however, the general form of these working arrangements is the same.

In noting the tendency for a participant to accept the definitional claims made by the others present, we can appreciate the crucial importance of the information that the individual *initially* possesses or acquires concerning his fellow participants, for it is on the basis of this initial information that the individual starts to define the situation and starts to build up lines of responsive action. The individual's initial projection commits him to what he is proposing to be and requires him to drop all pretences of being other things. As the interaction among the participants progresses, additions and modifications in this initial informational state will of course occur, but it is essential that these later developments be related without contradiction to, and even built up from, the initial positions taken by the several participants. It would seem that an individual can more easily make a choice as to what line of treatment to demand from and extend to the others present at the beginning of an encounter than he can alter the line of treatment that is being pursued once the interaction is under way.

In everyday life, of course, there is a clear understanding that first impressions are important. Thus, the work adjustment of those in service occupations will often hinge upon a capacity to seize and hold the initiative in the service relation, a capacity that will require subtle aggressiveness on the part of the server when he is of lower socio-economic status than his client. W. F. Whyte suggests the waitress as an example:

> The first point that stands out is that the waitress who bears up under pressure does not simply respond to her customers. She acts with some skill to control their behaviour. The first question to ask when we look at the customer relationship is, 'Does the waitress get the jump on the customer, or does the customer get the jump on the waitress?' The skilled waitress realizes the crucial nature of this question. . . .
> The skilled waitress tackles the customer with confidence and without hesitation. For example, she may find that a new customer has seated himself before she could clear off the dirty dishes and change the cloth. He is now leaning on the table studying the menu. She greets him, says, 'May I change the cover, please?' and, without waiting for an answer,

takes his menu away from him so that he moves back from the table, and she goes about her work. The relationship is handled politely but firmly, and there is never any question as to who is in charge.[8]

When the interaction that is initiated by 'first impressions' is itself merely the initial interaction in an extended series of interactions involving the same participants, we speak of 'getting off on the right foot' and feel that it is crucial that we do so. Thus, one learns that some teachers take the following view:

> You can't ever let them get the upper hand on you or you're through. So I start out tough. The first day I get a new class in, I let them know who's boss. . . . You've got to start off tough, then you can ease up as you go along. If you start out easy-going, when you try to get tough, they'll just look at you and laugh.[9]

Similarly, attendants in mental institutions may feel that if the new patient is sharply put in his place the first day on the ward and made to see who is boss, much future difficulty will be prevented.[10]

Given the fact that the individual effectively projects a definition of the situation when he enters the presence of others, we can assume that events may occur within the interaction which contradict, discredit, or otherwise throw doubt upon this projection. When these disruptive events occur, the interaction itself may come to a confused and embarrassed halt. Some of the assumptions upon which the responses of the participants had been predicated become untenable, and the participants find themselves lodged in an interaction for which the situation has been wrongly defined and is now no longer defined. At such moments the individual whose presentation has been discredited may feel ashamed while the others present may feel hostile, and all the participants may come to feel ill at ease, nonplussed, out of countenance, embarrassed, experiencing the kind of anomaly that is generated when the minute social system of face-to-face interaction breaks down.

In stressing the fact that the initial definition of the situation projected by an individual tends to provide a plan for the cooperative activity that follows—in stressing this action point of view—we must not overlook the crucial fact that any projected definition of the situation also has a distinctive moral character. It is this moral character of projections that will chiefly concern us in this report. Society is organized on the principle that any individual who possesses certain social characteristics has a moral right to expect that others will value and treat him in an appropriate way. Connected with this principle is a second, namely that an individual who implicitly or explicitly signifies that he has certain social characteristics ought in fact to be what he claims he is. In consequence, when an individual projects a definition of the situation and thereby makes an implicit or explicit claim to be a person of a particular kind, he automatically exerts a moral demand upon the others, obliging them to value and treat him in the manner that persons of his kind have a right to expect. He also implicitly forgoes all claims to be things he does not appear to be[11] and hence forgoes the treatment that would be appropriate for such individuals. The others find, then, that the individual has informed them as to what is and as to what they *ought* to see as the 'is'.

One cannot judge the importance of definitional disruptions by the frequency with which they occur, for apparently they would occur more frequently were not constant precautions taken. We find that preventive practices are constantly employed to avoid these embarrassments and that corrective practices are constantly employed to compensate for discrediting occurrences that have not been successfully avoided. When the individual employs these strategies and tactics to protect his own projections, we may refer to them as 'defensive practices'; when a participant employs them to save the definition of the situation projected by another, we speak of 'protective practices' or 'tact'. Together, defensive and protective practices comprise the techniques employed to safeguard the impression fostered by an individual during his presence before others. It should be added that while we may be ready to see that no fostered impression would survive if defensive practices were not employed, we are less ready perhaps to see that few impressions could survive if those who received the impression did not exert tact in their reception of it.

In addition to the fact that precautions are taken to prevent disruption of projected definitions, we may also note that an intense interest in these disruptions comes to play a significant role in the social life of the group. Practical jokes and social games are played in which embarrassments which are to be taken unseriously are purposely engineered.[12] Fantasies are created in which devastating exposures occur. Anecdotes from the past—real, embroidered, or fictitious—are told and retold, detailed disruptions which occurred, almost occurred, or occurred and were admirably resolved. There seems to be no grouping which does not have a ready supply of these games, reveries, and cautionary tales, to be used as a source of humour, a catharsis for anxieties, and a sanction for inducing individuals to be modest in their claims and reasonable in their projected expectations.

The individual may tell himself through dreams of getting into impossible positions. Families tell of the time a guest got his dates mixed and arrived when neither the house nor anyone in it was ready for him. Journalists tell of times when an all-too-meaningful misprint occurred, and the paper's assumption of objectivity or decorum was humorously discredited. Public servants tell of times a client ridiculously misunderstood form instructions, giving answers which implied an unanticipated and bizarre definition of the situation.[13] Seamen, whose home away from home is rigorously he-man, tell stories of coming back home and inadvertently asking mother to 'pass the fucking butter'.[14] Diplomats tell of the time a near-sighted queen asked a republican ambassador about the health of his king.[15]

To summarize, then, I assume that when an individual appears before others he will have many motives for trying to control the impression they receive of the situation. This report is concerned with some of the common techniques that persons employ to sustain such impressions and with some of the common contingencies associated with the employment of these techniques. The specific content of any activity presented by the individual participant, or the role it plays in the interdependent activities of an on-going social system, will not be at issue; I shall be concerned only with the participant's dramaturgical problems of presenting the activity before others. The issues dealt with by stage-craft and stage management are sometimes trivial but they are quite general; they seem to occur everywhere in social life, providing a clear-cut dimension for formal sociological analysis.

It will be convenient to end this introduction with some definitions that are implied in what has gone before and required for what is to follow. For the purpose of this report, interaction (that is, face-to-face interaction) may be roughly defined as the reciprocal influence of individuals upon one another's actions when in one another's immediate physical presence. *An* interaction may be defined as all the interaction which occurs throughout any one occasion when a given set of individuals are in one another's continuous presence; the term 'an encounter' would do as well. A 'performance' may be defined as all the activity of a given participant on a given occasion which serves to influence in any way any of the other participants. Taking a particular participant and his performance as a basic point of reference, we may refer to those who contribute the other performances as the audience, observers, or co-participants. The pre-established pattern of action which is unfolded during a performance and which may be presented or played through on other occasions may be called a 'part' or 'routine'.[16] These situational terms can easily be related to conventional structural ones. When an individual or performer plays the same part to the same audience on different occasions, a social relationship is likely to arise. Defining social role as the enactment of rights and duties attached to a given status, we can say that a social role will involve one or more parts and that each of these different parts may be presented by the performer on a series of occasions to the same kinds of audience or to an audience of the same persons.

20

The radio drama frame
Erving Goffman

From Goffman, Erving 1974: *Frame analysis*. New York: Harper & Row. Extract from
Penguin Books edition: Harmondsworth 1975, 144–9.

I have described some eight transcription practices which render stage
interaction systematically different from its real-life model. Still other
such conventions will be considered later. In any case, here is the first
illustration of what will be stressed throughout: the very remarkable
capacity of viewers to engross themselves in a transcription that
departs radically and systematically from an imaginable origin. An
automatic and systematic correction is involved, and it seems to be
made without its makers consciously appreciating the transformation
conventions they have employed.

As a further illustration of our ability to employ transformations,
look for a moment at the dramatic scriptings presented on the radio
stage—the radio drama frame.[1] Obviously, there are media restrictions that must be accepted: for example, in the early days, soprano
high notes could blow out transmitter tubes, so crooning came into
vogue;[2] and since a sharp increase in volume when volume was
already high could not be handled, many sound effects (for example,
gunshots) could not be employed.[3]

A basic feature of radio as the source of a strip of dramatic interaction is that transmitted sounds cannot be selectively disattended. For
example, at a real cocktail party, an intimate conversation can be sustained completely surrounded by a babble of extraneous sound. A
radio listener, however, cannot carve out his own area of attention.
What the participant does in real life, the director has to do in radio
and (to almost the same degree) on the stage. Therefore the following
convention has arisen:

> In radio drama, spatial information is characteristically introduced at
> the beginning of a scene, then faded down or eliminated entirely. Unlike
> the everyday experience of reverberation in a kitchen, we cannot dis-
> attend reverberation running under the dialogue on radio. It is therefore
> introduced in the first few lines and faded out. The same rule operates

for spatial transitions. Moving the scene from the city out to the country might be signalled by:

MAN: I'll bet Joe and Doris aren't so hot out there in the country. (Music fades in, SFX [sound effects] birds chirping, fade out music, birds chirping runs under dialogue)

JOE: Well, Doris, this country weather sure is pleasant.

Within three lines, the birds will be faded out, though they might return just before the transition back to the city.[4]

Similarly, there is the convention of allowing one or two low sounds to stand for what would ordinarily be the stream of accompanying sound. Again in both these examples the power of automatic correction is evident: the audience is not upset by listening in on a world in which many sounds are not sounded and a few are made to stand out momentarily; yet if these conditions suddenly appeared in the offstage world, consternation would abound.

Behind the need for these conventions is something worth examining in more detail, something that might be called the 'multiple-channel effect'. When an individual is an immediate witness to an actual scene, events tend to present themselves through multiple channels, the focus of the participant shifting from moment to moment from one channel to another. Further, these channels can function as they do because of the special role of sight. What is heard, felt, or smelled attracts the eye, and it is the seeing of the source of these stimuli that allows for a quick identification and definition—a quick framing—of what has occurred. The *staging* of someone's situation as an immediate participant therefore requires some replication of this multiplicity, yet very often replication cannot be fully managed. A protagonist in a radio drama will be in a realm in which things are presumably seen, and in which things that are heard, felt, and smelled can be located by sight; yet obviously the audience can only hear.

As might be expected, conventions became established in radio to provide functional equivalents of what could not otherwise be transmitted. Sound substitutes become conventionalized for what would ordinarily be conveyed visually. For example, the impression of distance from the centre of the stage is attained by a combination of volume control and angle and distance of speaker to microphone. Also:

By establishing a near sound, distant sounds, and intermediate sounds within a given scene, the production director can fairly accurately tell an audience the size of the scene they are hearing. If in a dramatic scene you hear a door open and a man's footsteps on a hollow wood porch, and then you hear him 'Hellooo' a loud call which comes echoing back after a few seconds, the routine says that the scene is taking place in a large space.[5]

A second solution has been to anchor by verbal accompaniment such sounds as are employed, this assuring that what might otherwise be an isolated sound is identified as to character and source. ('Well, Pete [sound of key turning], let them try to open that lock.') However, ordinarily, natural talk does not proceed in this manner. During broadcasts, then, comments that have been chosen, or at least tailored, to lock a sound into a context must therefore be dissembled as 'mere' talk; and again, this dissembling is systematically overlooked by the audience.

In addition to the 'multiple channel effect', another element in the organization of experience can be nicely seen in the radio frame: syntactically different functions are accorded to phenomenally similar events. The question is that of the realm status of an event; and some sort of frame-analytical perspective is required in order for this question to be put. Two examples.

First. Music in actual, everyday life can function as part of the background, as when an individual works while records play or suffers Muzak in its ever-increasing locations. Music can be accorded this in-frame background role in radio transcriptions of social activity—staged Muzak. (As might be expected, because in-frame music can also serve to set the scene for listeners, its first occurrence is likely to have foreground loudness; as the scene proceeds, however, the music will have to be progressively muted so that conversation can be heard.) But music can also be used as part of the radio drama frame to serve as a 'bridge', a signal that the scene is changing, music being to radio drama in part what curtain drops are to staged drama. Such music does not fit *into* a scene but fits *between* scenes, connecting one whole episode with another—part of the punctuation symbolism for managing material in this frame—and therefore at an entirely different level of application than music within a context. Furthermore, still another kind of music will be recognized: the kind that serves to foretell, then mark, the dramatic action, a sort of aural version of subtitles. This music pertains to particular events that are developing in a scene, and even though it may terminate at the same time as the kind serving to link scenes or close the stage, its reference is much less holistic. Unlike background music, however, the protagonists 'cannot', of course, hear it.[6] So syntactically there are at least three radically different kinds of music in radio drama; and yet, in fact, the same musical composition could be used in all three cases.[7] It would be correct to say here that the same piece of music is heard differently or defined differently or has different 'motivational relevancies', but this would be an *unnecessarily* vague answer. A specification in terms of frame function says more.[8]

The second example involves consideration of sound volume. The attenuation of sound is used in the radio frame as a means of signalling the termination of a scene or episode, leading to the re-establishment of the drama at what is taken to be a different time or place, or an 'instalment' termination—again, something handled on the stage by means of a curtain drop. This is done by a 'board fade', that is, a reduction of transmission power. But reduction in sound level can also be achieved by having an actor or other sound source move away from the microphone. Attenuation of sound created by moving away from the microphone can be aurally distinguished from a board fade and is used *within* a scene to indicate that an actor is leaving the scene.

Note, in both the fading out of background music (to eliminate interference with the speakers) and the attenuation of sound owing to someone's going off-mike (to express leave-taking), the auditor is meant to assume that the frame is still operative, still generating a stream of hopefully engrossing events—events that are part of the unfolding story. Music bridges and board fades, however, are not meant to be heard as part of the 'province of meaning' generated within a scene but rather as the beginning of what will be heard as between-scenes and out of frame.

Section V

Mass communication

Few if any sociologists would deny the importance of mass communication as a major factor in the production and distribution of social knowledge and social imagery in modern societies.

The press, discussed in the nineteenth century both as the potential agent of a democratic and public process of government and as a debaser and misleader of public opinion, has now been eclipsed in many of its classic functions and in its controversial nature by broadcasting, specifically national television services.

The potency of television's apparent ability to 'show the world' rather than simply to describe it, when coupled with the speed of international news-gathering and processing made possible by the newer electronic equipment, has made TV an influence to be noted and lived with in most areas of political and social life in industrialized societies.

There are a number of characteristics which distinguish mass-communication systems from other varieties of human communication, but perhaps the most important of these is their general nature as highly *institutionalized* forms of public message production and dissemination (though, of course, the 'messages' in question may be part of such very different media forms as, say, situation comedy, current-affairs studio debates or feature articles). Their operation on such a large scale together with the uniqueness of their products make 'The Media' a very special group of mass-production industries. It's worth pointing out too that it is their nature as mass-production and distribution systems rather than any notions about 'communicating to the masses' (a dubious and politically disturbing formulation at best) which justifies the use of the very term '*mass* communication'.

Another characteristic of mass communications is that they quite often involve not only a considerable division of labour in their production processes but also operate almost entirely through the complex mediations of print, photography, film and recording tape.

Production, transmission and reception are often considerably separated in time whilst producers and receivers are, by definition, almost always out of primary contact. Because of this it is very difficult to gauge the social context within which they operate without moving quickly to high levels of descriptive generality. Mass communications constitute a form of symbolic interaction, but the interaction is so removed from particular personal and social group contexts (though these are obviously a tremendously influential factor in audience interpretations and responses) that some special problems are posed for the student of media processes. Perhaps read or viewed nationally (maybe by a high percentage of the total population) the products of the mass-communications industry are nevertheless 'consumed' either individually or in small family groupings in the majority of cases. This allows the special styles and rhetorics of mass communication to display a quite astonishing mix of modes of address and of 'public' and 'informal' uses of language.

One has to be careful here to distinguish between the press and broadcasting (particularly television) since the latter has many powerful communicational tools at its command (for instance, 'live' direct speech to camera with the speaker in full-face framing) not available to even the most masterful of rhetoricians in print. It is difficult to gauge how far newspaper styles of presentation were modified by the development of news-photography or by the development of what we now see to be the dominant styles of television journalism and entertainment. Nevertheless, the emergence of carefully devised and highly professionalized modes of mass communicative 'informality' is a quite recent phenomenon much influenced by advances in photographic and television-studio technology and techniques.

A question we have to consider now is how best to study mass-communication processes given that their contribution to the construction of public knowledge and public meanings and their siting within modern political and economic systems is at once so complex and so crucial. The relationship between academic investigation into mass communication and the more general area of Communication Studies as it is, for instance, outlined in this Reader is not as simple as it might at first appear.

To start with, there has been a confusing use of terms which has concealed what are really quite important differences in methods of study and sometimes, indeed, in objects of study. A number of books and publications (perhaps taking their cue from Raymond Williams's very influential 1962 Penguin Special, *Communications*) have used the term 'communication' principally to refer to the operations of the press and broadcasting. However, this apparent relatedness of subject matter and academic perspective—mass communication as an important focus within Communication Studies—brings some problems with it. It should be clear from this Reader that we regard Communication Studies as covering a much wider ground than that of mass-communications study alone and, further, that it is not acceptable to claim the study of mass communication as somehow central to the whole of this wider range of studies.

Those who try to achieve such a neat fit may run into a number of difficulties. For, as we have suggested, mass communications are *industrial* activities, produced from within large organizations whose policies and professional routines are located within the political, economic and legal structures of the societies in which they operate. To study mass communications solely by reference to press and broadcasting output, in other words the 'messages' produced, is to leave out this important dimension or at least to remove it from direct inquiry. Communication Studies, centring as it does on language processes in the broadest sense, has shown a tendency to circumscribe media study within the realm of the textual and the linguistic. This tendency has brought criticism from sociologists and historians, who have protested at what they see as unwarranted claims about media operations being made from the evidence only of detailed but vulnerable in-depth analyses of media texts.

Yet despite this problem of relating mass-communications inquiry to work which quite often lacks a developed social or historical aspect (and Linguistics, Psychology and Visual Aesthetics, for instance, offer examples of such work) most researchers would perhaps agree that, whatever the approach adopted, the study of the media as agencies engaged quite centrally in *cultural production* is a vital aspect of mass-communications research. A notion of cultural production, moreover, keeps the expressive dimension of media systems in view whatever the specific focus of research might be.

The extracts and articles which we have chosen for this section all relate to broadcasting and all at some point address the question of the influence of broadcast communications.

Raymond Williams looks at how this issue has been tackled by different researchers and suggests some problems with dominant definitions and concepts. He points to the need to set the technology and institutions of television within the context of political and social power and he discusses the problem of making precise connections between television and other social phenomena. You will notice that he has some reservations about the usefulness of the term 'mass communications'; in explaining his disapproval he comments on the assumptions which often underlie research into the media.

Williams also tackles the notion of 'technology as cause' and criticizes the Canadian writer Marshall McLuhan for insufficiently relating his subtle studies of the formal properties of different media to any thorough social analysis. He sees McLuhan's influence (which for a period in the 1960s was very extensive) as an unfortunate one. It would be worth your while to follow this debate through in closer detail by using the references to McLuhan's work given at the end of the piece.

In the course of examining how notions of 'cause and effect' have been handled by researchers into television, Williams refers to the work of Jay Blumler. Our second piece is a statement by a research team which includes Dr Blumler. In it the authors argue that media study must engage with the idea of the individual viewer and his or her 'needs'. The thesis advanced in the article has had a considerable influence on recent audience studies in mass communication. As the writers point out, many early investigations of media influence were carried out both with a very limited idea of what constituted an 'effect' and a very underdeveloped sense of the relationship between media use and other social variables. The 'Uses and Gratifications' perspective is put forward as a way of maintaining an empirical research base (in contrast to more theoretical accounts, notably those deriving from Marxist theories of ideology) whilst at the same time registering the complexity of the interpretative processes involved in the 'use' of media products by audiences. The researchers here stress the idea of the 'active audience', one able to make its own mind up both about what it watches and about how it chooses to fit what it watches into the perspectives and knowledge gained from sources other than the media. It is argued that such a notion could lead to a viewpoint where the audience, far from being the dull, passive consumers of broadcasting output (this latter viewed either as intended opiate or businesslike response to demand) might be described more accurately as wanting a more varied and challenging diet than the television services have so far provided.

At times, we would want to query the authors' claims. For instance, the idea that value judgements should be suspended while audience orientations are explored on their own terms (p. 190) is a tricky one to put into practice given the difficulties of ever assessing objectively the audience's 'own terms'. This clearly ties in with the authors' earlier rejection of 'elitist' approaches—but the charge of elitism perhaps needs more specification. It would seem odd to label as elitist all researchers who were concerned to discuss matters of value and quality in broadcasting. Nevertheless, the piece goes on to offer a detailed argument about the 'active audience' and readers interested in following up matters of theoretical framework and substantive findings in audience research will be well served by the final bibliography.

One of the central debates both within public discussions of the media and in academic research into the area has concerned the extent to which the forms of mass communication somehow 'reflect' the varied circumstances and patterns of thought in a society and the extent to which they actually influence social processes in special and perhaps pervasive ways. As a straight either/or issue it is impossibly simplified but it still survives as a fundamental question underlying highly complex studies. In what one might term 'traditional' attempts at addressing this question, audience surveys of one kind or another have predominated (mass-communication research was at one time seen to be almost synonymous with audience research). Recently, however, a closer focusing on media forms themselves has led to arguments about how viewers and readers are, as it were, positioned by particular types of media discourse and format. This is to argue the case for media influence in a rather vulnerable way (it's the researcher's reading of the media text which produces the evidence of influential powers) but it offers some very important propositions as to how media 'languages' work to cue and constrain an audience's interpretations. As we argued earlier, such research could be more important still when connected both with empirical work on audience responses to particular programmes and with studies of production processes.

Colin McArthur works in the area of Film Studies and in the extract from his book which we have reprinted he discusses how television currently handles history and how viewers are put into certain 'relations of knowing' to historical material and not into others. We feel that McArthur's piece is a very clear and useful introduction to the study of television programme forms (particularly those forms to which the terms 'realism' and 'documentary' are often applied) and you will find that it links very directly with material in other sections of the Reader, notably in *Meaning and Interpretation* and in parts of *Language, Thought, Culture*.

McArthur is interested in developing his theories in terms of a notion of *ideology*—that is to say (although the term is a notoriously

difficult one) a structure of social cognitions and thought systematically generated by given economic and political conditions and often
having a very complex relation to social realities in so far as these are
ascertainable. As we said, the term is a difficult one!

In the final essay of this section, Stuart Hall develops a similar argument with regard to changes in news and current-affairs broadcasting.
He makes play with the title of a popular BBC radio programme
which introduced a new style of 'magazine' broadcast journalism
whilst he argues a thesis about news construction (the news as a cultural product) and about journalistic routines. He attempts to relate
ideas about political consensus to such professional touchstones as
objectivity and impartiality. Once again, the linguistic aspect of media
processes is highlighted as Hall concentrates critically on the production of news about 'violence' and 'law and order'.

Finally, we should point out that there are now available several
excellent Readers dealing specifically with mass communications (see
Further Reading). There is also an increasing number of works dealing with press and broadcasting history, policy and organization. In
this section, we can only suggest the range and complexity of argument and of research and study in the area.

Further reading
In the last few years mass-communication research has attracted much
attention from a variety of disciplines and there has been a huge
growth in the number of publications dealing with the area. Below
are listed a few of the general works (including Readers) which will
serve to introduce this complex and varied field of inquiry to the
student of communication.

Boyce, George *et al* (eds) 1978: *Newspaper history*. London: Constable.
   A collection of papers and essays on the history of the British press
   giving particular attention to the political and social character of
   the newspaper industry and of journalism.
Curran, James *et al* (eds) 1977: *Mass communication and society*. London:
   Edward Arnold.
   A very useful Reader produced for the Open University. It contains
   a number of articles which attempt to review recent work and these
   provide a helpful introduction to modern research and its findings.
Golding, Peter 1974: *The mass media*. London: Longman.
   A brief introduction to the history and structure of British mass

communications together with an account of current problems of policy and recent research findings. A recommended way of getting a sense of the whole field.

McQuail, Denis 1972: *Sociology of mass communications.* London: Penguin.

An indispensable collection of extracts and commissioned papers. Excellent references. Contains more strictly sociological approaches than does Curran, 1977 (above) and together with that volume provides the best range of material currently available.

McQuail, Denis 1969: *Towards a sociology of mass communications.* London: Collier Macmillan.

This short survey of what was, in 1969, a 'developing field' is still recommended for its clarity and its attention to problems of media research within the different and often conflicting perspectives of Sociology. Unlike Golding, 1974 (above) McQuail spends most of his time discussing how researchers have gone about their investigations and has only a very little to say in description of modern media. However, still essential reading for students.

Williams, Raymond. 1974: *Television: technology and cultural form.* London: Fontana.

A short but influential discussion of the relationship between the technological and the cultural in the development of modern television services. Williams considers the special forms of television output, developing an argument about the 'distribution and flow' of programming and its effects.

21

Effects of the technology and its uses

Raymond Williams

From Williams, Raymond 1974: *Television: technology and cultural form*. London: Fontana, 119–34.

A. Cause and effect in communications systems

Since television became a popular social form there has been widespread discussion of its effects. The most significant feature of this discussion has been the isolation of the medium. Especially in advanced industrial societies the near-universality and general social visibility of television have attracted simple cause-and-effect identifications of its agency in social and cultural change. What is significant is not the reliability of any of these particular identifications; as will be seen, there are very few such effects which come near to satisfying the criteria of scientific proof or even of general probability. What is really significant is the direction of attention to certain selected issues—on the one hand 'sex' and 'violence', on the other hand 'political manipulation' and 'cultural degradation'—which are of so general a kind that it ought to be obvious that they cannot be specialized to an isolated medium, but, in so far as television bears on them, have to be seen in a whole social and cultural process. Some part of the study of television's effects has then to be seen as an ideology: a way of interpreting general change through a displaced and abstracted cause.

Cultural science, when it emerged as a method in early classical sociology, was concerned with the necessary differentiation of its procedures from those of natural science. In its central concept of 'understanding', and in its sensitivity to the problems of judgement of value and of the participation and involvement of the investigator, it was radically different from the assumptions and methods of the 'sociology of mass communications' which is now orthodox and which at times even claims the authority of just this classical sociology. The change can be seen in one simple way, in the formula which was established by Lasswell as the methodological principle of studies of communication: the question 'who says what, how, to whom, with what effect?' For what this question has excluded is *intention*, and therefore all real social and cultural process.

Suppose we rephrase the question as 'who says what, how, to whom, with what effect and for what purpose?' This would at least direct our attention to the interests and agencies of communication, which the orthodox question excludes. But the exclusion is not accidental. It is part of a general social model which abstracts social and cultural processes to such concepts as 'socialization', 'social function' or 'interaction'. Thus socialization has been defined as 'learning the ways and becoming a functioning member of society', but while it is clear that in all societies this process occurs, it is for just this reason an indifferent concept when applied to any real and particular social and cultural process. What the process has in common, in many different societies, is given a theoretical priority over just the radical differences of 'ways' and 'functioning', and over the highly differential character of being a 'member' of the society, which in practice define the real process. The abstract notions of 'socialization' and 'social function' have the effect of conferring normality and in this sense legitimacy on any society in which a learning and relating process may occur. And when this is so, intention, in any full sense, cannot be recognized, let alone studied. To say that television is now a factor in socialization, or that its controllers and communicators are exercising a particular social function, is to say very little until the forms of the society which determine any particular socialization and which allocate the functions of control and communication have been precisely specified.

The central concepts of cultural science—understanding, value judgement, the involvement of the investigator—have thus been excluded or circumvented. This explains the consequent emphasis on 'effects', and the dissolution of causes into abstract notions of 'socialization' or 'social function' or into the false particularization of a self-directing technology. It explains also the orthodox description of such studies as the study of 'mass communications'. What is really involved in that descriptive word 'mass' is the whole contentious problem of the real social relations within which modern communications systems operate. Its merely descriptive and assumptive use is a way of avoiding the true sociology of communications, yet it is orthodox over a very wide range and in theories and studies which are otherwise sophisticated. A particular version of empiricism—not the general reliance on experience and evidence, but a particular reliance on evidence within the terms of these assumed functions (socialization, social function, mass communications)—has largely taken over the practice of social and cultural inquiry, and within the terms of its distortion of cultural science claims the abstract authority of 'social science' and 'scientific method' as against all other modes of experience and analysis. Against this confident and institutionalized practice it cannot be said too often that the work of social and cultural science is only secondarily a matter of methodological procedures; it is primarily the establishment of a consciousness of process, which will include consciousness of intentions as well as of methods and of working concepts.

Effects, after all, can only be studied in relation to real intentions, and these will often have to be as sharply distinguished from declared intentions as from assumed and indifferent general social processes. This will require the study of real agency, rather than of its apparent forms. As it is, however, the study of effects has mainly been rationalized in advance. It studies effects in 'the socialization process', that is to say in practice or breach of social norms—'violence', 'delinquency', 'permissiveness', or in 'mass reactions' (a mass, to be sure, that is then classified into sectors)—the reactions of political or cultural or economic consumers, in voting, ticket-buying or spending. With this distinction however: that the latter studies have been mainly financed by interested agencies (broadcasting organizations, market research and advertising agencies, political parties), while the former have been mainly financed by social-interest groups and political and cultural authorities. Some studies have escaped the definitions of interest which their true agencies have imposed; in some universities, while there has been hiving and blurring, there has also been some independent initiative. But very little has escaped the overall definitions, including the definitions of procedure, which are the real consequences of the social system and the ideology within which the inquiries are framed. If we are to begin to approach any real study of effects, we shall have to return to a scientific consideration of causes.

B. Some studies of effects

The case of 'violence on television' is a useful example. Here the experimental evidence is extraordinarily mixed (see the useful summary in Halloran, 1970 54–64). In majority it supports the view that 'the observation of mass-media violence' may be, while not a determining, a contributory factor to subsequent aggressive behaviour. A minority view is quite different: that the effect of observing violence on television is cathartic. A further minority view stresses the possibility of both provocative and cathartic effects. Useful attempts have been made to distinguish, as is crucially necessary, between different forms of violence, different levels of its portrayal or representation, and different groups of viewers. There has also been a necessary distinction between immediate and long-term effects.

It is important that this work should continue and be developed. But 'violence' is a notable example of the effects of the abstract concept of 'socialization'. It is assumed, for example, that violent behaviour is undesirable, in that it contradicts the norms of accepted social behaviour. But it must be immediately evident, if we look at real societies, that this is not the case. Each of the societies in which this work was done was at the time engaged in violent action—some of it of exceptional scale and intensity—which had been authorized by the norms of the society, in the sense of political decisions within normal procedures to undertake and continue it. At the same time, and for discoverable social reasons, certain other violent practices—notably 'violent protest' and armed robbery *within* the societies—had been identified and condemned. In what sense then are we to say that 'violence' is a breach of the socialization process? The real norm, in these actual societies, would seem rather to be: '*unauthorized* violence is impermissible'. This would depend on a precise set of distinctions, within a given social system, between approved and impermissible forms of behaviour, and at the level of this true agency the identifications would never be in doubt and would indeed be rationalized as 'law'. (The law may punish you if you refuse to kill in a foreign war; the law may punish you if you kill or assault in the course of domestic robbery or internal political struggle.) This rationalization corresponds to a particular social structure.

But then, while it may at that level be clear to the agency concerned, it may also, as it enters the communication process, be far from clear not only to the viewers but to the producers of its representations. Such confusion in viewers may indeed be separately studied: that is a discoverable and important effect. But it is at the level of agency and production that the real practices, and their implicit or possible confusions, require analysis. The ordinary assumption seems to run: 'this society discourages violent behaviour; violent behaviour is constantly represented and reported on television; we need to study its effects on people'. But surely anyone looking analytically at those first two statements would feel the need to examine their quite extraordinary relationship. Of course the apparent contradiction can be rationalized: the controllers of television are indifferent and greedy, governed only by the profit that can be made from programmes which show violence. (At a further level of rationalization the medium itself can be reified: 'television finds violence exciting'.) But this does not explain the odd relationship between 'discouragement by the society' and constant representation by a major social communications system. Are we to assume perhaps that the television organizations are outside the normal social structure? But in all the countries in which the research is done the control and ownership of television systems is centrally characteristic of general social control and ownership and (in part) authority. When this is realized, it would be as reasonable to say: 'this society encourages violent behaviour; violent behaviour is constantly represented and reported on television, its major communications system'. But the truth is that neither assumption will do. What we are really faced with is a contradiction within the social system itself. And it is then to the sociology of that contradiction that we should direct our primary scientific attention.

A different kind of problem arises when we look at studies of the effects of television on political behaviour. These have been usefully reviewed by Jay G. Blumler (1970, in Halloran, 1970 70–87). The centre of the problem is that a given society defines political behaviour in its own terms; in Britain and the United States, for example, as voting or as rating of political leaders. These have the additional advantage that they are relatively easy to count. Early studies seemed to show, moreover, that television had little discernible influence on either. Later studies, while not controverting this, found some measurable influence on information about party policies and, though it remains difficult to interpret, on the persuasibility of those with initially low party-political motivations or attachments.

But while it is useful to know these findings, and to look for similar further work, the most important question to ask is about the causes of these definitions of political effects. It is true that there is now beginning to be some study of 'system effects', as distinct from effects on countable individual voters. But this, too, has normally been undertaken within the terms of the political model from which the initial definitions were shaped. Thus it has been observed, correctly, that during elections but also at other times of general controversy, television as a system has become the most evident area in which political argument is conducted. Television interviews and commentators have become, in a sense, political figures in their own right, and there has been evident tension between them and orthodox (usually elected) political leaders. Yet to the degree that elected leaders depend, or believe they depend, on television coverage, this tension does not prevent leaders submitting themselves to more open and public questioning of their policies than has ever been the case in any comparable communications system. This much, at least, is clear gain.

Yet it remains true that this kind of effect is within the terms of a given political system and its definitions of political behaviour. The competitive assessment of leaders and through them (but normally only through them) of policies is taken as a norm. But this at once raises a question. In Britain at least, during the period of television as a majority service, this mode of political behaviour has in fact been declining, in the important sense that the proportion of people voting at elections has been steadily going down. In the same period, other forms of political behaviour—notably demonstrations and political strikes—have quite markedly increased. It would require a very different model of cause and effect to inquire into this. It could be argued that increased exposure to competitive assessment in these terms has weakened adherence to occasional election as a political mode, or even that (given other kinds of political stimulation by television—the reporting of demonstrations, the dramatization of certain issues) it has had some strengthening influence on alternative modes. Hardly anything is known about this, for the important reason that the assumption of effect was made, initially, in terms of the functioning of a given system.

Underlying orthodox investigation of the effects of television, whether on a matter like violence or on a quite different matter like voting, we can then see a particular cultural model, which tends to determine scope and method. What is usually asked about television is what influence it has by comparison with other influences. All these influences—television, the home, the school, the press, work—are assumed as discrete though then conceded to interact. Effects can then be measured, and techniques refined. But in an important sense there can be no inquiry about cause because the total social practice has been either disintegrated into these separable factors, or—an important condition for just this separation—has been assumed as normal: the *real* process of socialization or democratic politics or what may be. Thus effect is ordinarily studied at a tertiary level, as between competing or alternative factors, and in the breach or observance of given social, cultural and political norms. Yet just these factors and norms are themselves effects; they are the established institutions, relationships and values of a given order of society. Primary causes, in the given order of society, are then ordinarily displaced by a doubtful sphere of effects taken as causes, with the study of effects then becoming, in real terms, the isolable effects of effects.

The particular importance of this, in the case of television, is that it reinforces tendencies to think of a given cultural system—the intentions and uses of a technology—in limited or misleading ways. That is to say, it studies the symptoms of the operation of an otherwise unexamined agency or—for this is the position which the former position in part prepares—it studies an agency as a system, in extreme cases performing the final feat of abstraction when it is supposed that what is being studied is simply 'a medium', 'a technology', with its own quite internal laws of cause and effect.

C. The technology as a cause

Sociological and psychological studies of the effects of television, which in their limited terms have usually been serious and careful, were significantly overtaken, during the 1960s, by a fully developed theory of the technology—the medium—as determining. There had been, as we have seen, much implicit ideology in the sociological and psychological inquiries, but the new theory was explicitly ideological: not only a ratification, indeed a celebration, of the medium as such, but an attempted cancellation of all other questions about it and its uses. The work of McLuhan[1] was a particular culmination of an aesthetic theory which became, negatively, a social theory: a development and elaboration of formalism which can be seen in many fields, from literary criticism and linguistics to psychology and anthropology, but which acquired its most significant popular influence in an isolating theory of 'the media'.

Here, characteristically—and as explicit ratification of particular uses—there is an apparent sophistication in just the critical area of cause and effect which we have been discussing. It is an apparently sophisticated technological determinism which has the significant effect of indicating a social and cultural determinism: a determinism, that is to say, which ratifies the society and culture we now have, and especially its most powerful internal directions. For if the medium—whether print or television—is the cause, all other causes, all that men ordinarily see as history, are at once reduced to effects. Similarly, what are elsewhere seen as effects, and as such subject to social, cultural, psychological and moral questioning, are exluded as irrelevant by comparison with the direct physiological and therefore 'psychic' effects of the media as such. The initial formulation—'the medium is the message'—was a simple formalism. The subsequent formulation—'the medium is the massage'—is a direct and functioning ideology.

There are of course specific characteristics of different media, and these characteristics are related to specific historical and cultural situations and intentions. Much of the initial appeal of McLuhan's work was his apparent attention to the specificity of media: the differences in quality between speech, print, radio, television and so on. But in his work, as in the whole formalist tradition, the media were never really seen as practices. All specific practice was subsumed by an arbitrarily assigned psychic function, and this had the effect of dissolving not only specific but general intentions. If specific media are essentially psychic adjustments, coming not from relations between ourselves but between a generalized human organism and its general physical environment, then of course intention, in any general or particular case, is irrelevant, and with intention goes content, whether apparent or real. All media operations are in effect desocialized; they are simply physical events in an abstracted sensorium, and are distinguishable only by their variable sense-ratios. But it is then interesting that from this wholly unhistorical and asocial base McLuhan projects certain images of society: 'retribalization' by the 'electronic age'; the 'global village'. As descriptions of any observable social state or tendency, in the period in which electronic media have been dominant, these are so ludicrous as to raise a further question. The physical fact of instant transmission, as a technical possibility, has been uncritically raised to a social fact, without any pause to notice that virtually all such transmission is at once selected and controlled by existing social authorities. McLuhan, of course, would apparently do away with all such controls; the only controls he envisages are a kind of allocation and rationing of particular media for particular psychic effects, which he believes would dissolve or control any social problem that arises. But the technical abstractions, in their unnoticed projections into social models, have the effect of cancelling all attention to existing and developing (and already challenged) communications institutions. If the effect of the medium is the same, whoever controls or uses it, and whatever apparent content he may try to insert, then we can forget ordinary political and cultural argument and let the technology run itself. It is hardly surprising that this conclusion has been welcomed by the 'media-men' of the existing institutions. It gives the gloss of avant-garde theory to the crudest versions of their existing interests and practices, and assigns all their critics to pre-electronic irrelevance. Thus what began as pure formalism, and as speculation on human essence, ends as operative social theory and practice, in the heartland of the most dominative and aggressive communications institutions in the world.

The particular rhetoric of McLuhan's theory of communications is unlikely to last long. But it is significant mainly as an example of an ideological representation of technology as a cause, and in this sense it will have successors, as particular formulations lose their force. What has to be seen, by contrast, is the radically different position in which technology, including communication technology, and specifically television, is at once an intention and an effect of a particular social order.

D. Technology as an effect

If we cancel history, in the sense of real times and real places, we can conceive an abstract human nature which has specific psychic needs and which variable forms of technology and intercourse come to satisfy. This purely idealist model of human history may have variable specific culminations—the end of alienation, the rediscovery of the tribe—but within it technology is a simple human effusion, the extension of a limb or a sense. The destiny and the process can be believed in only if we assume a human essence waiting to come to realization, in these ways, with inbuilt if not yet realized metaphysical purposes. The model can be related to history only by endless retrospect, in which by selection such a process can be generalized or demonstrated. Characteristically, in such a model, there will be no more history: a culminating age has arrived.

Any cancellation of history, in the sense of real times and real places, is essentially a cancellation of the contemporary world, in which, within limits and under pressures, men act and react, struggle and concede, cooperate, conflict and compete. A technology, when it has been achieved, can be seen as a general human property, an extension of general human capacity. But all technologies have been developed and improved to help with known human practices or with foreseen and desired practices. This element of intention is fundamental, but it is not exclusive. Original intention corresponds with the known or desired practices of a particular social group, and the pace and scale of development will be radically affected by that group's specific intentions and its relative strength. Yet at many subsequent stages other social groups, sometimes with other intentions or at least with different scales of priority, will adopt and develop the technology, often with different purposes and effects. Further, there will be in many cases unforeseen uses and unforeseen effects which are again a real qualification of the original intention. Thus an explosive may be developed at the command or by the investment of a ruling class, or by the investment or for the profit of an industrial enterprise, yet come to be used also by a revolutionary group against that ruling class, or by criminals against the industrialist's property.

In other words, while we have to reject technological determinism, in all its forms, we must be careful not to substitute for it the notion of a determined technology. Technological determinism is an untenable notion because it substitutes for real social, political and economic intention, either the random autonomy of invention or an abstract human essence. But the notion of a determined technology has a similar one-sided, one-way version of human process. Determination is a real social process, but never (as in some theological and some Marxist versions) as a wholly controlling, wholly predicting set of causes. On the contrary, the reality of determination is the setting of limits and the exertion of pressures, within which variable social practices are profoundly affected but never necessarily controlled. We have to think of determination not as a single force, or a single abstraction of forces, but as a process in which real determining factors— the distribution of power or of capital, social and physical inheritance, relations of scale and size between groups—set limits and exert pressures, but neither wholly control nor wholly predict the outcome of complex activity within or at these limits, and under or against these pressures.

The case of television is an excellent example. We have seen that the complex process of its invention had specific military, administrative and commercial intentions, and each of these interacted with what were, for real if limited periods and in real if limited ways, scientific intentions. At the stage of transition from invention to technology, the process of its development came to be dominated by commercial intentions, though still with some real political and military interests. But then a primarily commercial intention acquired social and political intentions of a general kind, in notions of social training and social control which in part harmonized and in part conflicted with the driving commercial intention (the latter gaining ascendancy in the United States, though never an unqualified ascendancy; the former gaining but then losing ascendancy in Britain, though again the loss is not unqualified). Yet as intention became effect another dimension opened. It was not only ruling or commercial groups who recognized the problems of communication in conditions of complex or of privatized mobility. It was also the many people who were experiencing this process as subjects. To controllers and programmers they might seem merely objects: a viewing public or a market. But from their own side of the screen there was a different perspective; if they were exposed by need in new ways, they were also exposed to certain uncontrollable opportunities. This complicated interaction is still very much in the process of working itself out.

Literacy had shown similar complications. It is interesting that at the beginning of the industrial revolution in Britain, when education had to be reorganized, the ruling class decided to teach working people to read but not to write. If they could read they could understand new kinds of instructions and, moreover, they could read the Bible for their moral improvement. They did not need writing, however, since they would have no orders or instructions or lessons to communicate. At most they might struggle to produce simple signatures, which would be occasionally required for official purposes. The full range of writing came later, with further development of the society and the economy. But it is what happened to reading that is really significant. For there was no way to teach a mean to read the Bible which did not also enable him to read the radical press. A controlled intention became an uncontrolled effect. Yet the acquisition of literacy, then as now, almost always involved submission to a lengthy period of social training—education—in which quite other things than literacy or similar skills were taught; in which, in fact, values and norms were taught which became, very often, inextricable from the literacy.

The unique factor of broadcasting—first in sound, then even more clearly in television—has been that its communication is accessible to normal social development; it requires no specific training which brings people within the orbit of public authority. If we can watch and listen to people in our immediate circle, we can watch and listen to television. Much of the great popular appeal of radio and television has been due to this sense of apparently unmediated access. The real mediations will have to be noted, but again and again they are easy to miss. What is offered is a set with a tuner and a switch: we can turn it on or off, or vary what we are receiving. Throughout its history there has been this popular sense that broadcasting is a welcome alternative to the normal and recognizable social order of communications.

Many people who are aware of the manipulative powers of radio and television, or of its apparently inexhaustible appeal to children, react in ways which implicitly suppress all the other history of communication. Thus it is often indignantly said that television is a 'third parent', as if the children had not in all developed societies had third parents in the shape of priests, teachers and workmasters, to say nothing of the actual parents and relations who, in many periods and cultures, intervened to control or to instruct. Against those real alternatives this switchable communication has profound attractions. Or it is said that people are exposed to propaganda by television, as if there had never been masters, employers, judges, priests.

It is interesting that many of the contradictions of capitalist democracy have indeed come out in the argument about television control. The British version of 'public responsibility' was an emphasis, in new terms, of the priest and the teacher, with behind them a whole dominant and normative set of meanings and values. The American version of 'public freedom' was open broadcasting subject only to the purchase of facilities, which then settled freedom in direct relation to existing economic inequalities. In each case the control theoretically lost by the switchable receiver was regained by the assertion of paternalist or capitalist ownership of transmission. This explains the realities of contemporary mediation, but it explains also the apparently irrepressible search, by listeners and viewers, for other sources. Many British working-class people welcomed American culture, or the Americanized character of British commercial television, as an alternative to a British 'public' version which, from a subordinate position, they already knew too well. In many parts of the world this apparently free-floating and accessible culture was a welcome alternative to dominant local cultural patterns and restrictions. Young people all over Europe welcomed the pirate broadcasters, as an alternative to authorities they suspected or distrusted or were simply tired of. The irony was that what came free and easy and accessible was a planned operation by a distant and invisible authority—the American corporations. But in local and immediate terms, as in the other cases mentioned, this did not at first greatly matter; a choice was being exercised, here and now.

Television has now been a majority service for a whole generation. It has had certain intended effects corresponding to certain explicit intentions, essentially declared by the variable character of television institutions. But it has also had unforeseen effects, among them the desire to use the technology for oneself. In the young radical underground, and even more in the young cultural underground, there is

a familiarity with media, and an eager sense of experiment and practice, which is as much an effect as the more widely publicized and
predicted passivity. Indeed, by prolonged use of a technology which
had seemed to be contained and limited to commercial or paternal
or authoritarian ends, many people—we do not yet know whether
they are enough people—conceived quite different intentions and
uses. This is the critical answer to the notion of a determined technology as well as the more ordinary notion of a technological determinism. For these new uses are at least appropriate to the technology
as the uses and intentions which have hitherto defined it. It is from
this generation, raised on television, that we are continually getting
examples and proposals of electronic creation and communication
which are so different from orthodox television as to seem a quite new
technology and cultural form. The town-meeting by television is a
radically alternative definition of the relations between 'broadcasters'
and 'viewers'. The multi-screen play is a radically alternative definition of the framed projection or the framed flow. Just as television was
coming to seem a determined cultural form or a determined technology, there are these radically alternative definitions and practices,
trying to find their way through.

How the technology develops from now on is then not only a matter of some autonomous process directed by remote engineers. It is
a matter of social and cultural definition, according to the ends sought.
From a range of existing developments and possibilities, variable
priorities and variable institutions are now clearly on the agenda. Yet
this does not mean that the issue is undetermined; the limits and
pressures are real and powerful. Most technical development is in the
hands of corporations which express the contemporary interlock of
military, political and commercial intentions. Most policy development is in the hands of established broadcasting corporations and the
political bureaucracies of a few powerful states. All that has been established so far is that neither the theory nor the practice of television
as we know it is a necessary or a predicting cause. Current orthodox
theory and practice are, on the contrary, effects. Thus whether the
theory and the practice can be changed will depend not on the fixed
properties of the medium nor on the necessary character of its institutions, but on a continually renewable social action and struggle. It
is therefore to the immediate emergent problems of the technology
and the institutions that we must now turn.

22

Utilization of mass communication by the individual
Elihu Katz, Jay G. Blumler and
Michael Gurevitch

From Blumler, J. and Katz, E. (eds) 1974: *The uses of mass communication*. Beverly Hills, Ca: Sage.

Suppose that we were studying not broadcasting-and-society in mid-twentieth-century America but opera-and-society in mid-nineteenth-century Italy. After all, opera in Italy, during that period, was a 'mass' medium. What would we be studying? It seems likely, for one thing, that we would find interest in the attributes of the medium—what might today be called its 'grammar'—for example, the curious convention that makes it possible to sing contradictory emotions simultaneously. For another, we would be interested in the functions of the medium for the individual and society: perceptions of the values expressed and underlined; the phenomena of stardom, fanship, and connoisseurship; the festive ambience which the medium created; and so on. It seems quite unlikely that we would be studying the effects of the singing of a particular opera on opinions and attitudes, even though some operas were written with explicit political, social, and moral aims in mind. The study of short-run effects, in other words, would not have had a high priority, although it might have had a place. But the emphasis, by and large, would have been on the medium as a cultural institution with its own social and psychological functions and perhaps long-run effects.

We have all been over the reasons why much of mass-communication research took a different turn, preferring to look at specific programmes as specific messages with, possibly, specific effects. We were social psychologists interested in persuasion and attitude change. We were political scientists interested in new forms of social control. We

Authors' Note: A more extended version of this essay was first prepared for presentation in May 1973 to a conference at Arden House, Harriman, New York, on Directions in Mass Communication Research, which was arranged by the School of Journalism of Columbia University and supported by a grant from the John and Mary Markle Foundation. It may be consulted in full in W. Phillips Davison and Frederick T. C. Yu (eds) *Mass Communication Research: Major Issues and Future Directions* (New York: Praeger, 1974). The present text is a modified version of an abridgement that originally appeared in *Public Opinion Quarterly* (Winter 1973–1974).

were commissioned to measure message effectiveness for marketing organizations, or public health agencies, or churches, or political organizations, or for the broadcasting organizations themselves. And we were asked whether the media were not causes of violent and criminal behaviour.

Yet even in the early days of empirical mass-communication research this preoccupation with short-term effects was supplemented by the growth of an interest in the gratifications that the mass media provide their audiences. Such studies were well represented in the Lazarsfeld–Stanton collections (1942, 1944, 1949); Herzog (1942) on quiz programmes and the gratifications derived from listening to soap operas; Suchman (1942) on the motives for getting interested in serious music on radio; Wolfe and Fiske (1949) on the development of children's interest in comics; Berelson (1949) on the functions of newspaper reading; and so on. Each of these investigations came up with a list of functions served either by some specific contents or by the medium in question: to match one's wits against others, to get information or advice for daily living, to provide a framework for one's day, to prepare oneself culturally for the demands of upward mobility, or to be reassured about the dignity and usefulness of one's role.

What these early studies had in common was, first, a basically similar methodological approach whereby statements about media functions were elicited from the respondents in an essentially open-ended way. Second, they shared a qualitative approach in their attempt to group gratification statements into labelled categories, largely ignoring the distribution of their frequency in the population. Third, they did not attempt to explore the links between the gratifications thus detected and the psychological or sociological origins of the needs that were so satisfied. Fourth, they failed to search for the interrelationships among the various media functions, either quantitatively or conceptually, in a manner that might have led to the detection of the latent structure of media gratifications. Consequently, these studies did not result in a cumulatively more detailed picture of media gratifications conducive to the eventual formulation of theoretical statements.

The last few years have witnessed something of a revival of direct empirical investigations of audience uses and gratifications, not only in the United States but also in Britain, Sweden, Finland, Japan, and Israel. These more recent studies have a number of differing starting points, but each attempts to press towards a greater systematization of what is involved in conducting research in this field. Taken together, they make operational many of the logical steps that were only implicit in the earlier work. They are concerned with (1) the social and psychological origins of (2) needs, which generate (3) expectations of (4) the mass media or other sources, which lead to (5) differential patterns of media exposure (or engagement in other activities), resulting in (6) need gratifications and (7) other consequences, perhaps mostly unintended ones. Some of these investigations begin by specifying needs and then attempt to trace the extent to which they are gratified by the media or other sources. Others take observed gratifications as a starting point and attempt to reconstruct the needs that are being gratified. Yet others focus on the social origins of audience expectations and gratifications. But however varied their individual points of departure, they all strive towards an assessment of media consumption in audience-related terms, rather than in technological, aesthetic, ideological, or other more or less 'elitist' terms. The convergence of their foci, as well as of their findings, indicates that there is a clear agenda here—part methodological and part theoretical—for a discussion of the future directions of this approach.

Some basic assumptions of theory, method and value

Perhaps the place of 'theory' and 'method' in the study of audience uses and gratifications is not immediately apparent. The common tendency to attach the label 'uses and gratifications approach' to work in this field appears to virtually disclaim any theoretical pretensions or methodological commitment. From this point of view the approach simply represents an attempt to explain something of the way in which individuals use communications, among other resources in their environment, to satisfy their needs and to achieve their goals, and to do so by simply asking them. Nevertheless, this effort does rest on a body of assumptions, explicit or implicit, that have some degree of internal coherence and that are arguable in the sense that not everyone contemplating them would find them self-evident. Lundberg and Hultén (1968) refer to them as jointly constituting a 'uses and gratifications model'. Five elements of this model in particular may be singled out for comment:

(1) The audience is conceived of as active, that is, an important part of mass-media use is assumed to be goal directed (McQuail, Blumler and Brown, 1972). This assumption may be contrasted with Bogart's (1965) thesis to the effect that 'most mass-media

experiences represent pastime rather than purposeful activity, very often [reflecting] chance circumstances within the range of availabilities rather than the expression of psychological motivation or need'. Of course, it cannot be denied that media exposure often has a casual origin; the issue is whether, in addition, patterns of media use are shaped by more or less definite expectations of what certain kinds of content have to offer the audience member.

(2) In the mass-communication process much initiative in linking need gratification and media choice lies with the audience member. This places a strong limitation on theorizing about any form of straight-line effect of media content on attitudes and behaviour. As Schramm, Lyle and Parker (1961) said:

> In a sense the term 'effect' is misleading because it suggests that television 'does something' to children. . . . Nothing can be further from the fact. It is the children who are most active in this relationship. It is they who use television rather than television that uses them.

(3) The media compete with other sources of need satisfaction. The needs served by mass communication constitute but a segment of the wider range of human needs, and the degree to which they can be adequately met through mass-media consumption certainly varies. Consequently, a proper view of the role of the media in need satisfaction should take into account other functional alternatives—including different, more conventional, and 'older' ways of fulfilling needs.

(4) Methodologically speaking, many of the goals of mass-media use can be derived from data supplied by individual audience members themselves—that is, people are sufficiently self-aware to be able to report their interests and motives in particular cases, or at least recognize them when confronted with them in an intelligible and familiar verbal formulation.

(5) Value judgements about the cultural significance of mass communication should be suspended while audience orientations are explored on their own terms. It is from the perspective of this assumption that certain affinities and contrasts between the uses and gratifications approach and much speculative writing about popular culture may be considered.

State of the art: theoretical issues

From the few postulates outlined above, it is evident that further development of a theory of media gratification depends, first, on the clarification of its relationship to the theoretical traditions on which it so obviously draws and, second, on systematic efforts towards conceptual integration of empirical findings. Given the present state of the art, the following are priority issues in the development of an adequate theoretical basis.

Typologies of audience gratifications

Each major piece of uses and gratification research has yielded its own classification scheme of audience functions. When placed side by side, they reveal a mixture of shared gratification categories and notions peculiar to individual research teams. The differences are due in part to the fact that investigators have focused on different levels of study (e.g. medium or content) and different materials (e.g. different programmes or programme types on, say, television) in different cultures (e.g. Finland, Israel, Japan, Sweden, the United Kingdom, the United States, and Yugoslavia).

Unifunctional conceptions of audience interests have been expressed in various forms. Popular culture writers have often based their criticisms of the media on the ground that, in primarily serving the escapist desires of the audience, they deprived it of the more beneficial uses that might be made of communication (McDonald, 1957). Stephenson's analysis (1967) of mass communication exclusively in terms of 'play' may be interpreted as an extension, albeit in a transformed and expanded expression, of this same notion. A more recent example has been provided by Nordenstreng (1970), who, while breaking away from conventional formulations, still opts for a unifunctional view when he claims that, 'It has often been documented (e.g. during television and newspaper strikes in Finland in 1966–67) that perhaps the basic motivation for media use is just an unarticulated need for social contact.'

The wide currency secured for a bifunctional view of audience concerns is reflected in Weiss's (1971) summary, which states that, 'When ... studies of uses and gratifications are carried out, the media or media content are usually viewed dichotomously as predominantly fantasist-escapist or informational-educational in significance.' This dichotomy appears, for example, in Schramm's (1949) work (adopted subsequently by Schramm, Lyle and Parker, 1961; Pietila, 1969; and Furu, 1971), which distinguishes between sets of 'immediate' and 'deferred' gratifications, and in the distinction between informational and entertainment materials. In terms of audience gratifications specifically, it emerges in the distinction between surveillance and escape uses of the media.

The four-functional interpretation of the media was first proposed by Lasswell (1948) on a macro-sociological level and later developed by Wright (1960) on both the macro- and the micro-sociological levels. It postulated that the media served the functions of surveillance, correlation, entertainment, and cultural transmission (or socialization) for society as a whole, as well as for individuals and subgroups within society. An extension of the four-function approach can also be found in Wright's suggestive exploration of the potential dysfunctional equivalents of Lasswell's typology.

None of these statements, however, adequately reflects the full range of functions, which has been disclosed by the more recent investigations. McQuail, Blumler and Brown (1972) have put forward a typology consisting of the following categories: diversion (including escape from the constraints of routine and the burdens of problems, and emotional release); personal relationships (including substitute companionship as well as social utility); personal identity (including personal reference, reality exploration, and value reinforcement); and surveillance.

An effort to encompass the large variety of specific functions that have been proposed is made in the elaborate scheme of Katz, Gurevitch and Haas (1973). Their central notion is that mass communication is used by individuals to connect (or sometimes to disconnect) themselves—via instrumental, affective, or integrative relations—with different kinds of others (self, family, friends, nation, etc.). The scheme attempts to comprehend the whole range of individual gratifications of the many facets of the need 'to be connected'. And it finds empirical regularities in the preference for different media for different kinds of connections.

Gratification and needs

The study of mass-media use suffers at present from the absence of a relevant theory of social and psychological needs. It is not so much a catalogue of needs that is missing as a clustering of groups of needs, a sorting out of different levels of need, and a specification of hypotheses linking particular needs with particular media gratifications. It is true that the work of Schramm, Lyle and Parker (1961) draws on the distinction between the reality and pleasure principles in the socialization theories of Freud and others, but more recent studies suggest that those categories are too broad to be serviceable. Maslow's (1954) proposed hierarchy of human needs may hold more promise, but the relevance of his categories to expectations of communication has not yet been explored in detail. Lasswell's (1948) scheme to specify the needs that media satisfy has proved useful, and it may be helpful to examine Lasswell and Kaplan's (1950) broader classification of values as well.

Alternatively, students of uses and gratifications could try to work backwards, as it were, from gratifications to needs. In the informational field, for example, the surveillance function may be traced to a desire for security or the satisfaction of curiosity and the exploratory drive; seeking reinforcement of one's attitudes and values may derive from a need for reassurance that one is right; and attempts to correlate informational elements may stem from a more basic need to develop one's cognitive mastery of the environment. Similarly, the use of fictional (and other) media materials for 'personal reference' may spring from a need for self-esteem; social utility functions may be traced to the need for affiliation; and escape functions may be related to the need to release tension and reduce anxiety. But whichever way one proceeds, it is inescapable that what is at issue here is the long-standing problem of social and psychological science: how to (and whether to bother to) systematize the long lists of human and societal needs. Thus far, gratifications research has stayed close to what we have been calling media-related needs (in the sense that the media have been observed to satisfy them, at least in part), but one wonders whether all this should not be put in the broader context of systematic studies of needs.

Sources of media gratifications

Studies have shown that audience gratifications can be derived from at least three distinct sources: media content, exposure to the media *per se*, and the social context that typifies the situation of exposure to different media. Although recognition of media content as a source of gratifications has provided the basis for research in this area from its inception, less attention has been paid to the other sources. Nevertheless, it is clear that the need to relax or to kill time can be satisfied by the act of watching television, that the need to feel that one is spending one's time in a worthwhile way may be associated with the act of reading (Waples, Berelson and Bradshaw, 1940; Berelson, 1949), and that the need to structure one's day may be satisfied merely by having the radio 'on' (Mendelsohn, 1964). Similarly, a wish to spend time with one's family or friends can be served by watching television at home with the family or by going to the cinema with one's friends.

Each medium seems to offer a unique combination of (*a*) characteristic contents (at least stereotypically perceived in that way); (*b*) typical attributes (print vs broadcasting modes of transmission, iconic vs symbolic representation, reading vs audio or audio-visual modes of reception); and (*c*) typical exposure situations (at home vs out-of-home, alone vs with others, control over the temporal aspects of exposure vs absence of such control). The issue, then, is what combinations of attributes may render different media more or less adequate for the satisfaction of different needs (Katz, Gurevitch and Haas, 1973).

Gratifications and media attributes

Much uses and gratifications research has still barely advanced beyond a sort of charting and profiling activity: findings are still typically presented to show that certain bodies of content serve certain functions or that one medium is deemed better at satisfying certain needs than another. The further step, which has hardly been ventured, is one of explanation. At issue here is the relationship between the unique 'grammar' of different media—that is, their specific technological and aesthetic attributes—and the particular requirements of audience members that they are then capable, or incapable, of satisfying. Which, indeed, are the attributes that render some media more conducive than others to satisfying specific needs? And which elements of content help to attract the expectations for which they apparently cater?

It is possible to postulate the operation of some kind of division of labour among the media for the satisfaction of audience needs. This may be elaborated in two ways: taking media attributes as the starting point, the suggestion is that those media that differ (or are similar) in their attributes are more likely to serve different (or similar) needs; or, utilizing the latent structure of needs as a point of departure, the implication is that needs that are psychologically related or conceptually similar will be equally well served by the same media (or by media with similar attributes).

To illustrate the first approach, Robinson (1972) has demonstrated the interchangeability of television and print media for learning purposes. In the Israeli study, Katz, Gurevitch and Haas (1973) found five

media ordered in a circumplex with respect to their functional similarities: books–newspapers–radio–television–cinema–books. In other
words, books functioned most like newspapers, on the one hand, and
like cinema, on the other. Radio was most similar in its usage to newspapers, on the one hand, and to television, on the other. The explanation would seem to lie not only with certain technological attributes
that they have in common, but with similar aesthetic qualities as
well. Thus, books share a technology and an informational function
with newspapers, but are similar to films in their aesthetic function.
Radio shares a technology, as well as informational and entertainment content, with television, but it is also very much like newspapers—providing a heavy dose of information and an orientation
to reality.

An illustration of the second aspect of this division of labour may
also be drawn from the same study. Here, the argument is that structurally related needs will tend to be serviced by certain media more
often than by others. Thus, books and cinema have been found to
cater to needs concerned with self-fulfilment and self-gratification:
they help to 'connect' individuals to themselves. Newspapers, radio,
and television all seem to connect individuals to society. In fact, the
function of newspapers for those interested in following what is going
on in the world may have been grossly underestimated in the past
(Edelstein, 1973; Lundberg and Hultén, 1968). Television, however,
was found to be less frequently used as a medium of escape by Israeli
respondents than were books and films. And a Swedish study of the
'functional specialities of the respective media' reported that, 'A
retreat from the immediate environment and its demands—probably
mainly by the act of reading itself—was characteristic of audience
usage of weekly magazines' (Lundberg and Hultén, 1968).

Media attributes as perceived or intrinsic

When people associate book-reading, for example, with a desire to
know oneself, and newspapers with the need to feel connected to the
larger society, it is difficult to disentangle perceptions of the media
from their intrinsic qualities. Is there anything about the book as a
medium that breeds intimacy? Is there something about newspapers
that explains their centrality in socio-political integration? Or, is this
'something' simply an accepted image of the medium and its characteristic content?

In this connection, Rosengren (1972) has suggested that uses and gratifications research may be profitably connected with the long-established tradition of inquiry into public perceptions of the various media and the dimensions according to which their respective images and qualities are differentiated (cf. especially Nilsson [1971] and Edelstein [1973] and the literature cited therein). A merger of the two lines of investigation may show how far the attributes of the media, as perceived by their consumers, and their intrinsic qualities are correlated with the pursuit of certain gratifications. So far, however, this connection has only been partially discussed in the work of Lundberg and Hultén (1968).

The social origins of audience needs and their gratifications

The social and environmental circumstances that lead people to turn to the mass media for the satisfaction of certain needs are also little understood as yet. For example, what needs, if any, are created by routine work on an assembly line, and which forms of media exposure will satisfy them? What motivates some people to seek political information from the mass media and others to actively avoid it? Here one may postulate that it is the combined product of psychological dispositions, sociological factors, and environmental conditions that determines the specific uses of the media by members of the audience.

At certain levels it should not prove unduly difficult to formulate discrete hypotheses about such relationships. For example, we might expect 'substitute companionship' to be sought especially by individuals with limited opportunities for social contacts: invalids, the elderly, the single, the divorced or widowed living alone, the housewife who spends much time at home on her own, and so on.

At another level, however, it is more difficult to conceive of a general theory that might clarify the various processes that underlie any such specific relationships. A preliminary structuring of the possibilities suggests that social factors may be involved in the generation of media-related needs in any of the following five ways (each of which has attracted some comment in the literature):

(1) Social situation produces tensions and conflicts, leading to pressure for their easement via mass-media consumption (Katz and Foulkes, 1962).
(2) Social situation creates an awareness of problems that demand attention, information about which may be sought in the media (Edelstein, 1973).

(3) Social situation offers impoverished real-life opportunities to satisfy certain needs, which are then directed to the mass media for complementary, supplementary, or substitute servicing (Rosengren and Windahl, 1972).

(4) Social situation gives rise to certain values, the affirmation and reinforcement of which is facilitated by the consumption of congruent media materials (Dembo, 1972).

(5) Social situation provides a field of expectations of familiarity with certain media materials, which must then be monitored in order to sustain membership of valued social groupings (Atkins, 1972).

The versatility of sources of need satisfaction

Before becoming too sanguine about the possibility of relating social situations to psychological needs to media/content gratifications, it is important to bear in mind that gratifications studies based on specific media contents have demonstrated that one and the same set of media materials is capable of serving a multiplicity of needs and audience functions. Presumably, that is why Rosengren and Windahl (1972) have drawn attention to 'a growing consensus that almost any type of content may serve practically any type of function'. For example, Blumler, Brown and McQuail (1970) have found that the television serial *The Saint* serves functions of personal reference, identification with characters, and reality-exploration, in addition to its more obvious diversionary function. Similarly, their study of the gratifications involved in news viewing referred not only to the expected surveillance motive but also to functions of social utility, empathy, and even escape. In summarizing the implications of their evidence, McQuail, Blumler and Brown (1972) point out that:

> the relationship between content categories and audience needs is far less tidy and more complex than most commentators have appreciated.... One man's source of escape from the real world is a point of anchorage for another man's place in it.

Gratifications and effects

Pioneers in the study of uses and gratifications were moved chiefly by two aspirations. The first, which has largely been fulfilled, was to redress an imbalance evident in previous research: audience needs, they said, deserved as much attention in their own right as the persuasive aims of communicators with which so many of the early 'effects' studies have been preoccupied. The second major aim of uses and gratifications research, however, was to treat audience requirements as intervening variables in the study of traditional communication effects. Glaser's (1965) formulation offers a typical expression of the rationale behind this prospect:

> Since users approach the media with a variety of needs and predispositions ... any precise identification of the effects of television watching ... must identify the uses sought and made of television by the various types of viewers.

Despite this injunction, hardly any substantial empirical or theoretical effort has been devoted to connecting gratifications and effects. Some limited evidence from the political field suggests that combining functions and effects perspectives may be fruitful (Blumler and McQuail, 1968). But there are many other foci of traditional effects studies for which no detailed hypotheses about gratifications/effects interactions have yet been framed.

One obvious example is the field of media violence. Another might concern the impact on inhabitants of developing countries of exposure to television serials, films, and popular songs of foreign (predominantly American) origin. Yet another might relate to the wide range of materials, appearing especially in broadcast fiction, that purport simultaneously to entertain and to portray more or less faithfully some portion of social reality—e.g. the worlds of law enforcement, social work, hospital life, trade unionism, working-class neighbourhoods, and ways of life at the executive level in business corporations and civil-service departments.

Hypotheses about the cumulative effects of exposure to such materials on audience members' cognitive perceptions of these spheres of activity, and on the individuals engaged in them, might be formulated in awareness of the likely fact that some individuals will be viewing them primarily for purposes of escape, while others will be using them for reality-exploring gratifications. In these circumstances should we expect a readier acceptance of portrayed stereotypes by the escape seekers—the thesis of Festinger and Maccoby (1964) on persuasion via distraction might be relevant here—or by those viewers who are trusting enough to expect such programmes to offer genuine insights into the nature of social reality?

A similar body of recently analysed materials may be found in the television soap opera, with its postulated capacity to 'establish or reinforce value systems' (Katzman, 1972). In fact one cluster of gratifications that emerged from an English study of listeners to a long-running daytime radio serial (*The Dales*) centred on the tendency of the programme to uphold traditional family values (Blumler, Brown and McQuail, 1970). This suggests that an answer to Katzman's 'key question' ('to what degree do daytime serials change attitudes and norms and to what extent do they merely follow and reinforce their audience?') might initially be sought by distinguishing among the regular followers of such programmes those individuals who are avowedly seeking a reinforcement of certain values from those who are not.

In addition, however, the literature refers to some consequences of audience functions that conventional effects designs may be unable to capture. First, there is what Katz and Foulkes (1962) have termed the 'feedback' from media use to the individual's performance of his other social roles. Thus, Bailyn (1959) distinguished child uses of pictorial media that might 'preclude more realistic and lasting solutions' to problems from those that, at one level, were 'escapist' but that should more properly be categorized as 'supplementation'. Similarly, Schramm, Lyle and Parker (1961) maintained that child uses of the mass media for fantasizing might either drain off discontent caused by the hard blows of socialization or lead a child into withdrawal from the real world. And Lundberg and Hultén (1968) have suggested that for some individuals the substitute-companionship function may involve use of the media to replace real social ties, while for others it may facilitate an adjustment to reality.

Second, some authors have speculated on the connection between functions performed by the media for individuals and their functions (or dysfunctions) for other levels of society. This relationship is particularly crucial for its bearing on evaluative and ideological controversies about the role of mass communication in modern society. Thus, Enzenberger (1972) suggests that the eight-millimetre camera may satisfy the recreational and creative impulses of the individual and help to keep the family together while simultaneously atomizing and depoliticizing society. Or news viewing may gratify the individual's need for civic participation; but if the news, as presented, is a disjointed succession of staccato events, it may also leave him with the message that the world is a disconnected place. Similarly, many radical critics tend to regard television as part of a conspiracy to keep people content and politically quiescent—offering respite, para-social interaction with interesting and amusing people, and much food for gossip—while propagating a false social consciousness.

Implications for research policy and media policy

In reviewing the state of the art of gratifications research, we have focused on issues—theoretical, methodological, and ideological—rather than on systematized findings. We have also tried to make manifest our assumptions. Thus, we have confronted the image of the beery, house-slippered, casual viewer of television with the notion of a more 'active' audience—knowing that both images are true. We have asked whether a methodology based on respondents' introspection can be adequate. We have indicated the absence of satisfactory bridging concepts between the constraints arising from social situations and the gratifications sought from the media; or between particular patterns of use and likely effect.

These issues bear not only on the direction of future research, but also, echoing Nordenstreng (1970), on the relationship between research policy and media policy. Thus, we have raised the question of the extent to which the media create the needs that they satisfy. Even more fundamentally, we ask whether the media do actually satisfy their consumers—an assumption that radical critics of the media take more for granted than do gratification researchers (cf. Emmett, 1968–9). To assert that mass communication is a latter-day opiate of the masses presupposes a media–output audience-satisfaction nexus that gratifications research treats as hypothesis rather than fact.

In other words, our position is that media researchers ought to be studying human needs to discover how much the media do or do not contribute to their creation and satisfaction. Moreover, we believe it is our job to clarify the extent to which certain kinds of media and content favour certain kinds of use—to thereby set boundaries to the over-generalization that any kind of content can be bent to any kind of need. We believe it is part of our job to explore the social and individual conditions under which audiences find need or use for programme material aimed at changing their image of the *status quo* or 'broadening their cultural horizons' (Emmett, 1968–9).

From the point of view of media policy, then, we reject the view that an application of the uses and gratifications approach to policy questions must inevitably support or exonerate the producers of junk or the *status quo* of media content. That belief seems to require the acceptance of one or both of two other assumptions: existing patterns of audience needs support the prevailing patterns of media provision and no other; and audience concerns are in fact trivial and escapist. For reasons that should now be plain, we find these propositions dubious.

Though audience oriented, the uses and gratifications approach is not necessarily conservative. While taking account of what people look for from the media, it breaks away from a slavish dependence of content on audience propensities by bringing to light the great variety of needs and interests that are encompassed by the latter. As McQuail, Blumler and Brown (1972) have argued, uses and gratifications data suggest that the mass media may not, after all, be as 'constrained as the escapist theory makes out from performing a wider range of social functions than is generally assigned to them in western societies today'. In other words, instead of depicting the media as severely circumscribed by audience expectations, the uses and gratifications approach highlights the audience as a source of challenge to producers to cater more richly to the multiplicity of requirements and roles that it has disclosed.

23

The narrator as guarantor of truth
Colin McArthur

From McArthur, Colin 1978: *Television and history*. London: British Film Institute, 21–6.

> ... *the historian or relater of things important to mankind must, whoever he be, approve himself many ways to us ... ere we are bound to take anything on his authority.* (3rd Earl of Shaftesbury)

There is a justly famous sequence in *Letter from Siberia*, a film by the distinguished French documentarist Chris Marker, in which the series of images just seen by the audience is replayed twice with different commentaries which totally reverse the ideological meaning of the sequence as first shown. This illustrates starkly and directly what most of us know but constantly have to dredge up to the surface of our consciousness, i.e. that while filmed records of events are by no means ideologically neutral,[1] they nevertheless, in themselves, lack total explanatory force and require supplementing by other codes—usually musical or verbal or, most particularly, montage codes—before this explanatory force can *begin* to come into play.

So omnipresent is the phenomenon of narration and the (most usually disembodied) narrator, so *naturalized* has the process become, that considerable effort is required to distance oneself from it and interrogate its ideological import. This is true of documentary film practice in general and, within this, of 'factual' programmes about history. So prevalent is the fact of narration and the conception of history as narrative that the highly controversial issue[2] of the *necessity* of the relationship between narrative/narration and historiography has been (particularly with regard to tele-history) repressed.

It will readily be conceded that in 'real' life people's voices and verbal language use (like their dress and physical mannerisms) are coded, giving information of a complex kind. This, naturally, can become part of the film or television message (although it should be noted that the information 'urban, working-class Scot' passed by linguistic codes, while related to, is not the same as, the information 'actor *signifying* urban, working-class Scot'). This fact therefore should provoke reflection about the choices made as to which figures act as narrators in television programmes about history and what the ideological implications of these choices might be.

Right from the start of tele-history, narration has been the preserve primarily of the *actor* (significantly not the *actress* except in manifestly 'feminist' programmes such as *Women at War*) when the narration has been off-camera. When the narrator has been for a large part of the time on-camera (as in *Civilization*, *The Ascent of Man*, *America*, *The Age of Uncertainty*, etc.) then a somewhat different coding operation is at work, as will be discussed presently. The argument of this monograph is that the central ideological function of the narration is to confer *authority* on, and to elide *contradictions* in, the discourse. In a *patriarchal* society the narrator must therefore be a man and in a *bourgeois* society his voice must be one which signifies bourgeois authority. While few choices of narrator carry such flagrant ideological overtones as the use in the American series *Victory at Sea* of Richard Burton in his Churchillian dimension, the narration of tele-history has operated firmly, if not exclusively, within the linguistic parameters of the BBC and the London stage at an earlier point of their development (i.e. prior to the mid-fifties, when regional and non-upper-class accents increasingly penetrated the 'serious' productions of these institutions). This is exemplified by the choice as narrator[3] of Michael Redgrave (*The Great War*, BBC), Laurence Olivier (*World at War*, Thames), Iain Cuthbertson (*Destination America*, Thames)—using of course his Standard English voice rather than his *Sutherland's Law* (BBC) voice—and Robert Hardy (*The British Empire*, BBC). To be highly speculative, it is interesting to ponder what additional reasons might exist—apart from linguistic coding—as significatory of the ideological projects of these programmes. Could perhaps the Redgrave and Olivier knighthoods (and, in the latter's case, a peerage) have been relevant; could the choice of an actor associated in the public mind with regional roles be regarded as more fitting to the demotic aspirations of *Destination America*; and could the well-known association of Robert Hardy with English tradition (e.g. his narrating the series *Heritage*, BBC, on English pageantry and his book and television programme on the English long-bow) have been an added *cachet*?

Unquestionably, narration in tele-history has strong *denotative* features, i.e. the *matter* of what is said is crucially important: 'hard' information is given about which armies took part in particular battles, where the battles occurred, what the outcome was; how many of a particular nationality came to America and when, where they settled and what sort of space was allowed them, and so on. However, closely allied to the (subconscious?) class choices of narrator referred to above are the *connotative* aspects of narration, the *rhetoric* of narration. This is, of course, quite difficult to separate out from the rhetoric of other codes (pictorial, musical, sound) working simultaneously with it, but it might be argued that the rhetoric of narration in tele-history veers towards that of more heightened, stylized forms of verbal discourse such as blank verse and other *dramatic* forms. This would, of course, be consistent both with a view (whether conscious or otherwise) of *all* television as 'entertainment' and, at the same time, the apparently paradoxical impulse to signal the *difference* of tele-history from the comedy show which precedes it and the police series which comes after it, to signal its *seriousness*.

It is necessary, in its aspiration to drama, that the narration of tele-history be uneven, have troughs and *crescendi*, the latter being associated with the beginnings and endings of programmes, with structural features of the institution television such as commercial breaks, and with the impulses of narrative itself (e.g. the points of transition from stasis to action in a series about war). Needless to say, the *crescendi* of narration are supported by *crescendi* in the other codes, most notably those of music and cutting.

Take the complex codification of the opening of any episode from *The Great War*. The credit sequence consists basically of three extremely dramatic photographs from the First World War: a soldier standing beside a cross on the skyline; a half-decayed body in a trench; and a British soldier staring, as if shell-shocked, at the camera. The credit sequence is paced by Wilfred Josephs's bleak and evocative musical score and the photographs are connected by disturbing camera movements downwards and sideways. The sequence is clearly designed to evoke the sense of horror associated with certain aspects of the First World War which have registered in popular memory: its trench warfare; its dashed hopes; and its casualty lists in millions. However, the view of the war which the sequence evokes is of a time-less and metaphysical category prised free from history rather than as a conflagration which broke out as a result of the convergence of quite concrete historical forces. Given a recurrent opening motif of such dramatic force, the rhetoric of the narration could not then relapse into *pure* 'hard' information-giving or analysis: dramatic necessity requires that it aspire, from time to time at least, to the same register as the credit sequence. Thus, the episode entitled 'This Busi-

ness May Last a Long Time'—concerned with the change from classical to trench warfare—begins with shots of German soldiers in repose
accompanied by the cadenced narration of Sir Michael Redgrave:

> The pendulum of war had come to rest; the armies halted. Round the
> camp fires men were too weary to talk much, but they *could* wonder
> which way would they march tomorrow....

However, important as the 'hard' information-giving and the rhetorical features of narration are, far and away its most important function
is as organizer of the other discourses constituting the programme and
as guarantor of its 'truth'.

This feature of narration has been well described, with regard to
the nineteenth-century novel and the classical narrative fiction film
deriving so largely from it, by Colin MacCabe. The 'classic realist
text', as MacCabe calls it, is characterized by:

> a hierarchy amongst the discourses which compose the text and this hier-
> archy is defined in terms of an empirical notion of truth. Perhaps the
> easiest way to understand this is through a reflection on the use of inverted
> commas within the classic realist novel. While those sections in the text
> which are contained in inverted commas may cause a certain difficulty
> for the reader—a certain confusion *vis-à-vis* what really is the case—this
> difficulty is abolished by the unspoken (or more accurately the unwritten)
> prose that surrounds them.... Whereas other discourses within the text
> are considered as material which are open to reinterpretation, the narra-
> tive discourse simply allows reality to appear and denies its own status
> as articulation.....[4]

The analogous transparency of the narration in tele-history programmes gives it enormous ideological force, particularly since the
voice speaking the narration is—as has been suggested above—almost
invariably the voice of bourgeois authority.

The above quotation from MacCabe might have been written with
The Great War in mind, for the latter is constituted largely by attri-
buted texts with 'quotation marks' round them: 'As General X's order
of the day said...'; 'Colonel Y, writing home from the front, said
...'; 'As an editorial in the *Frankfurter-Zeitung* said...'; and so on.
Also in 'inverted commas', so to speak, are the on-screen recollections
of First World War veterans which form a recurrent discourse in the
series. Probably the only two discourses without 'inverted commas'
are the actuality footage round which the series is built and the narration. Both are presented as transparent, unarticulated, self-evidently
'true' and are presented as such for separate ideological reasons which
derive from the same philosophical basis.

It is worthwhile recalling the remarks of Stuart Hall [*not in this extract*]; particularly his suggestion that, in the received wisdom of television production, '"good television" must be either plain, simple and straight, *or* it requires the mediation of the explainer, guide, moderator, who "stands in" for the absent audience and makes the complicated plain, simple and straight'. In this latter category Hall had primarily in mind professional 'link-men' such as Robin Day and Michael Barratt, but the two types he poses fit the types of tele-history. If series such as *World at War*, *Destination America* and *The British Empire* constitute the former, *Civilization*, *The Ascent of Man* and *The Age of Uncertainty* constitute the latter. In one the authority is covert, in the other—by reason of the academic reputations of the narrators— it is overt, indeed *flaunted*. In each case the narrator guarantees *Truth*.

MacCabe makes the important argument that 'the classic realist text cannot deal with the real in its contradictions and ... in the same movement it fixes the subject [i.e. the spectator] in a point of view from which everything becomes obvious'.[5] He then goes on:

> There is, however, a level of contradiction into which the classic realist text can enter. This is the contradiction between the dominant discourse of the text and the dominant ideological discourses of the time. Thus a classic realist text in which a strike is represented as a just struggle in which oppressed workers attempt to gain some of their rightful wealth would be in contradiction with certain contemporary ideological discourses and as such might be classified as progressive. It is here that subject matter enters into the argument and where we can find the justification for Marx and Engels's praise of Balzac and Lenin's texts on the revolutionary force of Tolstoy's texts which ushered the Russian peasant onto the stage of history. Within contemporary films one can think of the films of Costa-Gavras [e.g., *Z*, *State of Siege*] or such television documentaries as *Cathy Come Home* [BBC]. What is, however, still impossible for the classic realist text is to offer any perspectives for struggle due to its inability to investigate contradiction. It is thus not surprising that these films tend either to be linked to a social democratic conception of progress—if we reveal injustices then they will go away—or certain *ouvrieriste* tendencies which tend to see the working-class, outside any dialectical movement, as the simple possessors of truth.[6]

Written primarily with narrative fiction in mind, this quotation is consequently entirely applicable to television historical drama with its discourse organized by the unseen writer and television director whereby, as MacCabe has put it, 'its end is guaranteed from its beginning and it is this certainty which enables the reader to place him or herself in a position of unity from which the material is dominated'.[7] But patently, it is also applicable to 'factual' television programmes about history where everything is filtered either covertly, through the absent writer and off-screen narrator, or flamboyantly through the sensibility of the on-screen writer/narrator.

The only 'progressive realist text' I am aware of in the area of historical drama on British television is *Days of Hope*, although its massive retention of the features of realist drama is, at the very least, problematic.[8] Such texts exist in other areas of television, e.g. *World in Action*[9] and the John Pilger documentaries which ATV nervously announced as constituting 'a personal view' and hastily followed with a programme by Auberon Waugh, certain of whose views are pronouncedly right-wing, for the sake of 'balance and impartiality'. But although the former are progressive, they are nevertheless still 'realist' and as such—in MacCabe's terms—they filter contradictions through a particular point of view and resolve them for the audience.

If the 'progressive realist text' is thin on the ground in the area of historical drama and 'factual' programmes about history, the 'revolutionary text' as canvassed by MacCabe—that text in which contradictions are not resolved for the spectator but which, through its critique or total abandonment of 'the hierarchy of discourses', leaves the spectator with a deal of work to do to resolve and act out the contradictions—that text is *absent* from the television screen, but some progressive answers to the central problem it poses are discussed [*later in the work*].

24

A world at one with itself
Stuart Hall

From Hall, Stuart 1970: A world at one with itself. *New Society* 18 June 1970, 1056–8.

The issue of violence in the mass media has been posed in the familiar terms of the fantasy or fictional portrayal of violence there. But if the media are playing a role in the alleged escalation of social violence, it is almost certainly not *Z Cars*, *The Virginian*, *Callan* or *Codename* which are 'responsible'. What is at issue is not the fantasy role of fictional violence, but the alleged real effects of real violence. The area of broadcasting in question is that traditionally defined as 'news/current affairs/features/documentaries'. It is, for example, the only too real bodies of only too real Vietnamese, floating down an all too real Cambodian river, which some as yet unstated informal theory of cause and effect links in the minds of television's critics with questions of 'law and order'. Thus it is to the question of *news* that we must turn.

As it happens, news has just undergone an enormous expansion in the new radio schedules. In the philosophy of streamed radio which underpins the BBC's *Broadcasting in the Seventies* (BBC 1969) news got a privileged place. Under the new dispensation, the avid listener is never more than half an hour away from the next news bulletin. But the really striking development is the growth of the news-magazine style of programme, on the *World At One* model.

What constitutes the definition of news currently employed on radio programmes of this new type? I put the point in this way, and not in the more familiar terms of 'coverage' or 'bias/objectivity', because this constitutes the heart of the matter. Journalists throughout the media are notoriously slippery and defensive when thus confronted. 'The news', they assume, is clearly what it is: newsworthy people and events, happening 'out there' in the real world, at home and abroad.

The relevant questions are always technical ones: 'How adequately can we cover these events?', 'Is the coverage biased or objective?' This view is legitimated by a body of journalistic folklore, with its ritual references to copy, deadlines and news angles. These sanction professional practice and keep non-professional busybodies at bay.

Of course, newsmen agree, the news can be either 'hard' or 'soft', graphically or neutrally presented (sensationalism/objectivity), a report from the front or a background analysis (actuality/depth). But these are matters of treatment—of form and 'flavour'—not of content or substance. It is worth observing that all these routine ways of setting up the problem are drawn from the press, reflecting both the common background of media newsmen in Fleet Street, and, more important, the powerful hold of models borrowed for radio or television from the press.

The notion that the news somehow discovers itself may be of service to the harassed newsgatherers and editors. Such professional 'commonsense constructs', such *ad hoc* routines, are employed in most large-scale organizations. They enable hard-pressed professionals to execute their tasks with the minimum of stress and role-conflict.

These idiomatic shorthands give the professional a map of the social system, just as the categories of classification in mental hospitals (Erving Goffman, 1961), the clinical records of hospitals (H. Garfinkel, 1967), and the notebooks and case records of police and probation officers (Aaron Cicourel, 1968) witness to the moral order and the system of meanings which other professionals use to give sense to their tasks.

But against this defensive strategy, it needs to be asserted that the news is a *product*, a human construction: a staple of that system of 'cultural production' (to use Theodor Adorno's phrase) we call the mass media. Journalists and editors select, from the mass of potential news items, the events which constitute 'news' for any day. In part, this is done by implicit reference to some unstated and unstatable criteria of *the significant*. News selection thus rests on inferred knowledge about the audience, inferred assumptions about society, and a professional code or ideology. The news is not a set of unrelated items: news stories are coded and classified, referred to their relevant contexts, assigned to different (and differently graded) spaces in the media, and ranked in terms of presentation, status and meaning.

The process of news production has its own structure. News items which infringe social norms, break the pattern of expectations and contrast with our sense of the everyday, or are dramatic, or have 'numerous and intimate contacts with the life of the recipients', have greater news salience for journalists than others. As a highly reputable reporter observed to an irate group of student militants, who were questioning her as to why her paper reported every vote cast during the period of a university occupation, but nothing of the weekend teach-in: 'Votes represent decisions: decisions are news: discussion is not.'

The role of the news journalist is to mediate—or act as the 'gate-keeper'—between different publics, between institutions and the individual, between the spheres of the public and the private, between the new and the old. News production is often a self-fulfilling activity. Categories of news, consistently produced over time, create public spaces in the media which have to be filled. The presence of the media at the birth of new events can affect their course and outcome. The news is not only a cultural product: it is the product of a set of institutional definitions and meanings, which, in the professional short-hand, is commonly referred to as *news values*.

Statistics of crime represent not only the real movement of the crime rate, but the changing definition of what constitutes crime, how it is recognized, labelled and dealt with. To label as 'violent' every incident from skinhead attacks on Pakistanis, to Ulster, to protests against the South African tour, is to establish a certain way of seeing and understanding a complex set of public events.

Once the category of 'law and order' has come into existence as a legitimate news category, whole different orders of meaning and association can be made to cluster together. Terms of understanding—such as the criminal categories reserved for acts of collective social delinquency ('hooligans', say, or 'layabouts')—become transferred to new events like the clashes between citizens and the army in Ulster. It may be that there has been some objective increase in real-world violence; but the effect on news values is *even greater* than that would justify.

This shift is difficult to pinpoint in the brief radio or television news bulletin, though if we take a long enough stretch of time, we can observe changes both in the profile and in the style of news reports. But in the format of the radio news magazine, which approximates more closely to the profile and treatment of a daily newspaper, the amplifying and interpretative function of the media comes into its own.

News magazines include studio interviews, reports from correspondents, replies to attacks, features and 'human interest' stories. This is where background classifying and interpretative schemes register most forcefully. In terms of direct bias, there seems less cause for concern. Within its limits, radio shows little direct evidence of intentional bias. It treats the spokesmen of the two major political parties with scrupulous fairness—more, in fact, than they deserve. But the troublesome question is the matter of unwitting bias: the institutional slanting, built-in not by the devious inclination of editors to the political right or left, but by the steady and unexamined play of attitudes which, via the mediating structure of professionally defined news values, inclines all the media towards the *status quo*.

The operation of unwitting bias is difficult either to locate or prove. Its manifestations are always indirect. It comes through in terms of who is or who is not accorded the status of an accredited witness: in tones of voice: in the set-up of studio confrontations: in the assumptions which underlie the questions asked or not asked: in terms of the analytical concepts which serve informally to link events to causes: in what passes for explanation.

Its incidence can be mapped by plotting the areas of *consensus* (where there is a mutual agreement about the terms in which a topic is to be treated), the areas of *toleration* (where the overlap is less great, and the terms have to be negotiated as between competing definitions) and the areas of *dis-sensus* or *conflict* (where competing definitions are in play).

Unwitting bias has nothing directly to do with the style of 'tough' interviewing, since, even in the areas of consensus issues, the professional ethic sanctions a quite aggressive, probing style (Hardcastle with Heath, Robin Day with Wilson), though the probe does not penetrate to underlying assumptions.

Areas of *consensus* cover the central issues of politics and power, the fundamental sanctions of society and the sacred British values. To this area belong the accredited witnesses—politicians of both parties, local councillors, experts, institutional spokesmen.

Areas of *toleration* cover what might be called 'Home Office issues'—social questions, prisoners who can't get employment after discharge, little men or women against the bureaucrats, unmarried mothers, and so on. The more maverick witnesses who turn up in this group get, on the whole, an off-beat but sympathetic 'human interest'—even at times a crusading—kind of treatment. Guidelines in this sector are less clear-cut. When such topics edge over into the 'permissive' category, they can arouse strong sectional disapproval. But here even the scrupulously objective news editor can presume (again, a matter of negotiation and judgement, not of objective fact) on a greater background of public sympathy, more room for manœuvre.

Areas of *conflict* have their un-accredited cast of witnesses too: protesters of all varieties; shop stewards, especially if militant, more especially if on unofficial strike; squatters; civil rights activists; hippies; students; hijackers; Stop the Seventy Tour-ers; and so on. In dealing with these issues and actors, interviewers are noticeably sharper, touchier, defending their flanks against any predisposition to softness.

One could plot the hidden constraints of this informal ideology in the media simply by noting the characteristic arguments advanced against each of these groups. Unofficial strikers are always confronted with 'the national interest', squatters with 'the rights of private property', civil rights militants in Ulster with the need for Protestant and Catholic to 'work together', Stop the Seventy Tour-ers with the way their minority actions 'limit the right of the majority to enjoy themselves as they wish'.

I am not arguing here that these arguments should not be accorded some weight. I am remarking how, in the handling of certain issues, the assumptions which shape an interview item are coincident with official ideologies of the *status quo*. I recall numerous instances when Ulster civil rights militants were confronted with the consequences of violence. But I cannot recall a single instance when an Ulster Moderate or politician was confronted with the equally tenable view, succinctly expressed by Conor O'Brien, that since Ulster society has for long been based on the dominance of a minority over a majority, no fundamental change in that structure can be expected without its accompanying release of the 'frozen violence' inherent in the situation.

I know that Ulster is a particularly sensitive matter, that the BBC's impartiality came under direct fire during the events of September 1969, and that in this period a close executive watch was maintained over the news output. But then, my criticism is not of the wilful, intentional bias of editors and newscasters, but of the institutionalized ethos of the news media as a whole. The influence exerted by this ethos over actual broadcast programmes is precisely to be found on those occasions when men of quite varying temperaments and political views are systematically constrained in a certain direction.

I recall William Hardcastle's phrase, when reporting the American Anti-Vietnam demonstrations last year: 'the so-called Vietnam Moratorium Committee'. William Hardcastle's objectivity is not in question. But I await, without much confidence, the day when *The World At One* will refer to 'the so-called Confederation of British Industries' or the 'so-called Trades Union Congress' or even the 'so-called Central Intelligence Agency'.

The sources for this hidden consensus must be located outside the broadcasting media proper, at the heart of the political culture itself. It is a view of politics based on the relative absence of violence in British political life, the relative degree of integration between the powerful corporate interest groups within the state. This negotiated consensus is both a historical fact and a source of ideological comfort. The sociologist, Paul Hirst, in a recent paper, 'Some problems of explaining student militancy' (Hirst, 1970) gave a succinct sketch of this political style:

> What is the nature of this consensus? It is that parliamentary democracy is founded upon legitimate procedures of political action, and that primary among these procedures is that parliament is the mode of pursuit and accommodating interests within the society. It provides legitimate means for the pursuance of interests without resort to open conflict.... British democracy raises the means of political action to the level of ends: the primary values of British political culture are specified by a body of existing institutions. These institutions and their maintenance have become the primary political goals.

We can only understand the limits and constraints within which 'objectivity' functions in the media when we have grasped the true sources of legitimation in the political culture itself.

We are now at the crunch. For the groups and events upon which, increasingly, the media are required to comment and report, are the groups in conflict with this consensual style of politics. *But* these are precisely the forms of political and civil action which the media, by virtue of their submission to the consensus, are consistently unable to deal with, comprehend or interpret. The nervousness one has observed in the treatment of these issues reflects the basic contradiction between the manifestations which the media are called on to explain and interpret, and the conceptual/evaluative/interpretative framework which they have available to them.

Whereas the core value of the political consensus is the adherence to 'legitimate means for the pursuance of interests without resort to open conflict', the highly heterogeneous groups I have mentioned are characterized either by political militancy, leading through extra-parliamentary politics to the varying types of 'confrontation', or by social disaffiliation, leading through collective and expressive acts of rebellion to the various types of civil disturbance. Civil righters, students, Black Power militants, political hijackers and kidnappers, shop stewards fall into the political militancy category. Skinheads, hippies, squatters, soccer hooligans, psychedelic freak-outs fall into the social disaffiliation category.

The collective label of 'violence'—and its twin metaphor, 'law and order'—is, at one and the same time, both a staggering confusion of new and old meanings and a penetrating insight. As symbolic categories they only make sense when the issues they refer to are shifted from the explanatory context of media to the content of *politics*.

The effective question about the role of the media, then, is not Callaghan's—'Do the media *cause* violence?'—nor Wedgwood Benn's—'Is politics too important to be left to the broadcasters?' (with its obvious retort); but rather, 'Do/can the media help us to understand these significant real events in the real world?' 'Do the media clarify them or mystify us about them?'

Actuality versus depth is not a simple technical choice. The distinction is already built into the structure of the national press. In the arena of news and foreign affairs, popular journalism does not permit systematic exploration in depth. In the 'quality' press, some measure of background interpretation and analysis is more regularly provided. Both these things are legitimated by the professional folk-wisdom. Thus, for the populars: 'The Great British Public is not interested in foreign news'—though how the regular reader of the *Mirror*, the *Express* or the *News of the World*, our circulation front-runners, could develop an intelligent interest in foreign affairs is a matter for speculation. And for the quality press there is 'the rigid separation of "hard" news from comment'.

Distinctions of format and depth of treatment flow, via the grooves of class and education, into the papers we get, and they are hardened and institutionalized in the social structure of the national press. But the relevance of this fragmented universe of press communication for a medium like radio at this time is highly questionable. The audience for news through the day is far less stratified by class and education than the readership of newspapers. Radio must operate as if its potential audience is *the whole nation*.

If follows that radio must find ways of making *both* the foreground event *and* the background context core aspects of its working definition of the news. Otherwise, the radio audience, whatever its range of interests, will be consigned effectively to getting a perpetual foreground.

This becomes a critical issue when the coverage is of groups and events which consistently challenge the built-in definitions and values enshrined in the political culture of broadcasters and audiences alike. This position redefines the concept of 'public service', in relation to radio, in a way which runs diametrically counter to the philosophy of rationalization which infected *Broadcasting in the Seventies*. The press has little to contribute to the development of appropriate models.

Judged in these terms, the manifest tendencies in radio are not encouraging. A heady, breathless immediacy now infects all of the news-magazine programmes. In terms of their profile of items, these programmes progressively affiliate to the model of the daily newspaper. As events like political confrontation and civil disturbance escalate, so the coverage is doubled, quadrupled. As coverage expands, so we become even more alive to the actual 'violent' events and overwhelmed by the vivid sound and image. But as this coverage takes the characteristic form of *actuality without context*, it directly feeds our general sense of a meaningless explosion of meaningless and violent acts—'out there' somewhere, in an unintelligible world where 'no legitimate means' have been devised 'for the pursuance of interests without resort to open conflict'.

'Out there', let us note, is a rapidly expanding area, covering most of the rest of the globe—Indo-China, Latin America, the Middle East, Africa, the Caribbean, Berkeley, Chicago, Tokyo—as well as some growing enclaves closer home. Events of this order play straight into an *ideological gap* in the media—and in public consciousness. That gap is not filled by the media—or, rather, it is now being filled in a systematically distorted way.

Let me conclude with two examples. Take the spate of kidnappings of foreign diplomats in Latin America. These events were endlessly covered on radio and television, usually by reporters on the spot. There was some studio discussion; but the thrust was consistently towards actuality coverage: has he been shot? will the government pay the ransom? will West Germany break off diplomatic relations? The model? Essentially: the front page of the *Daily Express*. What this coverage lacked was some framework which would make this bizarre series of events meaningful or intelligible.

I have been told that this kind of 'background piece' would be provided by the longer reports at the weekend by BBC foreign correspondents. But this is like telling a man whose regular and only newspaper is the *Mirror*, 'If you want to understand the politics of Guatemala, read the *Sunday Times*.' The example is not fortuitous. For during the kidnappings the *Sunday Times* did print a fairly full background article on Guatemala—and a hair-raising, all too intelligible, story it turned out to be.

An even better example, and one where the press performed as badly as radio and television (with the exception of *24 Hours*) was the recent Black Power rioting in Trinidad. The most generally agreed judgement among intelligent West Indians about Trinidad and Jamaica is that the political situation there is highly explosive. Indeed, the real question is why either society has not, before now, gone down in a wave of riots by underprivileged blacks against the privileged coloured middle class. The answer is not unconnected with the presence both of Cuba and of the American fleet within easy striking distance of Kingston and Port of Spain.

The background to the foreground-problem of riots in Trinidad is the persistent grinding poverty of the mass of the people, intensified by basic conflicts of interest between the coloured middle-class inheritors of the 'end of colonial rule' (one of the most conspicuous-consumption classes anywhere in the Third World) and the mass of peasants, workers and urban unemployed, who also happen to be black. Without this knowledge, the large-scale migration from the Caribbean to Britain, which has occupied so much 'foreground' space in recent months is, literally, unintelligible. It is another of those meaningless events, leading to the expected confrontations, and ultimately to 'violence'.

This gap between the urban and rural masses and a native bourgeoisie, grown flush in the hectic, post-colonial years of neo-imperialism, is *the* political fact about vast tracts of the Caribbean and Latin America. Yet radio discussions in studio uniformly expressed puzzlement at how Black Power could become an organizing slogan in a country where the government is 'black'. The fact which needs clarification, of course, is that in the West Indies (unlike the United States, where the permanent presence of a white power structure creates solidarity between all 'black brothers'), the emergent lines of social conflict are laid down precisely by the over-determined coalescence of class, power and gradations of colour.

Unfortunately, neither of the two accredited witnesses—Sir Learie Constantine, who regarded the riots as inexplicable, and Alva Clark, who regarded them as 'a tragedy'—contributed to this process of conceptual clarification. When faced with this sudden eruption of yet another incidence of political violence, the explanatory concepts of 'neo-colonialism' and 'native bourgeoisie' were not available—nor anything else which could do duty for them—in the world of radio.

Instead, the ingredients of the consensual view were quickly wheeled into place: 'The Prime Minister' ... 'resignations from the government' ... 'state of emergency' ... 'small groups of vandals roaming the streets' ... 'disaffection in the army' ... 'detachment of marines from nearby Puerto Rico' ... violence/law and order.

In one event after another, now, the same informal theories—supported by the same ideological commitments, and functioning as an 'objective' set of technical-professional routines—produce the same mysterious product with systematic regularity.

[Editors' note: given the frequent references to 'current events' in this article, and the statements about the 'present' circumstances in both politics and broadcasting, readers are reminded that the article was written in 1970.]

Notes and references

I 1: What is communication? (Colin Cherry)

Notes

1 But such reflexes do not form part of true human language; like the cries of animals they cannot be said to be *right* or *wrong* though, as signs, they can be interpreted by our fellows into the emotions they express.
2 John Donne, the Sixteenth Devotion.
3 See Reusch and Kees (1964) for many illustrations and examples of pictures, icons, motifs, gestures, manners, etc.
4 With kind permission of the Clarendon Press, Oxford.
5 With kind permission of the *Journal of the Acoustical Society of America*.
6 Locke used the word 'semeiotic' to denote the 'doctrine of signs'. See Locke (1689). For an appreciation and survey of Peirce's relevant work in digestible form, see Gallie (1952).

References

Gallie, W. B. 1952: *Peirce and pragmatism*. Harmondsworth: Pelican Books. An outline of Peirce's scattered work.

Locke, John 1689: *An essay concerning human understanding*. Numerous editions; e.g. London: Ward, Locke & Bowden.

McDougall, W. 1927: *The group mind*. London: The Cambridge University Press.

Morris, C. W. 1938: Foundations of the theory of signs. In *International encyclopedia of unified science series*, Vol. **1.2.** Chicago: University of Chicago Press. A brief introduction.

Morris, C. W. 1946: *Signs, language and behaviour*. New York: Prentice Hall Inc.

Reusch, J. and Kees, W. 1964: *Non-verbal communication*. Berkeley and Los Angeles: University of California Press.

Stevens, S. S. 1950: Introduction: a definition of communication. In Proceedings of the speech communication conference at MIT, *Journal of the Acoustical Society of America* **22,** 689–90.

1 2: Problems of terminology (Edmund Leach)

Notes

1 The technical literature on this topic is very large and reaches back for several centuries. The most frequently cited 'authorities' are C. S. Peirce, F. de Saussure, E. Cassirer, L. Hjelmslev, C. Morris, R. Jakobson, R. Barthes. These authors ring the changes with the terms *sign, symbol, index, signal, icon*, with very little agreement as to how the categories should be related but with ever-increasing complexity of argument. Firth (1973) follows Peirce and Morris in making *sign* a box category within which *symbol, signal, index* and *icon* are subdivisions. I have preferred the schema set out in Fig. 2.1 (p. 17) which is based on Mulder and Hervey (1972). Here *symbol* and *sign* are contrasted sub-sets of *index*. I have rejected Firth's usage because I need to take account of the major insights of de Saussure, Jakobson and Barthes. I have modified Mulder and Hervey, partly because I need a terminology which can be adapted to non-verbal as well as verbal communication, and partly I am more concerned to achieve comprehensibility than total rigour of argument. References to the authors mentioned above will be found below. Another helpful guide in this terminological maze is Fernandez (1965, 917–22; 1974).

References

Barthes, Roland 1967: *Elements of semiology*, trans. A. Lavers and C. Smith. London: Cape Editions.

Cassirer, Ernst 1953–7: *Philosophy of symbolic forms*, 3 vols, trans. R. Manheim. New Haven: Yale University Press.

Fernandez, J. W. 1965: Symbolic consensus in a Fang reformative cult. *American Anthropologist* **67**: 902–29.

Fernandez, J. W. 1974: The mission of metaphor in expressive culture. *Current Anthropology* **15**: 119–45.

Firth, Raymond 1973: *Symbols; public and private*. London: Allen & Unwin.

Hjelmslev, L. 1953: *Prolegomena to a theory of language*. Bloomington: Indiana University Press.

Jakobson, R. and Halle, M. 1956: *Fundamentals of language* (Janua Linguarum: Series Minor 1). The Hague: Mouton.

Lévi-Strauss, C. 1966: *The savage mind*. Chicago: University of Chicago Press.

Morris, Charles 1971: *Writings on the general theory of signs* (Approaches to Semiotics 16). The Hague: Mouton.

Mulder, J. W. F. and Hervey, S. G. J. 1972: *Theory of the linguistic sign* (Janua Linguarum: Series Minor 136). The Hague: Mouton.

Peirce, C. S. 1931–5: *Collected papers of Charles Sanders Peirce*. Ed. C. Harteshorne and P. Weiss. Cambridge (Mass.): Harvard University Press.

Saussure, F. de 1966: *Course in general linguistics*. Ed. C. Bally, A. Seche-haye, A. Riedlinger, trans. Wade Baskin. New York: McGraw-Hill Paperbacks.

I 3: The impossibility of not communicating (P. Watzlawick, J. Beavin and D. Jackson

Notes

1 It might be added that, even alone, it is possible to have dialogues in fantasy, with one's hallucinations (Bateson, 1961) or with life. Perhaps such internal 'communication' follows some of the same rules which govern interpersonal communication; such unobservable phenomena, however, are outside the scope of our meaning of the term.

2 Very interesting research in this field has been carried out by Luft (1962), who studied what he called 'social stimulus deprivation'. He brought two strangers together in a room, made them sit across from each other and instructed them 'not to talk or communicate in any way'. Subsequent interviews revealed the highly stressful nature of this situation. To quote the author:

> ... he has before him the other unique individual with his ongoing, though muted, behaviour. At this point, it is postulated, that true inter-personal testing takes place, and only part of this testing may be done consciously. For example, how does the other subject respond to him and to the small non-verbal cues he sends out? Is there an attempt at understanding his enquiring glance, or is it coldly ignored? Does the other subject display postural cues of tension, indicating some distress at confronting him? Does he grow increasingly comfortable, indi-cating some kind of acceptance, or will the other treat him as if he were a thing, which did not exist? These and many other kinds of readily discernible behaviour appear to take place....

References

Bateson, Gregory (ed.) 1961: *Perceval's narrative, a patient's account of his psychosis, 1830–1832*. Stanford: Stanford University Press.
Luft, Joseph, 1962: On non-verbal interaction. Paper presented at the West-ern Psychological Association Convention, San Francisco, April 1962.

I 4: Basic generalized graphic model of communication (George Gerbner)

Reference

Halloran, James 1969: The communicator in mass communication re-search. In Halmos, P. (ed), *The Sociological Review Monograph* **13.** Uni-versity of Keele, January 1969.

II 5: Cultural factors in human perception (A. R. Luria)

References

Allport, G. W. and Pettigrew, T. F. 1957: Cultural influence on the perception of movement: the trapezoidal illusion among Zulus. *Journal of Abnormal and Social Psychology* **55**, 104–13.

Deregowski, J. B. 1968a: Difficulties in pictorial depth perception in Africa. *British Journal of Psychology* **59**, 195–204.

Deregowski, J. B. 1968b: On perception of depicted orientation. *International Journal of Psychology* **3**, 149–56.

Rivers, W. H. R. 1901: Primitive color vision. *Popular Science Monthly* **59**, 44–58.

Segall, M. H., Campbell, D. T. and Herskovits, M. J. 1966: *The influence of culture on visual perception*. Indianapolis: Bobbs-Merrill.

Yarbus, A. L. 1967: *Eye movements and vision*. New York: Plenum.

II 6: Historical changes in gestural behaviour (David Efron)

Notes

1 For a fuller description, see our book, *Race and gesture*.

2 The Man in the Club Window, 1870: *The habits of good society: a handbook for ladies and gentlemen*. London: Low & Company, 284–5.

3 The following anecdote by Charles Lamb suggests that the habit of button-holding in gesticulation was also practised by Anglo-Saxons of a subsequent period.

> I was going from my house at Enfield to the India-house one morning, and was hurrying, for I was rather late, when I met Coleridge, on his way to pay me a visit; he was brimful of some new idea, and in spite of my assuring him that time was precious, he drew me within the door of an unoccupied garden by the roadside, and there, sheltered from observation by a hedge of evergreens, he took me by the button of my coat, and closing his eyes commenced an eloquent discourse, waving his right hand gently, as the musical words flowed in an unbroken stream from his lips. I listened entranced; but the striking of a church recalled me to a sense of duty. I saw it was of no use to attempt to break away, so taking advantage of his absorption in his subject I, with my penknife, quietly severed the button from my coat and decamped. (Richard W. Armour and Raymond F. Howes, *Coleridge the talker* [Cornell University Press, 1940] p. 279.)

With very slight alterations, Steele's description of the tactile gestures of the English coffee-house orators of the beginnings of the eighteenth century fits perfectly the gestural behaviour of a good many of the habitués of any café in the East Side Jewish ghetto of New York City today.

Button's was one of the rendezvous places of the upper and middle classes, and was kept by no less a lady than the Countess of Warwick. Cf., e.g., Addison: *The Spectator*, No 556: 'I was a Tory at Button's, and a Whig at Child's.' Also Johnson's *Lives of the most eminent English poets*, edition of 1801, II, 110–11.

4 Holden, S. M. 1925: *Fifty years of glorious oratory (1875–1925)*. Manchester: Weekly Advertiser Ltd, 97, 103, 186, 193, 201.

5 Estienne, Henri 1883: *Deux dialogues du nouveau langage François Italianizé et autrement desguizé, principalement entre les courtisans de ce temps*. Paris, Liseaux, I, 100 and 212; II, 99–100. [The first edition of the book saw its light in Geneva, in 1578.]

6 The last decade of the sixteenth century, and the first half of the seventeenth, mark the period during which the formation of the 'société polie' and the 'préciosité' takes place. It is, it will be recalled, the period in which the French nobility, having already lost a great part of its political power, undergoes a process of social domestication under the influence of the rising middle class. The standards of vigorous emotionality of the 'gentilhomme d'épée' fall into temporary discredit, and are superseded by a new set of affective and bodily norms ('grace', 'mesure', 'raison', etc.), proper of the new type of model-man which the middle class sets forth as its ideal: the 'honête homme'. D'Urfé's *Astrée*, the *Hotel de Rambouillet*, and, a few years later, Mlle de Scudery's 'ruelle', her *Grand Cyrus*, and her *Clélie*, are landmarks in the history of this change in the standards of emotional demeanour and bodily conduct of the upper strata of early seventeenth-century French society. The *mot d'ordre* of the 'honête homme' is *self-control* (maitrise de soi-même), always and everywhere. This standard pervades most of the writings—literary, moralistic, religious, and philosophical—of that period. It is found in the pastoral novel, from Montreux to D'Urfé; in the treatises of 'civilité', from Menage to Somaize; in the historical novel, from Scudery to La Caprenède; in Corneille's tragedies; in Camus's, François de Sales's and Vincent de Paul's religious treatises; in Descartes's *Les Passions de l'Ame* and in his letters. To give just one example among hundreds, the primacy of 'raison' in emotional behaviour is very seldom questioned by D'Urfé's characters. In fact, they are eager to declare again and again the rational character of their affective reactions. Symptomatic of this attitude are certain recurring expressions in their vocabulary, such as the word 'coldly': '... Je vous parle froidement ..., c'est pour vous fair entendre que la passion ne me transporte pas' (*Astrée*, I, 536). 'Ne croye pas, Hylas, repondit *froidement* Thamyra ...' (*ibid.*, IV, 382). '... le Druide luy repondit *froidement*' (*ibid.*, I, 25). 'Je voy bien, repondit *froidement* Hylas' (*ibid.*, I, 70). 'Je ne scay, repondit *froidement* Sylvandre' (*ibid.*, I, 269); etc., etc. 'Maitrise de soi-même' finds a concrete application in the realm of expressive bodily conduct, in general, and particularly in that of gestural behaviour. The manifestation of feeling and thought is reduced to a minimum in

the circles of the 'société polie'. An energetic play of features, a fiery glance, a vehement gesture, a loud tone of voice, are considered to be a violence to the spirit of 'bienséance', or, as Sarasin, one of the famous habitués of the Hotel de Rambouillet, used to say, things proper of 'the heap' (la tourbe), which is not rational enough to control its passions.

The two following statements are illustrative of the strong abhorrence that the 'société polié' felt for the unrestrained expression of the emotions. They represent the reactions of two of its prominent members to the vigorous affectivity of the Elizabethan stage which they witnessed in England. The statements are an interesting comment on the theory of 'racial' calmness of the Anglo-Saxon versus 'racial' excitability of the Frenchman. We see here Englishmen of the middle of the seventeenth century behaving like 'warm-blooded Mediterraneans' and Frenchmen of the same period reacting like 'cool Nordics'.

> Nos poètes, qui connoissent nostre douceur, n'ensanglentent point nostre scène et jamais il ne font paraistre les actions violentes. Tout au contraire, les poètes anglais, pour flatter l'inclination de leurs spectateurs, font toujours couler du sang sur le theatre et ne manquent jamais d'orner leur scène de catastrophes.... (LePays, *Lettre de l'Angleterre*, in *Lettres*, liv. 3.)

> [Les tragédies anglaises sont] un amas d'événements confus, sans aucun égard à la bienséance. Les yeux, avides de la cruauté du spectacle, y veulent voir des meurtres et des corps sanglants. En sauver l'horreur par les récits, comme on fait en France.... (Saint Evremond, *Sur les Tragédies*, 1677.) For standards of *self-restraint* of the 'société polie', cf. Henri Magendie, *La Politesse Mondaine et les Théories de l'Honnêteté*.

II 7: The perceptual process (Albert H. Hastorf, David J. Schneider and Judith Polefka)

References

Leeper, R. 1935: The role of motivation in learning: a study of the phenomenon of differential motivation control of the utilization of habits. *Journal of Genetic Psychology* **46**, 3–40.

II 8: Verbal and non-verbal communication (Michael Argyle)

References

Abercrombie, K. 1968: Paralanguage. *British Journal of Disorders in Communication* **3**, 55–9.

Argyle, M. 1972: Non-verbal communication in human social interaction.

In R. Hinde (ed.), *Non-verbal communication*. London: Royal Society and Cambridge University Press.

Argyle, M., Salter, V., Nicholson, H., Williams, M. and Burgess, P. 1970: The communication of inferior and superior attitudes by verbal and non-verbal signals. *British Journal of Social and Clinical Psychology* **9**, 221–31.

Brown, R. 1965: *Social psychology*. New York: Collier-Macmillan.

Burns, T. 1964: Non-verbal communication. *Discovery* **25(10)**, 30–7.

Chapple, E. D. 1956: *The interaction chronograph manual*. Moroton, Connecticut: E. D. Chapple Inc.

Cook, M. 1969: Anxiety, speech disturbances, and speech rate. *British Journal of Social and Clinical Psychology* **8**, 13–21.

Crystal, D. 1969: *Prosodic systems and intonation in English*. London: Cambridge University Press.

Davitz, J. R. 1964: *The communication of emotional meaning*. New York: McGraw-Hill.

Ekman, P. and Friesan, W. V. 1969: The repertoire of non-verbal behaviour: categories, origin, usage, and coding. *Semiotica* **I**, 49–98.

Hall, E. T. 1963: A system for the notation of proxemic behavior. *American Anthropologist* **65**, 1003–26.

Jourard, S. M. 1966: An exploratory study of body-accessibility. *British Journal of Social and Clinical Psychology* **5**, 221–31.

Kendon, A. 1972: Some relationships between body motion and speech: an analysis of an example. In A. Siegman and B. Pope (eds), *Studies in dyadic communication*. Elmsford, New York: Pergamon.

Lott, R. E., Clark, W. and Altman, I. 1969: *A propositional inventory of research on interpersonal space*. Washington: Naval Medical Research Institute.

Melly, G. 1965: Gesture goes classless. *New Society*, 17 June, 26–7.

Sarbin, T. R. and Hardyk, C. D. 1953: Contributions to role-taking theory: role-perception on the basis of postural cues. Unpublished, cited by T. R. Sarbin 1954: Role theory. In G. Lindzey (ed.), *Handbook of social psychology*. Cambridge, Mass.: Addison-Wesley.

Scheflen, A. E. 1965: *Stream and structure of communicational behavior*. Eastern Pennsylvania Psychiatric Institute.

Schlosberg, A. 1952: The description of facial expressions in terms of two dimensions. *Journal of Experimental Psychology* **44**, 229–37.

Sommer, R. 1965: Further studies of small group ecology. *Sociometry* **28**, 337–48.

III: Language, thought, culture

References

Jackson, L. 1974: The myth of elaborated and restricted code. *Higher Education Review* **6(2)**, 65–81.

Sampson, G. 1978: Linguistic universals as evidence for empiricism. *Journal of Linguistics* **14,** 183–206.

Vološinov, V. N. 1973: *Marxism and the philosophy of language.* Trans. Ladislav Matejka and I. R. Titunik. New York and London: Seminar Press.

III 9: Defining language (Jean Aitchison)

References

Evans, W. E. and Bastian, J. 1969: Marine mammal communication: social and ecological factors. In H. T. Anderson (ed.), *The biology of marine mammals.* New York: Academic Press.

Hockett, C. F. 1963: The problem of universals in language. In J. H. Greenberg (ed.), *Universals of language.* Cambridge, Mass.: MIT Press.

McNeill, D. 1966: Developmental psycholinguistics. In Smith, F. and Miller, G. A. 1966: *The genesis of language.* Cambridge, Mass: MIT Press.

Marshall, J. C. 1970: The biology of communication in man and animals. In Lyons, J. (ed.), 1970: *New horizons in linguistics.* Harmondsworth: Penguin.

Morton, J. 1971: What could possibly be innate? In Morton, J. (ed.), *Biological and social factors in psycholinguistics.* London: Logos Press.

Robins, L. 1971: *General linguistics: an introductory survey.* Second edition, London: Longmans.

Struhsaker, T. T. 1967: Auditory communication among vervet monkeys (*Cercopithecus aethiops*). In Altman, S. A. (ed.), *Social communication among primates.* Chicago: Chicago University Press.

Thorpe, W. H. 1961: *Bird song: the biology of vocal communication and expression in birds.* Cambridge: Cambridge University Press.

Thorpe, W. H. 1963: *Learning and instinct in animals.* Second edition, London: Methuen.

Von Frisch, K. 1950: *Bees: their vision, chemical sense and language.* Ithaca: Cornell University Press.

Von Frisch, K. 1954: *The dancing bees.* London: Methuen.

Von Frisch, K. 1967: *The dance and orientation of bees.* Translated by L. E. Chadwick, Cambridge, Mass.: Harvard University Press.

III 10: Language and speech (*langue* and *parole*) (Roland Barthes)

Notes

1 It should be noted that the first definition of the language (*langue*) is taxonomic: it is a principle of classification.

2 [Editorial note] Barthes refers his reader to a further section of *Elements of semiology* here: **II.5.1.**

3 *Acta linguistica* **I(1), 5.**

III 11 : Expressions, meaning and speech acts (J. R. Searle)
Notes

1 J. L. Austin, *How to do things with words* (Oxford, 1962). I employ the expression 'illocutionary act', with some misgivings, since I do not accept Austin's distinction between *locutionary* and *illocutionary* acts. Cf. J. R. Searle, 'Austin on Locutionary and Illocutionary Acts', *Philosophical Review*, forthcoming.

2 Austin, *op cit.*, p. 149.

3 G. Frege, *Die Grundlagen der Arithmetik* (Breslau, 1884), p. 73.

III 13 : Social class, language and socialization (Basil Bernstein)
References

Bernstein, B. 1962: Family role systems, socialization and communication. Manuscript, Sociological Research Unit, University of London Institute of Education. Also in: A socio-linguistic approach to socialization. In J. J. Gumpertz and D. Hymes (eds), *Directions in sociolinguistics*. New York: Holt, Rinehart & Winston.

Bernstein, B. 1970: Education cannot compensate for society. *New Society* **387,** February.

Bernstein, B. and Cook, J. 1965: Coding grid for maternal control. Available from Department of Sociology, University of London Institute of Education.

Bernstein, B. and Henderson, D. 1969: Social class differences in the relevance of language to socialization. *Sociology* **3(1).**

Bright, N. (ed.) 1966: *Sociolinguistics.* The Hague and Paris: Mouton.

Carroll, J. B. (ed.) 1956: *Language, thought and reality: selected writings of Benjamin Lee Whorf.* New York: Wiley.

Cazden, C. B. 1969: Sub-cultural differences in child language: an interdisciplinary review. *Merrill-Palmer Quarterly* **12.**

Chomsky, N. 1965: *Aspects of linguistic theory.* Cambridge, Mass.: MIT Press.

Cook, J. 1971: An enquiry into patterns of communication and control between mothers and their children in different social classes. PhD thesis, University of London.

Coulthard, M. 1969: A discussion of restricted and elaborated codes. *Educational Review* **22(1).**

Douglas, M. 1970: *Natural symbols.* London: Barrie & Rockliff, The Cresset Press.

Fishman, J. A. 1960: A systematization of the Whorfian hypothesis. *Behavioral Science* **5.**

Gumpertz, J. J. and Hymes, D. (eds) 1971: *Directions in sociolinguistics.* New York: Holt, Rinehart & Winston. [Volume published 1972.]

Halliday, M. A. K. 1969: Relevant models of language. *Educational Review* **22(1)**.

Hawkins, P. R. 1969: Social class, the nominal group and reference. *Language and Speech* **12(2)**.

Henderson, D. 1970: Contextual specificity, discretion and cognitive socialization: with special reference to language. *Sociology* **4(3)**.

Hoijer, H. (ed.) 1954: Language in culture. *American Anthropological Association Memoir* **79**. Also published by University of Chicago Press.

Hymes, D. 1966: On communicative competence. Research Planning Conference on Language Development among Disadvantaged Children. Ferkauf Graduate School: Yeshiva University.

Hymes, D. 1967: Models of the interaction of language and social setting. *Journal of Social Issues* **23**.

Labov, W. 1965: Stages in the acquisition of standard English. In W. Shuy (ed.), *Social dialects and language learning*. Champaign, Illinois: National Council of Teachers of English.

Labov, W. 1966: The social stratification of English in New York City. Washington DC Centre for Applied Linguistics.

Mandelbaum, D. (ed.) 1949: *Selected writings of Edward Sapir*. Berkeley and London: University of California Press.

Parsons, T. and Shils, E. A. (eds) 1962: *Toward a general theory of action*. New York: Harper Torchbooks. [Chapter 1 especially.]

Schatzman, L. and Strauss, A. L. 1955: Social class and modes of communication. *American Journal of Sociology* **60**.

Turner, G. and Pickvance, R. E. 1971: Social class differences in the expression of uncertainty in five-year-old children. *Language and Speech* [in press].

Williams, F. and Naremore, R.C. 1969: On the functional analysis of social class differences in modes of speech. *Speech Monographs* **36(2)**.

III 14 : Impossible discourse (Trevor Pateman)

Notes

1 This passage was published in 1956. But in his seminar of 1971–2, Barthes was still speaking of the 'social contract' of language.

2 If 'flower' and 'rose' are not hierarchically ordered, then there is no contradiction for the speaker in such statements as 'It's a rose, not a flower' or 'If it's not a flower, is it a rose?' Note that the speaker is not contradicting himself; there is no contradiction for him, only for the hearer.

3 Not all trees are alike. Whorf (Carroll, 1956, 136; see also the whole of the essay *The relation of habitual thought and behaviour to language*, 134–59) suggests that the word 'stone' logico-linguistically implies 'non-combustibility'. However, this implication seems to exist only as the result of belief in a particular theory, namely that stone is non-combus-

tible, and even to this theory there are exceptions (e.g. brimstone). The link between 'monarchy' and 'government' is different in nature. Here, the link is logico-linguistic. One could say that it is a synthetic truth (or falsehood) that 'stone' and 'non-combustibility' have the link they do or are supposed to have, whereas it is an analytic truth that 'government' and 'monarchy' have the relationship which they do. Whorf fails to come to terms with the fact that different theories can be developed within the same language (by speakers of the same language) and this, I presume, because of his identification of thought and language.

4 If I am correct in thinking that the conceptual understanding of a word requires reference to a superordinate term, then the most abstract words—those at the tops of trees—with no superordinate words of their own, would be doomed to remain the words for complexes; they could not be concepts. This seems to me paradoxical, for it is my conventional view that the most abstract words ought to be the most rigorously conceptually definable.

5 To a large degree, this was recognized by the students of schizophrenic thought being criticized. Thus, for instance, Kasanin writes that abstract or categorical thinking (the absence of which was regarded as a trait of schizophrenia) 'is a property of the educated adult person' (1944, 42). And Hanfmann and Kasanin write that 'the difference in [test] scores of this [group, largely composed of attendants at a state mental hospital] and of the college-educated group is sufficiently striking to warrant the conclusion that the highest performance level in the concept formation test is the prerogative of subjects who have had the benefit of college education' (1942, 59–60).

6 The question then arises, What are the specific features of schizophrenia? Some have concluded that there are none, that schizophrenia as a disease-entity does not exist.

7 Many of Wason and Johnson Laird's undergraduate samples do appallingly on reasoning tests. This cannot just be put down to the nature of the tests, for some do well on them. It could be put down to differential reactions to the test situation. Hudson has explored this (1970).

8 The opposition abstract/concrete helped me a great deal when I started in 1970 on the lines of thought developed here, though it has fallen into a secondary place in this chapter. I would still recommend the books which originally helped me, namely Cassirer (1944) and Goldstein (1963).

9 Compare from a different context the following criticism of Cameron: 'In our opinion all explanations [of failure on the Vygotsky blocks test] in terms of evasion or projection of blame on the task etc., misrepresent the situation of those patients who perform to the best of their ability but are unable even to conceive of the performance required from them' (1944, 96).

10 Based on a discussion in an evening class I once taught.

11 Vygotsky's child has an adequate understanding of both 'cow' and 'dog', otherwise he would not be able to make the particular mistake that he does.

12 This point was brought home to me by Chris Arthur.

13 Some people seek to solve political problems by spatial displacement, that is, by *emigration*. It would be interesting to study the political ideology of emigration, perhaps making use of Gabel's theories about spatialization (1969).

14 In contrast, Reich construes apathy as a defence mechanism against recognition of one's class position and interests (1970, 201).

15 'The masses' class consciousness does not consist of knowing the historical and economic laws which rule the existence of man, but: (1) knowing one's own needs in all spheres; (2) knowing the means and possibilities of satisfying them; (3) knowing the hindrances which the social order deriving from private enterprise puts in their way; (4) knowing which inhibitions and fears stand in the way of clearly recognizing one's vital needs and the factors preventing their fulfilment...; (5) knowing that the masses' strength would be invincible in relation to the power of the oppressors if only it were coordinated.' (Reich, 1971, 68–9.)

16 'If one wants to lead the mass of the population into the field against capitalism, develop their class consciousness and bring them to revolt, one recognizes the principle of renunciation as harmful, stupid and reactionary. Socialism, on the other hand, asserts that the productive forces of society are sufficiently well developed to assure the broadest masses of all lands a life corresponding to the cultural level attained by society.' (Reich, 1971, 23–4.)

17 Reich, in contrast, has a manipulative concept of song, dance and theatre: 'we must secure the emotional attachment of the masses. Emotional attachment signifies trust, such as the child has in its mother's protection and guidance, and confidence in being understood in its innermost worries and desires including the most secret ones, those relating to sex'. (1971, 58–9.) Apart from the last nine words, this reads more like Stalin than Reich.

18 The Maoist criticism of Stalin, that he made mistakes, is no criticism at all. For it does not challenge his right to have held the kind of power which *permitted him* to make such mistakes.

References

Bachelard, G. 1970: *La formation de l'esprit scientifique*. Paris: Bibliothèque des Textes Philosophiques.

Barthes, R. 1967: *Elements of semiology*. London: Cape.

Barthes, R. 1972: *Mythologies*. London: Cape.

Bernstein, B. 1971: *Class, codes and control: volume one: theoretical studies towards a sociology of language*. London: Routledge.

Carroll, J. B. (ed.) 1956: *Language, thought and reality: selected writings of Benjamin Lee Whorf.* Cambridge, Mass.: MIT Press.

Cassirer, E. 1944: *An essay on man.* New Haven, Conn.: Yale University Press.

Gabel, J. 1969: *La fausse conscience, essai sur la réification.* Third edition, Paris: Editions de Minuit.

Goldstein, K. 1963: *Human nature in the light of psychopathology.* New York: Schocken Books.

Halliday, M. A. K. 1969: Relevant models of language. *Educational Review* **22.**

Hanfmann, E. and Kasanin, J. 1942: *Conceptual thinking in schizophrenia.* Nervous and Mental Diseases Monograph Series number 67.

Hudson, L. 1970: *Frames of mind.* Harmondsworth: Penguin.

Kasanin, J. (ed.) 1944: *Language and thought in schizophrenia.* Stanford, Calif.: University of California Press.

Laing, R. D. and Esterson, A. 1970: *Sanity, madness and the family.* Harmondsworth: Penguin.

Lyons, J. 1968: *An introduction to theoretical linguistics.* Cambridge: Cambridge University Press.

McKenzie, R. and Silver, A. 1969: *Angels in marble.* London: Heinemann.

Marcuse, H. 1964: *One-dimensional man.* London: Routledge.

Pateman, T. 1973a: Review of R. Barthes, *Mythologies. Human Context* **5.**

Pateman, T. 1973b: The experience of politics. *Philosophy and Phenomenological Research* (USA) **33.**

Reich, W. 1970: *The mass psychology of fascism.* Trans. V. R. Carfagno. New York: Farrar, Straus & Giroux.

Reich, W. 1971: *What is class consciousness?* London: Socialist Reproduction.

Saussure, F. de 1966: *Course in general linguistics.* Trans. W. Baskin. New York: McGraw-Hill.

Vygotsky, L. 1962: *Thought and language.* Cambridge, Mass.: MIT Press.

Wason, P. and Laird, P. Johnson 1972: *Psychology of reasoning: structure and content.* London: Harvard University Press.

Wertheimer, M. 1961: *Productive thinking.* London: Tavistock.

Wittgenstein, L. 1958: *Philosophical investigations.* Second edition, Oxford: Blackwell.

Wood, J. (ed.) 1970: *Powell and the 1970 election.* Surrey: Elliot Right Way Books.

IV: Meaning and interpretation

Reference

Carey, James 1977: Mass communication research and cultural studies. In Curran, J. *et al.* (eds), *Mass communication and society.* London: Edward Arnold.

IV 15: Analysis of the Gerard Manley Hopkins poem 'Spring and Fall' (William Empson)

Reference

Richards, I. A. 1929: *Practical criticism: a study of literary judgement*. London: Routledge & Kegan Paul.

IV 18: Towards a semiotic inquiry into the television message (Umberto Eco)

Editors' notes and references

1 Mead, Margaret 1956: *New lives for old: cultural transformation—Manus 1928–1953*. New York: Morrow. Reprinted New York: Dell, 1968.
2 Eco, Umberto 1968: *La struttura assente*. Milan: Bompiani. No English translation of this work is available. However, Eco has published a more recent attempt at offering a comprehensive theory of semiotics in his *A theory of semiotics*. Bloomington: Indiana University Press, 1976. This latter work was, in its initial drafts, an attempted English translation of *La struttura assente*.
3 Both Robert K. Merton and P. F. Lazarsfeld conducted research into mass communication and its interaction with primary groups and group leaders. A useful introduction to their work is provided by their joint paper 'Mass communication, popular taste and organized social action' which is to be found in Schramm, W. (ed.) 1960: *Mass communication* (second edition) Urbana: University of Illinois Press.

IV 19: Introduction to the presentation of self in everyday life (Erving Goffman)

Notes

1 Gustav Ichheiser, 'Misunderstandings in Human Relations', Supplement to *The American Journal of Sociology* LV (September 1949), pp. 6–7.
2 Quoted in E. H. Volkart (ed.), *Social behaviour and personality*, contributions of W. I. Thomas to Theory and Social Research (New York: Social Science Research Council, 1951), p. 5.
3 Here I owe much to an unpublished paper by Tom Burns of the University of Edinburgh. He presents the argument that in all interaction a basic underlying theme is the desire of each participant to guide and control the responses made by the others present. A similar argument has been advanced by Jay Haley in a recent unpublished paper, but in regard to a special kind of control, that having to do with defining the nature of the relationship of those involved in the interaction.
4 Willard Waller, 'The Rating and Dating Complex', *American Sociology Review* II, p. 730.

5 William Sansom, *A contest of ladies* (London: Hogarth, 1956), pp. 230–2.

6 The widely read and rather sound writings of Stephen Potter are concerned in part with signs that can be engineered to give a shrewd observer the apparently incidental cues he needs to discover concealed virtues the gamesman does not in fact possess.

7 An interaction can be purposely set up as a time and place for voicing differences in opinion, but in such cases participants must be careful to agree not to disagree on the proper tone of voice, vocabulary, and degree of seriousness in which all arguments are to be phrased, and upon the mutual respect which disagreeing participants must carefully continue to express towards one another. This debaters' or academic definition of the situation may also be invoked suddenly and judiciously as a way of translating a serious conflict of views into one that can be handled within a framework acceptable to all present.

8 W. F. Whyte, 'When Workers and Customers Meet', chap. vii, *Industry and society*, edited by W. F. Whyte (New York: McGraw-Hill, 1946), pp. 132–3.

9 Teacher interview quoted by Howard S. Becker, 'Social Class Variations in the Teacher–Pupil Relationship', *Journal of Educational Sociology* XXV, p. 459.

10 Harold Taxel, 'Authority Structure in a Mental Hospital Ward' (unpublished Master's thesis, Department of Sociology, University of Chicago, 1953).

11 This role of the witness in limiting what it is the individual can be has been stressed by the Existentialists, who see it as a basic threat to individual freedom. See Jean-Paul Sartre, *Being and nothingness* (London: Methuen, 1957).

12 Goffman, 'Communication Conduct in an Island Community', pp. 319–27.

13 Peter Blau, 'Dynamics of Bureaucracy' (PhD dissertation, Department of Sociology, Columbia University, University of Chicago Press, 1955), pp. 127–9.

14 Walter M. Beattie, Jr, 'The Merchant Seaman' (unpublished MA Report, Department of Sociology, University of Chicago, 1950), p. 35.

15 Sir Frederick Ponsonby, *Recollections of three reigns* (London: Eyre & Spottiswoode, 1951).

16 For comments on the importance of distinguishing between a routine of interaction and any particular instance when this routine is played through, see John von Neumann and Oscar Morgenstern, *The theory of games and economic behaviour* (second edition; Princeton University Press, 1947), p. 49.

IV 20: The radio drama frame (Erving Goffman)

Notes

1 Here I draw extensively on the previously cited unpublished paper by John Carey, 'Framing Mechanisms in Radio Drama'.

2 *Ibid.*

3 *Ibid.*

4 *Ibid.*

5 Albert Crews, *Radio production directory* (New York: Houghton Mifflin Co., 1944), p. 67, cited in Carey, 'Framing Mechanisms in Radio Drama'.

6 Eileen Hsü, 'Conflicting Frames in Soap Opera' (unpublished paper, University of Pennsylvania, 1970). Carey, 'Framing Mechanisms in Radio Drama', provides a comment on the mechanics of this multiple level of use:

> The board fade also told the listener if music was a vehicle for transition; if it was to act as mood lighting; or if it was part of the action on stage. For example, by establishing a perspective between music and a microphone, the director suggests that the music is on stage; by keeping mike distance constant and board fading, in the context of a cross fade between two characters, the director suggests that music is helping to make the transition; and by keeping mike distance constant while board fading in and out of a scene, the director suggests that the music indicates how the people in the scene feel or how you should feel about them.

7 The form of scripted drama called a musical provides a fourth role for music. A character may not only enact a performance of song or music (this having the same realm status as background music, merely a more prominent place), but may also 'break into' musical expression as though this could be interposed in the flow of action without requiring a formal shift into the performer role. The lyrics and especially the mood of these songs will have something to do with the drama in progress, but how much is an awesomely open question. What the remaining characters do during these musical flights is itself complex and no less a departure from dramatic action than the offering itself. Here, then, is the Nelson Eddy syndrome. That we can suffer it (or almost) attests again to the immense flexibility of framing practices. Observe that the same suspension-of-action arrangement allows for the interposition of other delights—a dance turn, an instrumental rendition—accompanied or unaccompanied by voice.

8 There is an instructive parallel here in the organization of cartoons. As already suggested, the space enclosed in a response balloon is taken to be radically different from the space employed in depicting a scene, and the former can be enclosed in the latter without taking up any scenically real space.

V 21 : Effects of the technology and its uses (Raymond Williams)

Editors' note

1 Marshall McLuhan's most useful work for the student of mass communications is *Understanding media*. London: Routledge & Kegan Paul, 1964, Abacus edition 1973.

Other important publications by McLuhan include *The mechanical bride: folklore of industrial man*. London: Routledge & Kegan Paul, 1951, and *The Gutenburg galaxy: the making of typographic man*. London: Routledge & Kegan Paul, 1962.

References

Blumler, Jay 1970: The political effects of television. In Halloran 1970.
Halloran, James (ed.) 1970: *The effects of television*. London: Panther books.

V 22 : Utilization of mass communication by the individual (Elihu Katz, Jay G. Blumler and Michael Gurevitch)

References

Atkin, C. K. 1972: 'Anticipated communication and mass media information-seeking'. *Public Opinion Quarterly* **36**.
Bailyn, L. 1959: 'Mass media and children'. *Psychological Monographs* **71**.
Berelson, B. 1949: 'What "missing the newspaper" means', in P. F. Lazarsfeld and F. N. Stanton (eds), *Communication research, 1948-9*. New York: Duell, Sloan & Pearce.
Blumler, J. G., Brown, J. R. and McQuail, D. 1970: 'The social origins of the gratifications associated with television viewing'. Leeds: The University of Leeds. (mimeo)
Blumler, J. G. and McQuail, D. 1969: *Television in politics*. Chicago: University of Chicago Press.
Bogart, L. 1965: 'The mass media and the blue-collar worker', in A. Bennett and W. Gomberg (eds), *Blue-collar world: Studies of the American worker*. Englewood Cliffs, NJ: Prentice-Hall.
Dembo, R. 1972: 'Life style and media use among English working-class youths'. *Gazette* **18**.
Edelstein, A. 1973: 'An alternative approach to the study of source effects in mass communication'. *Studies of Broadcasting* **9**.
Emmett, B. 1968-9: 'A new role for research in broadcasting'. *Public Opinion Quarterly* **32**.
Enzenberger, H. M. 1972: 'Constituents of a theory of the media', in D. McQuail (ed.), *Sociology of mass communications*. Harmondsworth: Penguin.
Festinger, L. and Maccoby, N. 1964: 'On resistance to persuasive communication'. *Journal of Abnormal and Social Psychology* **60**.

Furu, T. 1971: *The function of television for children and adolescents*. Tokyo: Sophia University.

Glaser, W. A. 1965: 'Television and voting turnout'. *Public Opinion Quarterly* **29**.

Herzog, H. 1942: 'Professor quiz: a gratification study', in P. F. Lazarsfeld and F. N. Stanton (eds), *Radio research*, 1941. New York: Duell, Sloan & Pearce.

Katz, E. and Foulkes, D. 1962: 'On the use of the mass media for "escape": clarification of a concept'. *Public Opinion Quarterly* **26**.

Katz, E., Gurevitch, M. and Haas, H. 1973: 'On the use of mass media for important things'. *American Sociological Review* **38**.

Katzman, N. 1972: 'Television soap operas: what's been going on anyway?' *Public Opinion Quarterly* **36**.

Lasswell, H. 1948: 'The structure and function of communications in society', in L. Bryson (ed.), *The Communication of ideas*. New York: Harper.

Lasswell, H. and Kaplan A. 1950: *Power and society*. New Haven: Yale University Press.

Lazarsfeld, P. F. and Stanton, F. N. (eds) 1949: *Communications research, 1948–9*. New York: Harper.

Lazarsfeld, P. F. and Stanton, F. N. 1944: *Radio research, 1942–3*. New York: Duell, Sloan & Pearce.

Lazarsfeld, P. F. and Stanton, F. N. 1942: *Radio research, 1941*. New York: Duell, Sloan & Pearce.

Lundberg, D. and Hultén, O. 1968: *Individen och Massmedia*. Stockholm: EFI.

McDonald, D. 1957: 'A theory of mass culture', in D. M. White and B. Rosenberg (eds), *Mass culture: the popular arts in America*. Glencoe: Free Press.

McQuail, D., Blumler, J. G. and Brown, J. R. 1972: 'The television audience: a revised perspective', in D. McQuail (ed.), *Sociology of mass communications*. Harmondsworth: Penguin.

Maslow, A. H. 1954: *Motivation and personality*. New York: Harper.

Mendelsohn, H. 1964: 'Listening to radio', in L. A. Dexter and D. M. White (eds), *People, society and mass communications*. Glencoe: Free Press.

Nilsson, S. 1971: 'Publikens upplevelse av tv-program'. Stockholm: Sveriges Radio PUB. (mimeo)

Nordenstreng, K. 1970: 'Comments on "gratifications research" in broadcasting'. *Public Opinion Quarterly* **34**.

Pietila, V. 1969: 'Immediate versus delayed reward in newspaper reading'. *Acta Sociologica* **12**.

Robinson, J. P. 1972: 'Toward defining the functions of television', in *Television and social behavior*, Vol. 4. Rockville, Md: National Institute of Mental Health.

Rosengren, K. E. 1972: 'Uses and gratifications: an overview'. Sweden: University of Lund. (mimeo)

Rosengren, K. E. and Windahl, S. 1972: 'Mass media consumption as a functional alternative', in D. McQuail (ed.), *Sociology of mass communications*. Harmondsworth: Penguin.

Schramm, W. (1949): 'The nature of news'. *Journalism Quarterly* **26.**

Schramm, W., Lyle, J. and Parker, E. B. 1961: *Television in the lives of our children*. Stanford: Stanford University Press.

Stephenson, W. 1967: *The play theory of mass communication*. Chicago: University of Chicago Press.

Suchman, E. 1942: 'An invitation to music', in P. F. Lazarsfeld and F. N. Stanton (eds), *Radio research, 1941.* New York: Duell, Sloan & Pearce.

Waples, D., Berelson, B. and Bradshaw, F. R. 1940: *What reading does to people*. Chicago: University of Chicago Press.

Weiss, W. 1971: 'Mass communication'. *Annual Review of Psychology* **22.**

Wolfe, K. M. and Fiske, M. 1949: 'Why children read comics', in P. F. Lazarsfeld and F. N. Stanton (eds), *Communication research, 1948–9.* New York: Harper.

Wright, C. 1960: 'Functional analysis and mass communication'. *Public Opinion Quarterly* **24.**

V 23 : The narrator as guarantor of truth (Colin McArthur)

Notes

1 This is a difficult and complex question but some of the issues which have to be thought about are whether the construction of lenses so as to give monocular, Renaissance perspective constitutes an ideological choice and whether the use of certain filming practices (e.g. hand-held camera) constitute acts of coding. For instance, the exterior sequence in Kubrick's *Dr Strangelove* (1963) showing the infantry attack on General Ripper's base, seems to have been coded (through the particular film stock, lack of 'composition', and jerky camera movements) to evoke in the audience the sense of watching a Second World War newsreel, a strategy also used in Godard's *Les Carabiniers* (1963).

2 See the journal *History and Theory* intermittently over the past fifteen years, but particularly Vols VI, VIII, X and XV; and—more recently—Leon J. Goldstein, *Historical knowing*, University of Texas Press, 1976.

3 It is of the essence of ideology that its operations are masked from those within it. I would expect the programme makers to claim (nor would I disbelieve them) that the choice of narrator is made on the grounds of lucidity of speech and capacity for 'drama'. The latter reason would throw interesting light on the running argument of this monograph about the aspiration of *all* television—'factual' as well as 'fictional'—towards the condition of entertainment.

4 Colin MacCabe, 'Realism and the Cinema: Notes on some Brechtian Theses', in *Screen*, Summer 1974, pp. 8–9.
5 *Ibid.*, p. 16.
6 *Ibid.*
7 Colin MacCabe, 'Days of Hope', in *Screen*, Spring 1976, p. 100.
8 See the argument on *Days of Hope* between the present writer and Colin MacCabe in *Screen*, Winter 1975/6 and Spring 1976; and (also relevant to the issue of Realism) the generous text by Raymond Williams—'A Lecture on Realism'—in *Screen*, Spring 1977.
9 See, for example, the article by Stephen Heath and Gillian Skirrow, *op. cit.*

V 24: A world at one with itself

References

BBC 1969: *Broadcasting in the seventies*. London: BBC.

Berger, P. and Luckmann, T. 1967: *The social construction of reality*. New York: Doubleday Anchor.

Breed, W. 1956: Analysing news: some questions for research. *Journalism Quarterly* 33.

Cicourel, A. 1968: *The social organization of juvenile justice*. New York: John Wiley & Sons.

Clausse, R. 1963: *Les nouvelles*. Brussels: Centre National d'Etude des Techniques de Diffusion Collective.

Garfinkel, H. 1967: *Ethnomethodology*. New Jersey: Prentice-Hall.

Goffman, E. 1961: *Asylums*. New York: Doubleday. Harmondsworth: Penguin 1968.

Hirst, P. 1970: Some problems of explaining student militancy. Paper delivered to the British Sociological Association conference at the University of Durham (unpublished).

Hughes, H. 1942: The social interpretation of news. *Annals* 219.

Lang, K. and Lang, G. 1965: The inferential structure of political communications. *Public Opinion Quarterly* 19.

Saxer, U. 1969: News and publicity. *Diogenes* 68.

White, D. 1950: The 'gatekeeper': a case study in the selection of news. *Journalism Quarterly* 27.4 Fall 1950. Reprinted in Dexter and White (eds), 1964: *People, society and mass communications*. Glencoe: The Free Press.

Index

Index